ANDREW THOMPSON
UNIVERSITY OF GLAMORGAN   2009

D1477729

Identity as Ideology

Also by Siniša Malešević

THE SOCIOLOGY OF ETHNICITY

IDEOLOGY, LEGITIMACY AND THE NEW STATE: Yugoslavia, Serbia and Croatia

CULTURE IN CENTRAL AND EASTERN EUROPE: Institutional and Value Changes (*edited*)

MAKING SENSE OF COLLECTIVITY: Ethnicity, Nationalism and Globalization (*edited with M. Haugaard*)

IDEOLOGY AFTER POSTSTRUCTURALISM (*edited with I. MacKenzie*)

Identity as Ideology

Understanding Ethnicity and Nationalism

Siniša Malešević
National University of Ireland, Galway

First published in 2006 by
PALGRAVE MACMILLAN
Houndmills, Basingstoke, Hampshire RG21 6XS and
175 Fifth Avenue, New York, N.Y. 10010
Companies and representatives throughout the world.

PALGRAVE MACMILLAN is the global academic imprint of the Palgrave
Macmillan division of St. Martin's Press, LLC and of Palgrave Macmillan Ltd.
Macmillan® is a registered trademark in the United States, United Kingdom
and other countries. Palgrave is a registered trademark in the European
Union and other countries.

ISBN-13: 978–1–4039–8786–0 hardback
ISBN-10: 1–4039–8786–6 hardback

This book is printed on paper suitable for recycling and made from fully
managed and sustained forest sources.

A catalogue record for this book is available from the British Library.

Library of Congress Cataloging-in-Publication Data

Malešević, Siniša.
    Identity as ideology : understanding ethnicity and nationalism / Siniša
Malešević.
        p. cm.
    Includes bibliographical references and index.
    ISBN 1–4039–8786–6 (cloth)
        1. Group identity. 2. Nationalism. 3. Ethnicity. I. Title.
HM753.M347 2006
305.8009—dc22   2006045981

10 9 8 7 6 5 4 3 2 1
15 14 13 12 11 10 09 08 07 06

Printed and bound in Great Britain by
Antony Rowe Ltd, Chippenham and Eastbourne

For my sister Snježana

Contents

List of Tables

Acknowledgements

There are many colleagues to thank for their invaluable help in putting this book together. As the book draws to a greater or lesser extent from previous essays and papers I owe gratitude to all those who commented on its contents at different occasions: Nicholas Abercrombie, Michael Banton, John Breuilly, Gerard Delanty, Michael Donnelly, Thomas Hyland Erikson, Michael Freeden, Yash Ghai, Mark Haugaard, John Hutchinson, Atsuko Ichijo, Krishan Kumar, Michael Lessnoff, Alan Macfarlane, Iain Mackenzie, Michael Mann, Nicos Mouzelis, and Anthony D. Smith. As the final version of the manuscript was completed while I was a visiting academic at the Department of Government at the London School of Economics I also want to thank all the participants of the Department's weekly nationalism workshop from whose discussions I have greatly benefited and to John Hutchinson for inviting me to spend a semester at the LSE.

I am particularly indebted to unfailing support and inspiring and enlightening suggestions of John A. Hall and, despite our obvious disagreements, Richard Jenkins. Finally I reserve special thanks for my close friends and colleagues Kevin Ryan and Gordana Uzelac who have read and discussed with me the earlier versions of the manuscript. I am also grateful to Kevin for his thorough editing.

Chapters 1 and 2 draw in parts on (2002) 'Identity: Conceptual, Operational and Historical Critique', in S. Malešević and M. Haugaard (eds) *Making Sense of Collectivity*. London: Pluto and (2003) 'Researching Social and Ethnic Identity: A Sceptical View', *Journal of Language and Politics* 2 (2): 265–87.

Chapter 3 is a substantially revised version of (2002) 'Rehabilitating Ideology after Poststructuralism', in S. Malešević and I. MacKenzie (eds) *Ideology after Poststructuralism*. London: Pluto.

Chapter 4 draws in part on (2006) 'Nationalism and the Power of Ideology', in G. Delanty and K. Kumar (eds) *The Sage Handbook of Nations and Nationalism*. London: Sage.

Chapter 5 is a revised version of (2004) ' "Divine Ethnies" and "Sacred Nations": Anthony D. Smith and the Neo-Durkhemian Theory of Nationalism', *Nationalism and Ethnic Politics* 10 (4): 561–93.

Chapter 7 draws in small part on (2000) 'Ethnicity and Federalism in Communist Yugoslavia and its Successor States', in Y. Ghai (ed.) *Autonomy and Ethnicity*. Cambridge: Cambridge University Press.

Chapter 8 is a revised and expanded version of (2002) 'From Organic Legislators to Organicistic Interpreters: Intellectuals in Yugoslavia and Post-Yugoslav Sates, *Government and Opposition* 37 (1): 55–75.

Chapters 6, 9, introduction and the conclusion were not previously published in any form. I am thankful to various publishers for their permission to draw upon these essays.

Introduction

Despite many claims to the contrary most sociologists and social theorists are the victims of fashion. Although many of us in the academic world tend to believe, even if not explicitly proclaim, that our analyses are somehow beyond the banalities, trivialities and ever changing silliness of everyday life, we are far from being immune to the latest intellectual trends and scholarly fads. We may detest, scorn or even ridicule the newest craze and popular obsession with celebrity entertainers, but our world too has its own pop idols and hip acts. Although, as a rule, our idols tend to be more often dead than alive and our fashions change in a matter of decades or centuries rather than months or weeks, we too have our Beckhams and Byonces as well as our Mammas and Pappas. If this was not the case we would not look at the highly influential Miliband-Poulantzas debate of the 1970s as something irrelevant if not obscure by today's standards, or at the structural-functionalist icons of the 1950s and early 1960s, such as Davis and Moore, as outdated relics of the past. As soon as old icons are discarded new ones are embraced: Althusser is passé, Foucault is in; Marcuse is out-of-date, Bourdieu is trendy; Žižek and Butler are chic, Sartre and de Beauvoir are yesterday's news. As academic celebrities fade so do their concepts: hence instead of ideological state apparatuses and interpolation we prefer discourses, archaeologies and genealogies, instead of class consciousness and repressive desublimation we favour *jouissance, différance* and so on. Some may argue that this is inevitable, as our knowledge increases we move on and abandon outdated ideas and obsolete conceptual apparatuses. However, sociology, just as most of social sciences and humanities, is not a straightforwardly cumulative discipline. Unfortunately we do not have the privilege of physics or chemistry of looking at our academic predecessors as pioneers whose discoveries changed the direction of the

1

discipline but who can no longer teach us anything new. As Alexander (1987) rightly argues, sociologists cannot dispense with their classics, as foundational paradigm shifts in this field happen only when new empirical evidence is matched with a Kuhnian-like shift in the theoretical realm. Since the principal empiricist distinction between fact and theory is not ontological but analytical, as empirical data in the social world is always tainted by theory, so modern day sociologists cannot but treat their classics as an unlimited source of insightful and fresh concepts and ideas. Instead of discarding classics as archaic and superseded we are bound to treat them as our contemporaries engaged in an ongoing dialogue with us. This reality is in itself a good indicator of the extent to which we are engaged in intellectual fashions: we continue to admire Plato and Aristotle, Weber and Durkheim and many other classics, but we have little patience for yesterday's icons and yesterday's concepts. And this is exactly how all fashions work. There remains a great admiration for the old past but only ridicule for the more recent past: we appreciate the music, code of dress or behaviour from the 1920s or 1960s but we laugh at the aggressive make-up, hairstyle and manners of the late 1970s, 1980s or early 1990s. It is cool to know how to dance Charleston but highly uncool to sport a mullet hairstyle.

The academic equivalent of a mullet is the concept of ideology. Whereas in the 1970s and 1980s this was an almost requisite idiom in any analyst's toolbox, since the 1990s the term has been relegated to the third division, suddenly replaced by the proliferation of new hip analytical concepts – 'discourse', 'meta-narrative', 'simulacra', and most of all 'identity'. As 'ideology' became almost universally identified as a research tool from a Marxist toolbox, and as Marxist inspired theories of social change lost their popular appeal, so the concept of ideology has been demoted. The conspirational, conflictual and pessimistic undertones with which the concept of ideology was associated gave way to consensual, cheerful and optimistic idioms that were meant to reflect the changes inaugurated between the 1970s and the beginning of the new century. Hence instead of the highly polarised and class ridden world of the 1980s, together with the strong echoes of the Cold War, the new brave world was seen as trans-ideological and oriented much more towards individual self-actualisation than the old collectivisms of yesteryears. Among the new conceptual tools created in this period, 'identity' emerged as a dominant idiom to come to terms with the realities of the new post-cold and post-class world. More than any other concept 'identity' is almost universally regarded as capable of accounting for the direction of the unprecedented social change that has hit our planet. Moreover, this popularity quickly extended beyond academia to politics, economy, culture, the advertising industry and many other spheres of everyday life. 'Identity' has become more popular than any other social concept.

As a result of this conceptual shift and the inherent logic of fashion today almost nobody would take lightly the accusation that he or she is 'ideological', while nearly everybody would claim to have or be proud of having some kind of identity. Even those, or in particular those, who were renowned in the 1970s and 1980s for their erudite Marxist analyses of ideology, now prefer to hide away their mullet sporting photos and rather talk about discourses and identities. Clinging to the concept of ideology is highly uncool given the vogue in multiple identities, identity crisis and identity politics. My aim in this book is to be distinctly uncool by opting for ideology over identity. This however is not done for the sake of resisting a fashion or out of some personal rebellion. On the contrary, my initial research objective was identity: trying to conceptualise, operationalise and explore its forms and expressions in a variety of empirical contexts. As I have tried to show in Chapters 1 and 2 this has proved highly problematic due to the fact that the concept of identity is conceptually and operationally deeply porous. Moreover these early doubts, coupled with the unparalleled popularity of this concept, suggested something sociologically more significant: identity has become a powerful ideological device wielded as much by academics as political entrepreneurs, social movements or state institutions. The fact that until very recently identity was almost unquestioned as a categorical apparatus of social analysis, as well as in ordinary life, is itself a good indicator of its omnipotent ideological status. As Barthes (1993: 143) rightly argued so long ago, the success of ideology is to be measured by the degree of its naturalisation, that is, by how certain meanings and practices are almost universally seen as normal and natural. Myths and ideologies rarely rely on deliberate lies or even on Socrates's noble lies, instead they purify meanings, making them look obvious and innocent; instead of denying things they give them 'natural and eternal justification', bestowing 'clarity which is not that of an explanation but of a statement of fact'. The concept of identity has acquired this naturalist glaze.

Arguing that identity is an ideological device does not automatically imply deceit. On the contrary many individual claims to a particular ethnic, national or gender identity are profoundly sincere. As I elaborate in Chapters 3 and 6, employing the concept of ideology as a primary heuristic and analytical device does not necessarily imply clinging to its traditional Marxist articulations. On the contrary, following the approach

I have outlined in my previous work (Malešević, 2002), the principal aim here is to utilise a model of ideology analysis which does not link dominant belief systems to modes of economic production, or counterpoise ideological views to those of science. Instead ideology is conceptualised as a relatively universal thought-action conveyed in the distinct conjectural arrangements of a particular social order that routinely surpasses ordinary experience. As emphasised in Chapter 6 ideologies appeal to individual or group interests, moral norms or superior knowledge claims in order to justify actual or potential social action.

The principal meta-ideology under scrutiny here is identitarianism. The focal point of this book goes beyond psychological, anthropological or micro sociological theories of self and social identification. Stretching from Tajfel's (1981) social identity theory, to Goffman's (1968,1969, 1975) dramaturgical approach, to the symbolic interactionism of Mead (1934) and Blumer (1969), Frederick Barth's (1969) studies on boundaries and group interaction, Berger and Luckman's (1966) theories of social construction of reality, to Anthony Cohen's (1985) and Richard Jenkins's (1996, 1997, 2004) illuminative analyses of inter- and intra-group categorisation, embodiment and group perceptions, much of this work is extremely valuable and indispensable to our understanding of group formation and self-articulation. In contrast to this corpus of works, the core of my analysis is 'identity talk' or identitarianism, a leading ideological paradigm of our age. Under the guise of 'need to belong' identity often becomes a mystical phrase, a new name for the old Herderian *volksgeist*, a praise for 'roots' and an imagined conflict-less social order.

In this book I problematise the conceptual and methodological uses and misuses of 'identity'. However my preoccupation is firmly with the sociological and political implications of identitarinism. Despite all the talk about identity politics, the celebration of cultural difference, and self-actualisation, identity is, in analytic terms largely framed as a profoundly de-politicising concept. Since identitarians speak in the culturalist language of group difference while simultaneously acting along the existing political tracks, their nominally culturalist discourses acquire implicit political weight and hence easily become a potent device for mass mobilisation. Once we are on the terrain of mass political mobilisation then what is required is analytical engagement with the specific ideological projects articulated by dominant social actors, and little is to be gained by simply taking social actors at their word and assuming that 'it is all about identity'. This is important because identitarian discourses often soothe, naturalise and normalise the ideological currents of our everyday social reality. Instead of coming to grips with the overwhelming force of nationalism, that dominant ideology of modernity, identity talk pacifies and makes obvious something that is distinctly extraordinary, historically novel, structurally contingent and human-made. As repeatedly emphasised in the book these ideological realities under which we all live are not necessarily a product of human intent bent on mass brainwashing and nor are they caused principally by the workings of world capitalism or any other gigantic mega force. Rather as argued in Chapters 4, 5 and 6 this unusual outcome had more to do with the peculiarities of European historical development that gave birth to the modernist ethos of Enlightenment and Romanticism and the specific geopolitical arrangements from which the contemporary nation-state was created.

Hence the concepts we use in social analysis often influence our perception of social reality as well as the nature of the research questions we pose. So if one looks only inwardly for the psychological or even biological basis of 'identity claims' one may miss the outward structural, historical and ideological underpinnings of how, when and why such claims exist at the particular moment in time. As ethnicity and nationess are distinct articulations of politicised culture, so any relatively coherent claim to possessing, maintaining or acquiring particular ethnic or national identity is always an ideological statement. Thus as researchers and social analysts our job is to dissect, analyse and attempt to explain the social origins, the intensity or the popular appeal of such statements rather than taking them at face value or even celebrating them. This is not to say that there is something inherently wrong with one's attachment to a particular ethnic or national collectivity. Not at all. What is argued here is that as social scientists we have a certain responsibility towards the concepts we use, concepts that very often enter public policy discourses and find their application in the everyday practice and institutions of the modern nation-state. Chapters 7, 8 and 9 illustrate how far these processes can go when ethnicity and nationess become institutionalised and are deployed as a device of elite power struggles. In its most radical form 'identity as ideology' lands itself with relative ease to the extremist political projects and genocidial policies.

The layout of the book

Although the general argument of this study is framed around the question of whether identity talk is a form of ideological practice, the core of the book is focused on the workings of a very specific, but highly versatile, identitarian ideology – nationalism. I explore both theoretically and empirically the facets of nationalist ideology in its ethnic, civic and banal forms. Through the critical engagement with the leading approaches in this field I argue not only that nationalism, in all its diverse forms, is a dominant ideological narrative of the modern age, but also that to understand it fully one needs to analyse it as a dominant *operative* ideology of our times. Whether ethnic, civic or banal, nationalism remains the most potent source of state legitimacy and the most reliable mechanism for mass mobilisation. No social movement, left, right or centre, and no political agent who aspires either to state control or popular mobilisation outside of regular institutional channels can be triumphant without, at the very least, implicitly invoking on the nationalist rhetoric and practice. Hence the main question remains: Why and how has such a distinctly novel and modern ideology of popular sovereignty and cultural homogeneity managed to acquire the global hegemonic position that it enjoys today? In this book I examine the most influential explanations of this puzzle both in terms of their strengths and weaknesses and also ask what this means in the practicalities of everyday life in a nation-state.

First I look at the conceptual problems in accounting for the nature of this historical process of formational change asking: whether ethnicity and nationess are better conceptualised as questions of identity or ideology. Second I critically analyse two paramount theories of nationalism, those of Ernest Gellner and Anthony Smith, tracing the contours of alternative understandings of nation-formation processes, focusing on two different layers of ideology articulation and examining the role of coercion in nation-state building. Finally I explore the workings of ethnicity and nationalism in practice: the making and breaking of the nation-state in the context of the former Yugoslavia and Rwanda.

It should be noted that while the book is organised as three sections, focusing on conceptual, theoretical and empirical issues respectively, it is also the case that all chapters will, of necessity, engage in occasional discussion of all three dimensions: concepts, theories and empirical material.

In Chapter 1 I assess the analytical strength of the concepts of 'identity', 'ethnic identity' and 'national identity' by looking at the non-sociological roots of these idioms. It is argued that these three concepts are traditionally adopted either in an overly weak or excessively strong sense, allowing either for a vague and overly inclusive use or else a reified and extremely inflexible use, neither of which is helpful in social analysis. Despite this problematic conceptual nature, identity talk has proliferated inside, as much as, outside academic circles. Hence the chapter explores some historical and sociological reasons why identitarianism has acquired such a conceptual supremacy and global popularity. I argue that 'identity' has filled the vacuum created by the demise of three other master concepts – 'race' (after the collapse of Nazi project), the 'national character', and 'social consciousness' (with the end of the Cold War). In the contemporary environment of dramatic social, political, economic and cultural change 'identity' has become an umbrella term for anything and everything, a shortcut which evades the rigour of explanation.

Chapter 2 focuses on the relationship between conceptual and methodological problems in the empirical study of ethnic and national identity. In particular the analysis explores the issues of operationalisation and 'measuring' ethnic and national identity claims. By scrutinising a number of representative quantitative/empiricist and qualitative/interpretativist models of ethnic and national identity, I argue that despite their valuable contribution on the nature of ethnicity and nationess neither of the two research strategies proves fruitful in capturing the chimera of 'ethnic and national identity'.

In Chapter 3 I look at the analytical relevance of the concept of ideology in the wake of recent criticisms. The focal point is contemporary post-essentialist perspectives inspired by Foucault, post-modernism, and post-Marxism, all of which operate with a poststructuralist understanding of ideology. I argue that although poststructuralism correctly challenges the totalising ambitions of ideology critique, by focusing exclusively on the Marxist understanding of ideology it fails to account for the contributions of other theoretical traditions. Poststructuralist and postmodernist preference for the concepts of 'discourse', 'identity' or 'meta-narrative' over that of ideology has been criticised as being too relativist and analytically insufficient for empirical purposes. I argue that the concept of ideology can be rehabilitated by moving it from structure-centred approaches towards more agency-centred theories of ideology and by shifting the emphasis from the function to the form and content of ideology. It is claimed that the subtlety of micro approaches are better suited to the study of those issues postructuralism challenges while also giving a new life to the concept of ideology.

Apart from postmodernist critiques, the concept and theory of ideology has also endured equally harsh treatment by modernist historical and political sociology. Since the publication of the Dominant Ideology Thesis (1980) by Abercrombie *et al.* it has become common place to accept the view that there is no and never was 'dominant ideology'. Chapter 4 explores the depth of these assessments and while accepting some aspects of these criticisms the chapter aims to contest the wholesale rejection of the role ideology plays in modernity. I argue that the concept of dominant ideology is still an essential heuristic device for the analysis of the principal ideological narrative of modernity, that is nationalism. Rather than treating dominant ideology as a static thing, the chapter makes a case for a view of ideology as a dynamic process operating at two different levels – the normative and the operative. To illustrate the main argument a brief analysis of key ideological texts from the three very different societies (Iran, Yugoslavia and United Kingdom) is provided. On the basis of this analysis the chapter aims to show how, despite the striking and mutually exclusive teachings on the normative level, in all three cases the operative layers of ideology exhibit a great deal of similarity and congruence, indicating that nationalism remains a dominant ideology of the modern age.

Chapter 5 provides an analysis of the most sophisticated identitarian theory of nationalism – Anthony D. Smith's ethno-symbolism. By assessing the epistemological foundations of this approach I argue that Smith's theory can be properly understood only when one engages more directly with the broader sociological worldview that his position is an integral part of – Durkheimianism. The link with Durkheim is most evident in Smith's conceptualisation of ethnies and nations as historically evolving solidary groups, his view of such groups as moral communities underpinned by the shared sense of a collective past, and finally in his understanding of ethnic and national collectivities as sacred unions developing in the context of the profane nature of modernity. Although Smith's vision of the social world goes a step beyond classical Durkheimianism, the evolutionist, identitarian/collectivist and idealist nature of his argument is still chained to the Durkheimian legacy, which prevents it from developing an all-inclusive account of nations and nationalism.

As Ernest Gellner is regularly counterposed to Anthony Smith as epitomising the modernist, materialist and almost anti-identitarian theory of nationalism, Chapter 6 scrutinises key aspects of his approach. However, just as with the case of Smith I examine the broader epistemological bases of Gellner's historical sociology which rests on a simple but profound understanding of the radical structural transformations that have shaped the nature of human collectivity. His focus is on the tectonic structural changes which have transformed a deeply hierarchical, economically stagnant, inegalitarian and violent world into one characterised by an intensive social mobility, perpetual economic growth, (principled) egalitarianism and relatively peaceful social conditions. Despite Gellner's pronounced normative and epistemological antipathy to identitarianism his account of social change is found to underestimate the role of both ideology and violence (in its internal and external form) in the modern, and particularly late modern, era. This chapter challenges Gellnerian view of modernity in its privileging of production over ideology and coercion. Not only is it that modernity was born through and with violence, but violence has dramatically intensified and undergone transformation with modernity, requiring more potent and subtle sources of self-justification articulated in the proliferation and development of powerful and pervasive ideological doctrines.

Chapter 7 explores the organisational implications of identitarianism in practice through the example of Yugoslav break-up. Contrary to the widely shared view that the state disintegrated because it was an artificial multi-ethnic federation, with the long history of mutual animosities kept under control only by the iron fist of communist government, I argue that exactly the opposite was the case. Not only is there no evidence of any 'deep ancient hatreds' or suppression of ethnicity under state socialism, but also more importantly it was the peculiar character of the state's own ideologically articulated institutional structure that was at the heart of its future collapse. As a result the power elite of socialist Yugoslavia used decentralisation as a means of avoiding democratisation and liberalisation. Under pressures from below for further democratisation the government of socialist Yugoslavia shifted the question of popular political participation to the level of inter-republic relations and in this way unwittingly created conditions for the concentrated institutionalisation, and later extensive politicisation, of cultural difference.

In addition to the structural causes of state collapse and the role of political elites Chapter 8 looks at the responsibility of a state created organic, identitarian cultural elite – the intellectuals. Drawing critically on Zygmunt Bauman's typologies of interpreters and legislators and Antonio Gramsci's organic and traditional intellectuals the chapter identifies and assesses the profile of the intelligentsia in communist and post-communist period. I argue that Yugoslavia lacked the category of traditional intellectuals (be they legislators or interpreters) and that the dominant type of a Yugoslav intellectual was an organic, identitarian legislator. As a result, the post Yugoslav states are also characterised by the lack of traditional intelligentsia and what has happened in the early post-communist period is that only the former organic legislators have become organicistic interpreters.

Finally in Chapter 9 the darkest side of identitarian ideology and policy are investigated. Although ethnic cleansing and genocide are still generally seen as a prerogative of despotic and backward regimes, most recent research has forcefully made the case that systematic mass scale extermination was rarely the aim of the traditional rulers. A fully fledged genocidal enterprise requires both the technology and ideology of modernity. Drawing critically on Zygmunt Bauman's and Michael Mann's theories of ethnic cleansing this chapter analyses the relationships between modernity, nation-building and the systematic mass scale violence in Bosnia and Rwanda. While the synthesis of Mann's and Bauman's theories proves highly useful in the explanation of many aspects of Rwandan and Bosnian experience on the macro level, the micro level of analysis is largely neglected. To rectify this one-sidedness and thus to enhance our understanding of links between genocide and modernity, the emphasis is placed on the role transformations in social status play in the process of ethnic mobilisation.

As Randall Collins (1992: 25) insightfully argues 'an individual can dominate other people mainly by taking advantage of their feelings of solidarity'. Even though identity talk relies on individualist terms such as selfhood, personality or individual autonomy, its ideological power is rooted in its implicit collectivist clarion-call to group solidarity. The omnipotence of nationalism in modernity, whether as ethnic, civic or banal, owes a great deal to this popular solidaristic appeal to collective morality. As humans we are cultural beings dependent on the familiarity and warmth of our close group bonds. However the very ties that sustain us as human beings are the same ones that turn us into mass killers, with an excessive love for our 'culture and identity' regularly exhibiting an inverse relationship to our appreciation of other 'cultures and identities'. As Gellner (1998: 5) puts it 'cultures freeze associations, and endow them with a feel of necessity' by turning ordinary social worlds into homes, 'where men can feel comfortable and where they belong rather than explore'. It is exactly these pleasant, gullible, sultry feelings and succulent scents of group belonging that can, in the hands of skilful and callous political entrepreneurs, turn easily into a stench of human flesh.

Part I
Concepts

1
Ethnic and National Identity: The Conceptual Critique

Introduction

Identity is not something tangible or visible: you cannot touch, smell, taste or see it. Yet many claim that its presence is so prevalent today that nearly everything has become a matter of identity. Television, radio and newspapers bombard us on everyday basis with information on how 'the very identities of numerous cultures or ethnic groups are threatened'. We hear over and over again, explicitly or covertly, how our national identity has to be preserved either from the 'the floods of immigrants' or polluting influences of culturally or morally inferior Others: the West, the Imperialists, the Muslim fundamentalists, the Americans, the uncivilised barbarians, the EU bureaucrats, the terrorists, the Asians, the Africans, and so on. Romanticist writers and organic intellectuals demand that we discover and respond to our cultural identities. Advertising seduces us daily with consumerist messages that sell us distinct status identities. As numerous studies and publications demonstrate 'identity' has become a dominant idiom in popular, activist, and contemporary academic discourse. This near absolute dominance can best be illustrated by the simple fact that Google search lists over 93 million sites linked to the key word 'identity'.[1]

This concept has not only acquired almost universal acceptance, it has also become a normative strait jacket. Today, a person is expected and required to have an identity. Even though there is profound popular disagreement on whether identities are essential or existential, primordial or constructed, singular or multiple there is almost no dispute over the question of whether identities exist or not. It is assumed that 'an identity' constitutes an indispensable ingredient of every human being so that making the claim of not having or wanting an identity might be regarded at best as bizarre and at worst as suspicious, immoral or sinister. For the keepers of today's moral order being identity-impaired might be perceived socially as more problematic than being mentally or physically impaired.

In this and Chapter 2 I intend to question this unproblematic use of the concept of 'identity', and in particular 'ethnic and national identity'. I argue that the vague and porous nature of these concepts creates profound methodological problems in the study of human life. I also look briefly at the historical and geographical underpinnings of these concepts to evaluate their analytical utility. Finally I sketch some possible sociological reasons as to why these concepts have acquired such a hegemonic position today and I briefly explore the political implications of their use. While Chapter 2 provides detail scrutiny of operational and methodological problems, the focus here is on the conceptual and theoretical issues.

The idea of identity

Social scientists in general and sociologists in particular are renowned for their inexhaustible appetite for analogies, metaphors and images, seeking the means to capture the 'essence' of social reality in a single word. In order to interpret and explain the nature of social change, the individual and group behaviour or the outcome of unpredictable social events, social scientists are very often eager to look for meaningful and generalisable categories outside of their respective disciplines. Sometimes these concepts are found in art (i.e. Lyotard's 'post-modern'), literature (Goffman's dramaturgical sociology of 'frames', 'performances', or 'theatre'), theology (Weber's 'charismatic authority') or architecture (Mumford's necropolis). However the most resonant categories of generalisibility are found in natural or technical sciences (with examples ranging from Durkheim's mechanical and organic solidarity to Parsons's equilibrium to Castells' network society or Beck's risk society). The concept of 'identity', and hence its derivative, ethnic and national identities, also have their origins outside the social sciences – more precisely in mathematics, logics and analytical philosophy. This mathematical term has entered sociological discourse via neo-Freudian psychoanalysis, psychology and psychiatry.

Despite some pronounced differences mathematical, logical and philosophical understandings of 'identity' are similar in the sense that they all operate with a formal strict and precise concept. In modern logic and set theory identity refers to a symmetrical, transitive, relation. It is the 'two-place predicate' (=) that holds only between a thing and itself (i.e. for all x and y, 'x = y' holds true if x is y) (Copi, 1979: 140–9). Analytical philosophy operates with two standard concepts of identity – qualitative and numerical identity. While qualitative identity relates to arbitrary objects that are duplicates, exactly similar in all respects (i.e. two blue navy shirts produced in the same military factory on the same day), numerical identity refers to object's irreplaceable uniqueness (i.e. despite the different clothes they wear, Spiderman and Peter Parker are only one person). Derek Parfit (1995: 14) illustrates this distinction in the following terms:

> I may believe that, after my marriage, I shall be a different person. But that does not make marriage death. However much I change, I shall still be alive if there will be someone living who will be me. Similarly, if I was teletransported [to Mars], my Replica on Mars would be qualitatively identical to me; but, on the sceptic's view, he wouldn't be me. I shall have ceased to exist.

Finally, in mathematics identity refers to several things – in algebra identity is an element in a set of numbers that when combined with another number in an operation leaves that number unchanged (i.e. $b + 0 = b$). It also has more specific meanings such as 'an equality that remains true regardless of the values of any variables that appear within it' or 'a function f from a set S to itself' (i.e. $f(x) = x$ for all x in S) (Cori and Lascar, 2000: 31–4). Goddard (1998) has recently summarised all these mathematico-logical understandings of identity as something that basically refers simultaneously[2] to two distinct forms of difference: absolute, zero difference, and relative, non-zero difference. Absolute definition of identity relates to 'the unconditional nature of a thing that is not derived from external relation – the product of internal self-similarity', while relative definition of identity implies 'the conditional nature of a thing, n, derived from the difference between n and not (n) – the product of external other-difference'. The example of zero difference is logical statement 'he must be Peter since he is the same as Peter' whereas the example of non-zero difference is 'Peter is best since he earned more than the others'.

Since its incorporation into the discourse of social science the concept 'identity' preserved its dualistic mathematico-logical meaning. Having an 'identity' meant being on the hand identical (or in less extreme versions, similar) to a group/category and on the other hand it also meant being different from another group/category (Peter = Peter, Peter ≠ Nancy).

For example a working-class identity simultaneously implied that individuals who share this form of identity have a more or less identical class position (e.g. being manual workers, dependent on similar wages, living in the similar housing estates, having the same educational qualifications, sharing the same cultural values etc.) and at the same time that this group differs from the other classes (e.g. middle or upper classes) and their respective identities.

However, this dual application of the concept in social science was paradoxical from the very beginning. While mathematics, logics and analytical philosophy can operate with an absolute, rigid and total concept (e.g. absolute zero) which cannot be reduced further to anything else ($3 = 3$), sociology and the social sciences do not have such a privilege. On the contrary, events and actors in the social world are, as most social scientists now agree, highly dynamic, flexible, constantly changing, fuzzy, unpredictable and in the continuous process of creating unintended consequences of their action (Boudon, 1982). As Harris (1995: 47–50) rightly argues identity is a formalist category and formal models are ill suited to deal with the complexities and fluctuations of social reality. Identity as conceptualised in mathematics, logics and analytical philosophy relates to questions of equivalence and substitution. 'Experimentalists have no problem with substitutivity in formal systems, but their main interest in such systems lies in their ability to illuminate the structure of the material world'. While formalist models are highly appealing for their precision, clarity and certainty, in social research their use is extremely limited. In other words, since there is no absolute zero difference in the world of humans applying formalist concepts here seems rather futile. However this was no obstacle to the dramatic proliferation of identity discourse in social science and the humanities. As Gleason (1983) points out, the concept of identity was introduced into this field of study only in the late 1950s and 1960s, primarily through the work of the psychologist Erik Erikson. Although there were almost no references to 'identity' in social science dictionaries and encyclopaedias before the 1950s, since then this concept has attained almost indisputable recognition. Such an overextensive use of the term also creates a cacophonic confusion with many mutually competing understandings of 'identity'.

The concepts of 'Identity'

Brubaker and Cooper (2000: 6–8) have recently tried to bring some order to this conceptual cacophony by identifying five dominant ways in which the concept of identity is currently used in social science and the humanities: (a) identities as non-instrumental forms of social action; (b) identities as a collective phenomena of group sameness; (c) identities as deep and foundational forms of selfhood; (d) identities as interactive, processual, contingent products of social action; and (e) identities as fluctuating, unstable and fragmented modes of the 'self'. They argue that these five understandings of identity range from 'strong' to 'weak' uses of the concept – while the first two conceptions operate with the common-sense, 'hard' uses of the term, the remaining three, which are often found in the social constructivist approaches (particularly in cultural studies, anthropology and sociology) work with very 'soft', flexible and contingent understandings of identity. However, despite pronounced differences, all of these understandings of identity have a firm footing in their mathematico-logical and philosophical origins. Hence, whereas the use of identity as 'non-instrumental forms of social action' and 'interactive, processual, contingent products of social action' refer in our mathematico-logical classification to relative non-zero difference, the 'collective phenomenon of group sameness', 'deep and foundational forms of selfhood' and fluctuating and fragmented modes of the 'self' refer in a literal or metaphoric sense to absolute zero difference.

Relating identity to social and political action means defining a group or category from the outside. In mathematical terms the conditional nature of a thing, n is derived from the external relation which in this case is social action. The authors who operate with the concept of identity in this tradition define identity in firm opposition to self-interests or alternatively as a ground for possible social action. The idea is that the actions of individuals and groups are not determined only by their instrumental rationality but also by shared cultural values reflected in common cultural or political identities. In contemporary sociology of ethnicity and nationalism one can find numerous examples of this form of identity use.

A typical example is a relatively recent debate on 'national identity, citizenship and multicultural society' between J. Rex and G. Delanty (1996). While the authors express profound disagreement on whether interests or identities are at the core of 'new nationalism' in Europe, they both share the understanding that identities are something opposed to interests. So for example, Rex speaks how

> Delanty also seems to want to argue that the banal nationalism of the masses is now no longer about the pursuit of interests as, I think, was the case with classes, but is now primarily concerned with identity ... therefore [they] become concerned above all to achieve identity.

They will surely still have interests which they pursue and which affect the structure of their organizations. (Rex, 1996: 1.5)

And Furthermore 'Whether we are talking about interests or identity, however, we should be clear that the "banal" interpretation of the immigrants' role may be challenged' (Rex, 1996: 1.8). In addition, Delanty also operates with the concept of identity as a base for social action arguing that 'identity' not 'ideology' is a key motive of social action. So we can read that

> Nationalism no longer appeals to ideology but to identity. ... this of course does not mean that ideology has come to an end, but that it has fragmented into a politics of identity: ideology is being refracted through identity. (Delanty, 1996: 2.3)

There are three crucial problems with this form of 'identity' use. First, there is no obvious reason why all forms of non-instrumental motivation and action should be categorised as being based on 'identity'. As we could learn from Weber (1968) and others social action can originate from a variety of motives: those that are predominantly rational (instrumental or value rational), traditional, habitual, emotional and so on. The use of the term 'identity' here is extremely counterproductive because by not differentiating between all these different forms of action it explains very little. Instead of pinpointing the exact type of motive or action taking place and thus providing an explanation, it obscures the entire explanatory process by simply conjuring up the word 'identity', like pulling a rabbit out of a hat.

Second, there is no self-evident reason why any form of social action should be characterised as having basis in 'identity'. One can straightforwardly explain a variety of forms of social and political action with the use of less ambiguous concepts and without making any reference to 'identity'. If we look at our previous example of 'new nationalisms' in Europe one can develop a similar argument to Delanty's without invoking the concept of identity at all. So one could argue that nationalism no longer appeals to ideology but to sociologically or psychologically less troubling categories, such as group membership, self-understanding, self- or group-perception, sense of commonality, shared values, emotions, or status hierarchy.

Third, there is no empirical evidence that it is 'identity' that motivates individuals to form groups. If identity is understood as a form of value driven action than one has little reliable empirical tools to measure the intensity of values. As Hechter (1995: 56) argues on the basis of his empirical work 'values can not readily be imputed from behaviour ... usually we do not know if such behaviours result from the fear of sanctions (...), or directly from deeply held value commitments. Since both mechanisms produce the same outcome, it is impossible to tell which of them is responsible in the usual case'.

The uses of identity in relation to 'group sameness', 'foundational forms of selfhood' and as 'fluctuating modes of the self' mean defining a group or category from the inside out. The strategy used here is a literal or metaphoric understanding of identity in reference to its unconditional nature which is not derived from an external relation. This is most clearly visible in the work of authors who operate with the strong concepts of group membership and thus write about 'gender', 'cultural' 'ethnic', 'national' and other identities. For example H. Isaacs and A. Smith operate with very strong and definite concepts of cultural, ethnic and national identity. While Isaacs's conceptual framework incorporates the relation to 'group sameness' and 'foundational forms of selfhood', Smith's theory works with all three understandings of identity ('group sameness', 'foundational forms of selfhood' and as 'fluctuating modes of the self') as an absolute zero difference. Isaacs's concept of 'basic group identity' represents the most straightforward case of understanding identity as an absolute zero difference. According to Isaacs (1975: 29–30, italics mine): 'this is the identity derived from belonging to what is generally and loosely called an "ethnic group". It is composed of what has been called "primordial affinities and attachments". It is the identity made up of *what a person is born with* or *acquires at birth*.' Even though A. Smith uses more subtle concepts his terminology is still firmly rooted in understanding identity as an absolute zero difference. In clear reference to 'group sameness' and 'foundational forms of selfhood' he writes how 'the *attempt to create new* communities and *cultural identities* is likely to prove painfully slow and arduous, especially where the *new identities lack clear boundaries* and must compete with *well established and deep rooted identities* and communities' (Smith, 1999: 19, italics mine); or how 'identities are forged out of shared experiences, memories and myths in relation to those of other collective identities' (Smith 1999: 247). Furthermore he defines nationalism as 'an ideological movement for *attaining and maintaining identity*, unity and autonomy of a social group some of whose members deem it to constitute an actual or potential nation' (Smith, 1999: 18, italics mine). Smith finally incorporates the third understanding of identity ('fluctuating modes of the self') by making a distinction between individual identities which are seen as changeable, situational and optional, and collective identities (e.g. ethnic, religious and national identities) which 'tend to be pervasive and persistent' (Smith, 1999: 230).

This form of identity use is even more problematic than the previous one. First, the concept is reified to the extreme. Both Smith and Isaacs operate with the idea of identity as something tangible, visible or touchable. As we could read in their works identities, as with other material things, have 'clear boundaries', they are 'acquired' and 'well routed', should be 'attained and maintained' and so on. Identities are truly perceived as things. They are seen as something firm, stable and given and not as a product of social action, contingent events, or human agency. In this way a concept (of 'identity') acquires attributes and property that only the material world can have – boundaries, action or will. This view is not only analytically problematic but it can also have serious practical implications when used within the realm of popular discourse for the political mobilisation of groups or individuals (as demonstrated in Chapter 9). Hence, people are incited to kill or die in order to 'preserve, maintain or acquire their identities'.

Second, by using the concept of identity in reference to 'group sameness' and 'foundational forms of selfhood' in such a reified way we are unable to provide an explanation of individual or group behaviour. Instead on focusing on what our job is, to explain why individuals reify their group membership and perceive other groups and categories as homogenous things with single wills, we engage in the creation, maintaining or reproduction of the reified view of the social world. As Brubaker and Cooper (2000: 5) following Bourdieu (1990) rightly point out, academics who take on this type of reasoning do not distinguish between the categories of practice ('lay', 'folk', 'native' concepts) and the categories of analysis. If the social actors in their every day life operate with the terms such as 'identity', 'ethnic identity' or 'national identity' as something self-evident and unproblematic this does not mean that a researcher should treat these categories in the same manner.

Third, even when researchers such as Smith (1999: 230) occasionally acknowledge that some forms of 'identity' are contingent, situational and instrumental (as typical in 'fluctuating modes of the self'), there is no self-evident rationale as to why, or justification of how, the concept of identity is necessary to explain individual's and group's multiple and fragmented perceptions and understandings of 'selves'. What some theorists and researches do here is invoke 'identity' to explain 'modernity', 'post-modernity' and other grand abstract concepts. Thus, one (reified) metaphor is used as a shortcut to explain the other (grand) abstraction.

This strategy leads to a very soft understanding of the concept which produces extreme vagueness and as such is empirically of very little value. If the concept of 'identity' is used theoretically to mean anything and everything (as in some works from post-structuralism and cultural studies) then it empirically means nothing.

To recap, neither one of the two original theoretical models (relative non-zero difference and absolute zero difference) and five conceptual approaches derived from them ('non-instrumental forms of social action', 'interactive and contingent products of social action', 'collective phenomenon of group sameness', 'deep and foundational forms of selfhood' and 'fluctuating and fragmented modes of the "self" ') to the study of identity has much analytical or heuristic legitimacy. On the one hand the concept is not indispensable nor necessary while on the other hand it is either vague and all-inclusive or reified and excessively inflexible.

'Identity' in space and time

The formalist conceptual origins of 'identity' have profound analytical implications for its use in social science. Despite the astonishing variety of uses to which 'identity' is put in contemporary sociology and beyond, this remains, as some researchers have recently started realising, a theoretically thin and unarticulated concept. As Bendle (2002: 1–4) rightly argues and documents it well on his analysis of Castells's and Giddens's theories, the leading accounts of identity are 'radically under-theorised and incapable of bearing the analytical load that the contemporary situation requires'. Instead of often invoked journalistic clichés such as 'identity crisis', what one encounters here is a conceptual crisis in sociology where sociological analyses are 'profoundly weakened by an excessive and uncritical reliance on what has become a politicised, residual and under-theorised concept'. A simple and crude assimilation of a formalist, and hence analytically intransigent concept, in many ways alien to sociology has created the environment where some sociological answers to contemporary problems differ little from popular common sense comprehension: 'it is all about identity crisis'. The contemporary resurgence of so-called identity politics is a good indicator of such an essentialist misuse of this concept where 'one's hidden injury becomes the ground for a claim of valued identity' (Rose, 1999: 268). In more extreme circumstances this form of reasoning leads to situations such as those of mass extermination in Rwanda and Bosnia (see Chapter 9) where as Helen Hintjens (2001) puts it 'identity becomes a knife'.

The recent and unprecedented popularity of this concept hides its historical novelty and geographical exclusivity. Despite some authoritative claims to the contrary (i.e Jenkins, 2004) 'identity' as well as its derivatives 'ethnic and national identity' have very specific and narrow spatial and temporal origins. As many anthropological studies show (e.g. Daniel, 1984, Roland, 1988, Ewing, 1990, Douglas, 1992) the concept of identity is largely a European and Western creation. Concepts such as 'self', 'personality', 'character' or 'person' carry a set of fairly distinct meanings and images in different social worlds. In many non-Western contexts human collectivities are not conceptualised as presuming a bounded sense of social or individual agency. Unlike the Western or European concept of identity which is profoundly individualist and visualises collective behaviour in an individual, conscious, purposeful way, many non-Europeans operate with a very different understanding of collective and individual action. Handler (1994: 31–3) gives examples of North American Indians whose conception of personhood is not confined to bounded and tangible self. Instead Ojibwa Indians perceive supernatural creatures, animals and even stones as being equivalent to human personality. No entity is conceived as finite and material, and a bear and a stone alike can transform into a human beings and vice versa. For this worldview the idea of personal or group demarcated identity may seem equally strange and bizarre as it may look incomprehensible and of no use. Similarly for Hopi Indians human thoughts are not located and enclosed within the confines of one's head but are rather visualised as floating openly in the outside world, on an equal footing not only with the thoughts and images of other creatures, but also the real creatures themselves: 'A Hopi would naturally suppose that his thought (or he himself) traffics with the ... corn plant ... that he is thinking about' (Handler, 1994: 31). Douglas (1992: 82–3) reports how Tellensi and many other West Africans conceive individuals as inborn multiple personalities 'whose component parts act like separate persons. One part of the personality speaks the life-course of the individual before he is born'. Geertz's (1973) example of the irrelevance of personal names in Bali where 'persons orient themselves to a divine and unchanging cosmic realm in which the details of an individual's unique personality have no importance' (Handler, 1994: 33) just confirms the geographical specificity of 'identity'. Many non-European social milieus operate with a concept of self that has very little in common with their modern European counterparts where 'identity' is conceptually located in a linear vision of time with the strong sense of continuity and progression and within concrete material boundaries.

In addition to its spatial exclusivity 'identity' has also very recent and thus limited temporal foundations. As Handler (1994), Baumeister (1986) and Bauman (1996, 2004) show 'identity' is largely an invention of the modern age. The decline of the feudal order, intensive industralisation, urbanisation, decline of religious authority and a parallel erosion of political legitimacy couched in terms of the divine origins of rulers have all had a decisive impact on the discovery of self. Modernity has diminished traditional social structure and its stable logic of differentiation and continuity. As Bendle (2002: 16) argues 'factors that underpinned a sense of continuity (geography, community, employment, class, etc.) were destabilised; whilst those that provided a sense of differentiation (ancestry, social rank, gender, moral virtue, religion, etc.) were delegitimised'. Hence 'identity' was born when traditional communal ties started to weaken, when old hierarchies started to collapse and when the sense of individuality was re-discovered as something valuable but also dynamic, mobile and creative. Industrial capitalism and secularisation have helped redirect attention away from the medieval obsession with an after-life to self-actualisation and the accomplishments of individual goals in earthly settings. Analysing Jane Austen's novels Handler and Seagal (1990, 1994) shows how understandings of social relations and a logic of individuality differ starkly in distinct historical epochs: there is no sense of 'identity' in late eighteenth- and early nineteenth-century England since this is 'a world in which individuality is complexly balanced with non-individualistic social forms of rank and patriarchal family' (Handler, 1994: 36). 'Identity' is a historical product of modernity which discovered the depths, potentials and ingenuity of the human self created on the ruins of the traditional order.

The fact that the origins of 'identity' are predominantly modern and Western tells us a great deal about the concept's wrongly assumed 'normality', its analytical fragility, and ultimately its dispensability. However it does not tell us much about the reasons for its near universal and worldwide popularity today. Further investigation is required: Why is this global appeal of 'identity' regularly articulated in ethno-national terms?

Ethnicity + nation + identity = ethnic and national identity?

This brief genealogy of 'identity' suggests a novel and in many respects unprecedented break in direction concerning the obsession with individual autonomy which characterised the birth of (European) modernity.

However despite its Enlightenment inspired preoccupation with the development and articulation of individuality, a unique sense of personhood or self-actualisation, the post-Enlightenment discourses of identity have for the most part acquired collectivist overtones. Instead of the individual 'discovery of the self', or psychological sense of personality, 'identity' has become associated with cultural, thus inevitably group-centric, difference. As clearly recognised now (i.e. Yack, 1996, Hall, 2002) it was not only a Romanticist backlash that was responsible for this articulation and later institutionalisation of cultural difference in uncompromising collectivist and exclusivist terms, the Enlightenment bears as much responsibility, since civic forms of group association were often as rigid. In other words despite its initial focus on individual autonomy and self-affirmation, the post-Enlightenment era gave birth to a variety of group centric discourses of identity. Among these diverse discourses associated with the representation of cultural difference two concepts stand out in terms of their influence on academic as well as public life – ethnic and national identity.

The common sense notions of 'ethnic and national identity' which are also widespread among some academics imply that ethnicity + identity = ethnic identity and nation + identity = national identity. In other words, all three concepts are seen as largely unproblematic and the simple mechanical addition of one to the other allows us to speak of and research 'ethnic or national identities'. Sometimes the distinction is made between ethnicity and ethnic identity or nation and national identity (i.e. Liebkind, 1989, Smith, 1999) but most often these concepts are used interchangeably (i.e. Cameron, 1999, Edensor, 2002, Kumar, 2003). However this is a deeply flawed strategy since, as with the concept of 'identity', so do the concepts of 'ethnicity' and 'nation' carry a lot of problematic baggage. Adding one profoundly problematic concept to another just as problematic idiom can only create more misunderstanding and confusion and prevent the pursuit of sober research. Similarly, treating them all as synonyms brings even more analytical turmoil. Before accounting for the difficulties of applying arduous constructions such as 'ethnic or national identity' (see Chapter 2) let us briefly explore the conceptual meanings of ethnicity and nation.

There is no need to look in great details at the etymological roots of these two concepts as this has been done on numerous occasions (Guibernau, 1996, Malešević, 2004, Smith, 2004). What is essential here is that despite their ancient origins in the Greek and Latin worlds and their sporadic use in the past, both concepts are, as with 'identity', fairly modern acquiring their contemporary meanings in the last two hundred (nation) or fifty years (ethnicity). They are also both, again as with 'identity', associated with a particular form of cultural difference and all three, as used in their contemporary parlance, are undoubtedly Western creations. Finally, despite their supposed straightforwardness and unproblematic use these two concepts, as with identity, have acquired multiple sets of meanings. As Uzelac (1999, 2006) and Fenton (2003) document there are dozens and dozens of (often mutually exclusive definitions) of nations and ethnicity. They range from objectivist to subjectivist (Renan), from cultural to political, from essentialist to existentialist from agency-centred to structure-centred. Outside academia, in popular and bureaucratic discourses there is also great variety of uses which are often dependent on geographical location, particular social context or historical contingencies (Hroch and Maleckova, 2001).

Thus, in the English speaking world nation and nationality are often used as synonyms for state or nominal citizenship, while in Central and Eastern Europe these terms imply symbolic or real link with ethnic ancestry. Thus what makes one British or French is the possession of a British or French passport and a degree of loyalty to their respective states whereas to be German or Croat one also requires at least one German or Croat grandmother. This situation is similar for ethnicity: the North American public regularly uses 'ethnicity' as a synonym for cultural minority with no salient physical group difference, where Italian or Polish Americans were defined as 'ethnic groups' while African Americans or Amerasians were denoted as 'racial groups'. Due to a very different historical heritage the European audience is more inclined to adopt ethnicity as a substitute for nationhood which is articulated in terms of a presumed commonality in shared territory or descent: what makes one Albanian is not determined by the place of her birth, be that Kosovo, Albania or Sweden, but by her ethnic origins, and living as Welsh or Scot in England does not make one necessarily an ethnic minority.

The problem with most definitions of ethnicity and nation and consequently with ethnic and national identity is their static view of something which is in fact an extremely dynamic set of relationships. Typical definitions of these two concepts list a set of required attributes that a social group has to possess in order to be deemed 'an ethnic group' or 'nation'. For example Bulmer (2001: 69–70) defines an ethnic group as 'a collectivity within larger society which has real or imagined common ancestry, memories of a shared historical past, and a cultural focus upon one or more common elements which distinguish the members of the group form other members of the society ... [and these] include: area of origin, language, religion, nationality, kinship patterns, physical appearance such as skin colour'. In a similar inflexible way Smith (2003a: 24–5) defines a nation as 'a named human population occupying an historic territory and sharing common myths and memories, a public culture, and common laws and customs for all members'. Both of these definitions operate with what Wolf (1982: 6) and after him Carrithers (1992) call a 'billiard ball view of social groups', that is they posit human collectivities as either-or fixed and overly structured entities with stable and almost unchangeable features. Does this mean that if a number of individuals who do not believe in common ancestry or memories of a shared past or do not actively participate in public culture, break common laws and do not observe common customs are by default cast outside of the particular ethnic group or nation? If this is so how come that in times of war or an 'ethnic' conflict one regularly encounters new leaders of ethnic groups and nations many of whom prior to the conflict were indifferent to law and custom, with little knowledge or interest in common myths and memories or public culture. For example the siege of Sarajevo in early 1990s reversed all social hierarchies with well-known street gangsters and criminals with no link with any ethnic or national movements and with no previous interest in ethnic politics, such as Jusuf Prazina-Juka, Musan Topalović-Caco and Ramiz Delalić-Ćelo, transformed overnight into national heroes and popular symbols of ethno-national resistance (Selimbegović, 2000).

Furthermore, do these definitions imply that if members of a group suddenly lose or change some of these attributes that the nation or an ethnic group has stopped being such a group? For example imagine a hypothetical case where a great majority of members of a particular nation subscribe to a myth of common descent which after successful and indisputable archaeological discovery turns out to be an absolute and incontrovertible fabrication. Let's say the common shared belief is that group's origins were traditionally traced back to Tumleks and after the archaeological discovery it becomes obvious that every single Tumlek was poisoned on 4 August 366. What happens then? Would that particular social collective stop being a nation? Of course it would not. Its historians and nation builders would quickly find an adequate replacement from an unlimited repertoire of potential myths and memories which would prove as good as the Tumlek origins of their nation. It is similar with common laws and public culture: the fact that German Democratic Republic and Federal Republic of Germany had incompatible legal systems and distinct public culture did not affect the well ingrained, and nineteenth century induced, collective perceptions that there is one single and indivisible German nation. The situation is almost identical with two Koreas.

These objectivist and objectifying definitions are extremely limited in accounting for diverse forms of cultural difference. Ethnic groups and nations are not billiard balls, they do not and could never exist on their own. They emerge as specific group labels in a particular moment of time and with a particular social and political reason. In both cases they ideologically cling on the notion of culture, whether as an anthropologically understood lived culture (culture as a distinct way of collective existence) in ethnic relations, or a socio-political understanding of high culture (culture as civilisational refinement expressed in artistic excellence) in nation-formation. What is vital here is to understand that instead of speaking of ethnic groups and nations as collective assets of a particular group and consequently about externally presumed 'ethnic and national identities' it is much more fruitful to treat these entities as categories of social practice. 'Ethnic group' and 'nation' just as 'ethnic and national identities' are not particularly useful concepts as they inevitably imply stability, rigidity and staticism which does not reflect the realities of the social world. Instead as Brubaker (1998, 2004) cogently argues it is more useful to talk about 'ethnicity without groups', or about nationess as set of contingencies, discursive frames, political projects or organisational routines. Just as ethnicity is not a group but a form of social relationship, similarly nationess is a dynamic set of historically framed processes. This is not to say that there are no objective cultural differences in the world of humans. Of course there are. It is precisely because cultural differences are so real and so vivid that they can easily become objects of ethnicisation and nationalism. For unlike cultures which are complex expressions of real human differences (i.e. distinct ways of collective existence) ethnicity is not, as Blumer and many others wrongly suggest, the expression of objective characteristics such as language, religion or origin. Similarly ethnicity is not the representation of a nebulous 'ethnic identity'. Ethnicity is, as I have argued elsewhere (Malešević, 2004), politicised social action, a process whereby elements of real, actual, lived cultural differences are politicised in the context of intensive group interaction. Ethnicity is not a synonym for cultural diversity as a great majority of our cultural practices and beliefs are rarely if ever politicised. Whereas culture is about real, lived collective difference, ethnicity is often about segments of that broad cultural repertoire which does not have to be real or lived experience. In an intensive social conflict just as in milder forms of group competition, as Weber (1968) was well aware, any cultural trait can become politicised and hence serve as an object of group mobilisation.

For nationess this is even more so, being a peculiar and novel historical creation. Nation is not, as some analysts (i.e van den Berghe, 1981, 2005: 115) suggest simply a politicised ethnicity. Not only is such an understanding tautological given that ethnicity is already a politicised culture, but more importantly such a view does not clearly distinguish between the near universal and trans-historical processes of politicisation of collective difference at work in all ethnic relations, and the historically specific series of events and practices that characterise nation-formation. Nationess is a complete historical and profoundly contingent novelty, a complex process whereby a patch of relatively arbitrary territory becomes firmly demarcated, centrally organised and run while simultaneously growing into an indisputable source of authority and group loyalty for the great majority of those who inhabit it. Nationhood is a modern ideological construct reinforced equally by the institutions of the modern state (education system, mass media, public culture) as well as by civil society and family and kinship networks. The fact that something is ideological does not imply that is false. On the contrary as Gellner (1983) rightly points out modern human beings are sincere in their nationalist feelings. Nationalism is a powerful political ideology that although dependent on continuous institutional reinforcement does not go against the grain of public opinion. However this has little to do with some mystically ingrained 'identity' and a great deal with the socio-historical context of post-Westphalian world where not being national is scarcely an option any more. In other words, nationalism is not as Connor (2005: 40) claims 'identity and loyalty to the nation', it is the particular, historically created, ideological condition that most human beings now find themselves in. There is nothing normal or self-evident to it. It is a symptom of a particular historical epoch and an indicator of a particular direction that modernity took at the end of eighteenth century. Thus when Smith (2001b: 30) defines national identity as 'the maintenance and continuous reproduction of the patterns of values, symbols, memories, myths and traditions that compose the distinctive heritage of nations, and the identifications of individuals with that particular heritage and those values, symbols, memories, myths and traditions', he provides us with an almost tautological statement with little heuristic value. National identity is linked to the maintenance and reproduction of values that compose national heritage, yet it is far from clear who does the 'maintenance and reproduction' as well as who decides what a 'heritage of nation' is. What does it mean when individuals make a claim of identifying with a particular national heritage? Such a static definition does not make obvious that there are always different individual and inter-group understandings of what and how it means to be a Serb or Norwegian; it also does not make apparent that there are different intensities of such feeling or that there are different individual or social contexts that certain feelings inspire which at the surface may all look the same. Furthermore the expressions of popular pride in national heritage can also be no more than stereotypical answers of conformity with the dominant ideological narrative that nationalism is; or a banal expression of inertia of everyday routine and habit. Such a definition tells us little about the real depth of such individual or collective sentiment (about the relationship between cognitive, affective and conative rationale behind this view); or it can be just an expression of plain instrumentalism. Most of all such understanding of 'national identity' is overly inward looking and too psychological as it presumes that expressions of particular views and feelings are uncontaminated by the workings of state institutions, civil society movements and influences of other forms of social structure.

Therefore as with 'identity', 'ethnicity' and 'nation' contain a multiplicity of meanings. The plasticity and ambiguity of the concepts allows for deep misunderstandings as well as political misuses. However, unlike 'identity' ethnicity and nation have also acquired legislative and institutional underpinnings through formulations such as 'ethnic minority', 'ethnic group', 'nationhood' or 'nationality' which have had even more destructive effects. Institutionalised and bureaucratised definitions of the situation such as the idea that a particular individual legally belongs to an 'ethnic minority' or one 'ethnic group' or nation, for instance as formulated in census, passports and other state and inter-state and UN documents, not only reifies group and individual relations which are always dynamic, but it also becomes a form of oppression by caging individuals into involuntary associations. In such a situation cultural difference which is by definition mobile, flexible and hazy is arrested and codified, thus preventing social change. Hence most popular and legislative understandings of ethnicity and nation are severely problematic since they operate with unsociological views of cultural difference perceiving it from the inside out. It is assumed, as Bulmer's definition testifies, that social groups possess different cultural characteristics which make them unique and distinct (common language, life style, descent, religion or physical markers). In such a perspective culture is perceived as something relatively or firmly stable, persistent and definite. Cultural difference is viewed in terms of a group's property (e.g. Germans posses a distinct culture to that of Serbs). However since the publication of F. Barth's 'Ethnic Groups and Boundaries' (1969) and more recently Brubaker's vigorous conceptual criticisms (1996, 1998, 2004) of the terminology used in this field, social science is adopting radically different concepts of ethnicity and nationess. Barth stood the traditional understanding of cultural difference on its head, that is, he defined and explained ethnicity from the outside in: it is not the 'possession' of cultural characteristics that makes social groups distinct but rather the social interaction with other groups that makes that difference possible, visible and socially meaningful. Brubaker (2004: 3) has expanded this view even further by attacking the clichéd constructivism which dominates the analyses of cultural difference where one finds 'constructivist and groupist language casually conjoined' and where some academics are ridden by tension of maintaining their scholarly cool headedness while simultaneously shifting to essentialist foundationalism that political mobilisation requires. It is almost impossible to uphold this 'dual orientation of many academic identitarians as both analysts and protagonists of identity politics' (Brubaker, 2004: 33).

Therefore, popular and legislative understandings of ethnicity which are unfortunately shared by some academics in their attempt to research 'ethnic and national identities' have little analytical value. When ethnicity is understood in a reflexive way as a meeting point of social action rather than in terms of hard cultural contents, than the contrived construction 'ethnic identity' makes very little sense. Similarly when nationess is conceptualised as a set of historically articulated and still ongoing process of ideological construction instead of some presumably fixed and everlasting attachments to symbols of national heritage then there is no need for 'national identity'. A claim to possessing 'ethnic or national identity' is by definition an essentialist claim which aims to simultaneously reify all three categories – 'identity', 'ethnicity' and 'nation'. This problem is perhaps most discernible in attempts to operationalise and apply the concepts of 'ethnic and national identity' in empirical research which will be analysed in the next chapter. However before that an explanation is required to address the question: Why have problematic concepts such as identity, together with its derivatives, ethnic and national identity, acquired an almost unquestioned popularity? Though Brubaker (2004) provides us with a powerful criticism of identitarianism in practice he does not tell us much about the sociological reasons for such popularity.

Why such popularity?

Although, as argued in this chapter, the concepts of ethnic and national identity appear to be theoretically and conceptually deficient one cannot dispute their astonishing popularity within and outside of academia. Although the concept of identity gained prominence from the 1960s, it was really in the late 1980s and through the 1990s to the beginning of this century that 'identity' acquired an almost hegemonic position in both academic and popular discourse. While mass media and scholarly journals and books made very sporadic references to 'identity' or 'ethnic identity' in the 1940s and 1950s, today it is impossible to skim through articles, news bulletins or books on cultural or political difference without noticing hundreds and often thousands of references to 'identity'. Although, as demonstrated above, there was a sociological call for 'identity' as early as the nineteenth century, the recognition of such a concept had to wait until the end of the twentieth century for 'identity' to became a dominant concept in both popular and academic discourse. This fact in itself begs a question: Why has such clearly ambiguous concept become so dominant in popular and academic discourse at this time?

There are probably many sociological and historical reasons why the concept of identity has acquired such a dominant position. However, I will focus here only on one which I consider to be the most important. The astonishing popularity of the concept comes primarily from the fact that 'identity' has historically and ideologically filled the role that the three other major social concepts have vacated – the concepts of 'race' 'national character' and 'social consciousness'.

The master ideological concept used to make sense of human difference and similarity from the late eighteenth until the first half of the twentieth century was the concept of 'race'. Charles Linne's was the first use of the concept in an academic and rigorous way to produce the following (at the time influential) typology of human races: (1) Americans – reddish, obstinate, and regulated by custom; (2) Europeans – white, gentle, and governed by law; (3) Asians – sallow, severe, and ruled by opinion; and (4) Africans – black, crafty, and governed by caprice (Wolf, 1994: 4). What Linne started, in his use of quasi-biological concepts to define, select and order human difference, the social science of the nineteenth and early twentieth century developed to perfection. As Banton (1983: 35–50) explains the use of the concept 'race' has shifted from the initial emphasis on descent to taxonomic and eventually explanatory level: it was very much the responsibility of scientific discourse that race became conceived as a stable, permanent, definite and unchangeable biological and cultural entity. De Gobineau, Lubbock, Morton, Knox and other 'scientific racists' perceived races as different species (in a zoological sense) and had a belief that a 'person's outward appearance was an indicator of his place in a natural order'. Darwin's theory of evolution only strengthened the authority of 'a scientific concept of race', while social Darwinism co-opted the concept for the social sciences and more general use. Banton (1983: 52) and Dickens (2000) document how the concepts of race and racial inequality were dominating public discourse of the nineteenth and early twentieth century and how very few if any intellectuals were immune to belief in the superiority of their ('white') race. The general belief was that one should 'preserve racial hygiene', races had to be 'maintained' and their purity 'attained', it was seen as legitimate to 'fight for one's race' or to 'awaken racial consciousness'. It was only the military defeat of the Nazi state and its racist ideology that has largely delegitimised academic and consequently popular concepts of race. Although the term has survived the Second World War and is still used it has lost most of the scientific and popular appeal it had before the Second World War. Post-Nuremberg world had to look for and adopt another social concept that would deal with cultural and physical difference and would at the same time dissociate their users from any resemblance to the Nazi project.

In the 1950s and 1960s there was no clear winner to replace 'race' – whereas the European and left-leaning intellectuals and after them journalists, and the general public in the Eastern (but also in Western) Europe, switched to the new ideological master concept of 'social consciousness', centre and right wing intellectuals as well as the general public in America opted for the ideological master concept of 'national character'.

Just as 'race' these two concepts provided enough elasticity to cover many distinct processes and forms of cultural, political or physical difference. The Hegelian/Marxist inspired idea of 'social consciousness' gained prominence together with the discourse of class politics. While racial unity and racial consciousness were now seen as dangerous concepts, proletarian unity and class consciousness were not only accepted but also considered highly desirable ideas throughout the communist and many parts of non-communist Europe. Following Marx it was regularly argued that classes can fully exist only when they develop 'full class consciousness' (class 'fuer sich' as opposed to class 'an sich'). Class consciousness and workers unity had to be 'awakened', 'attained' and 'maintained'. One had to fight using revolutionary means to 'preserve and acquire' social consciousness. Class consciousness was also regarded as superior to 'national consciousness'. Marcuse (1964) and other Frankfurt School theorists believed that capitalism and mass culture produce 'false needs' and false, or in Marcuse's terms 'unhappy consciousness', and that proletariat and other disadvantaged groups have to liberate themselves to discover their 'true consciousness'.

Similarly, following the influential culture-and-personality school of anthropology (M. Mead, R. Benedict) the concept of 'national character' has largely replaced race in a quasi-biological sense in America in the 1960s. As Gleason (1983: 24) emphasises

> the new era of scientifically respectable study of national character was inaugurated in WW II by a group of scholars who were called upon by agencies of the United States government to apply their skills to such questions as how civilian morale could best be maintained or what kind of propaganda could be most effectively employed against the enemy.

The term caught on in the public eye and academics, politicians and journalists embraced phrases such as 'national character has to be preserved', that nations strongly differ in terms of their 'characters', McCarthy's Committee on Non-American Activities revealed how 'communism is not part of an American national character', one had again 'to fight for the true national character', and prove ones worth by being 'a part of American national character', and so on.

Although fairly different the ideological master concepts of 'social consciousness' and 'national character' had a great deal in common. They were both vague and inclusive enough to accommodate many distinct processes, events or social actors and as such quickly secured popularity. They both answered the need of the Cold War politics to present a unified front to the enemy by perceiving its citizens as closely bound by singular and clearly recognisable will – 'we all maybe different individuals but we all share an American/British/French national character' or 'Soviet class consciousness is above petty individual differences'. As such these concepts were both also deeply collectivist, analytically inflexible and strongly prone to reification. Hence, whereas the master concept of 'race' was now abandoned in form (rejecting only the term) it fully persisted in its content, meaning and function – as 'character' or 'consciousness'.

With the emergence of youth, ethnic, gender and other radical politics in the late 1960s and 1970s in the West and Gorbachev's policies of openness in the East in the mid-1980s the domination of 'the national character' and 'social consciousness' has started to erode. The new social movements could not easily fit into the old Cold War concepts of class and nation-state. 'Identity' politics was slowly taking over. The absolute collapse of communist ideology and the break-up of supranational federal states in Eastern Europe has ultimately delegitimised the notions of class consciousness in the East and of stable and predictable national character in the West. 'Identity' emerged as a new and an all-inclusive ideological master concept to simultaneously define and 'explain' the current situation of dramatic social change. The popularity of this master concept has come exactly from its ambiguity and ability to accommodate different processes, structures, actions and events. 'Identity' provided an illusion that dramatic social change was under control: we know what is happening – 'only people are fighting to preserve, awake, maintain etc. their identities'. Identity has thus emerged as a grand umbrella term to contain all the unexplained and constantly emerging phenomena of our times in a single word. 'Identity' transpired as a simple universal answer to all unanswered complexities and problems of contemporary social life.

As with 'race', 'national character' or 'social consciousness', 'identity' possesses elasticity and aloofness, quickly making sense of difference and similarity. 'Identity' and its derivatives, ethnic and national identity, have today become a legitimate political tool in the academic and popular discourse just as 'race' was at the end of nineteenth and the beginning of the twentieth century and as 'national character' and 'social consciousness' were during the Cold War. This time again the form ('national character/social consciousness') has been sacrificed to the content. One communitarian, reifying, stultifying concept has just been replaced with another similar one.

Furthermore, the vagueness and aloofness of this ideological master concept corresponds even more with the times than the previous three master concepts. 'Identity' is a fuzzy term for fuzzy times. The speed and intensity of social and political change has prevented development of more analytical, more precise or empirically useful concepts. In the postmodern spirit of these times every social problem is easily and quickly labelled and 'explained' as an identity problem, and since it is now commonly acknowledged (at least in academia) that identities are fluid, complex, multiple and dynamic, then no full explanation of this or that social problem is possible. 'Identity' is a tautology for our times.

However, what is important to emphasise here is that just as 'race', 'national character', or 'social consciousness', 'identity' is not an innocent concept. Exactly as 'race' was uncritically borrowed from biology where the theory of evolution was crudely applied to the world of humans to justify political goals – colonialism or Nazi expansion, and 'national character' and 'social consciousness' were borrowed from medicine (psychiatry in particular) and used to delegitimise ideological (class or national) enemies, so was 'identity' appropriated from mathematics and logics to serve ideological goals. These goals may now be multiple – to acquire political autonomy or an independent state for an ethnic group ('to maintain cultural identity'), to gain the power or to uphold the political status quo in the state ('to attain or keep democratic political identity'), to win the public or media support against the asylum seekers ('to preserve national identity') and so on, but the reason for this appropriation remains as before, political. Individuals and groups are still politically mobilised to fight for, to die or to kill for the preservation and defence of their 'identities' just as they were for the protection of racial hygiene or class unity.

Conclusion

Most general studies of identity emphasise that identity implies sameness and difference at the same time. So, for example, Jenkins (1996: 3–4) argues that 'the notion of identity simultaneously establishes two possible relations of comparison between persons and things: similarity, on the one hand, and difference, on the other'. And indeed this is exactly what the original mathematical and logical meaning of the terms is all about. However, as argued in this chapter, the definitional simplicity and seductive crispness of the concept as developed in analytical philosophy, logics and mathematics is, for better or worse, unachievable in social sciences. Both attempts to transfer the concept, either in its original mathematical way or in a more popular metaphoric manner, have proved futile. The term 'identity' (as well as its derivatives 'ethnic' or 'national identity') covers too much ground to be analytically useful. Instead of theoretical and methodological clarity the concept has brought upon us more confusion and opened up a door for possible manipulation. Its conceptual ambiguity prevents clear and transparent operationalisation which, as we will see in Chapter 2, has profound methodological implications, whereas its methodological aloofness leads to analytical paralysis. And finally its quasi-scientific use through popular appeal has a potential for devastating political outcomes. The enormous popularity of this concept is to be located in its ability to summarise the state of unbridled self in an age of high modernity. This summary of self with all its ambiguities and uncertainties provides an imaginary sense of control and direction in a world 'gone mad'.

'Identity' is no more than a common name for many different and distinct processes that need to be explained. Wrapping all these diverse forms of action, events, actors under a single expression can only generate more misunderstanding and will not help us in any way to explain the extraordinary social change that has been taking place in a last few decades. 'Identity' is an ill-suited concept for such a giant task.

2
An Operational Phantom

Introduction

Chapter 1 explored briefly the conceptual origins and the current use to which idioms of ethnic and national identity are placed in sociology and beyond the academic world. The analysis established that the notion of 'identity' in most of its contemporary uses suffers from acute conceptual weaknesses – it is either utilised in a restricted and essentialist or an all-embracing and vague way – which makes it dispensable and possibly redundant as a categorical apparatus for sociological analysis. However, indicating conceptual flaws may not be sufficient in discrediting what has become a highly popular. Indeed many sociological concepts from 'culture', 'state', 'community' to 'socialisation' or 'capitalism' have endured a much longer history of contention and remain a regular feature of sociological analyses. As Jenkins (2004: 9) argues identity has become 'an established part of the sociological tool kit' and cannot be easily discarded. A more damning critique would be to show that ethnic and national identities are concepts of limited use in empirical research. The aim of this chapter is to do exactly that – to demonstrate that neither of the two dominant research traditions (quantitative-empiricist and qualitative-interpretativist/historicist) generated successful operational models to 'measure' ethnic and national identity. This is not to say that astonishing amount of research done in this field is of little use. On the contrary, many studies of this kind have produced important findings and have collected precious information on the nature of ethnicity and nationess. What is questioned here is the claim on the part of some researchers working in this field that they can investigate or measure ethnic and national identity.

37

The first part of this chapter explores some representative attempts at quantitative analysis of 'ethnic identities' while the second part addresses a range of qualitative endeavours to study 'national identities'. Thus the focus of the first section is on the ability to utilise very strict methodological procedures of sampling, surveying or validation in order to develop reliable and testable tools to generate verifiable findings on the nature of 'ethnic identity'. This research strategy is a direct offshoot of the original logical and mathematical understanding of identity which operates with a strict and formalist conceptualisation. The qualitative tradition of research is its epistemological counterpart where the principal strategy of analysis is historical, comparative or metaphorical-interpretative, and where the ambition is not to produce statistically reliable and testable hypotheses but to pinpoint and investigate what is typical and substantial about 'national identities'.

In this chapter I argue that although these studies do tell us a great deal about ethnic relations and nationalism they are unable to generate, as they often claim, any specific findings on 'ethnic or national identities'. The chapter attempts to demonstrate that since neither one of the two research strategies is very productive then we are left with the decision to either abandon the concept of (ethnic and national) identity – which due to its enormous popularity is probably unrealistic – or demote its status as a major research tool in sociological theory and empirical practice.

Gauging 'ethnic identity': the poverty of quantitative strategy

The conceptual problems which arise in the use of 'identity' and thus 'ethnic and national identity' discussed in Chapter 1 have a direct bearing on the research strategies and methodology. In other words, in order to explain, analyse and 'measure' identity claims one needs to have a clearly defined understanding of what identity is. Generally speaking quantitative empirical studies on identity and ethnic and national identities are for the most part conducted relying on strictly formulated social surveys. A great number of surveys on 'identity' claims were devised and under-taken on the basis of common sense assumptions of identity, as if this is unproblematic. A typical example is the highly influential and often cited study by J. Linz and A. Stepan (1992, 1996) on national and ethnic identities in Spain, Soviet Union and Yugoslavia. The main argument of the authors (the crucial importance of holding first democratic elections at the all state/federal level before the regional ones for the preservation of multiethnic states emerging from the authoritarian regimes) is based on the results of a survey employing simplified and stereotypical distinctions; more specifically the authors draw their conclusions about the salience of ethnic and national identities on the basis of respondents answers to questions such as the following: 'Do you feel proud of being Spanish, Catalan or Basque?'. The authors obviously operate on one hand with a very strict and essentialist concept of ethno/national identity as something everybody necessarily possesses and on the other the entire concept has been reduced to a single variable – 'being proud of'. Why should this particular variable be regarded as measuring 'identity' at all and not the intensity (proud-ness) of being a member of a particular category/group? If identity is to be understood as a complex set of processes articulating an individual and/or collective sense of similarity and difference (as defined by Jenkins, 2004, or Bauman, 2004) then how can one make such sweeping generalisations about multifaceted human condition on the basis of a single idiomatic question? And furthermore how do we know that the respondents's answers are not just a stereotypical, routine or inertia driven reaction to a most colloquial query? Even if one intends to find out about the intensity of 'being proud to be Spanish' this information can certainly not be acquired from a single question.

However this example is only the tip of the iceberg. Most quantitative oriented research on 'ethnic identity' focuses on identifying a degree of individual attachment to a particular group. Relying on these results sees many researchers making unsubstantiated claims about existence, salience or strength of ethnic identities. Some of these studies focus on a single ethnic collectivity (i.e. Paul and Fischer, 1980, Parham and Helms, 1981), while others attempt to identify the differences between levels of commitment to one's ethnic group among individuals with diverse ethnic backgrounds (i.e. Phinney, 1992 and Phinney and Alipuria, 1996, M.S. Spencer *et al.*, 2000). Nevertheless both types of research are predominantly concerned with the intensity of group attachment and only sporadically, if at all, analyse the form, content or structure of such attachments. Hence one can find out whether 'Latinos' have lower 'ethnic identity scores' than 'Blacks' or 'Asians' or vice versa without learning much at all about the types and forms that ethnic identification can take. Such a rigid positivist approach to the study of 'ethnic identity' operates with an extremely narrow understanding of cultural difference and an individual or collective sense of belonging. When 'ethnic identity' is conceptualised in such crude terms – you are or you are not Latino or Black or Asian or whatever – there is no space for identifying and analysing subtle forms of individual and group self-perceptions. Such rigid 'either-or' or 'to what degree' models are unable to analytically deal with different individual or collective, external or internal understandings of Blackness, Latinoness, etc. the result being that one can set such approaches aside. Hence in order to illustrate the difficulties involved in employing the concept of 'ethnic identity' in social research one has to engage with more ambitious theoretical and operational attempts which take the many subtleties of cultural difference into account. The following analysis will concentrate on two such models – Peter Wenreich's concept of ethnic identity and Wsevolod W. Isajiw's model of ethnic identity retention – demonstrating that even such comprehensive models are doomed to fail.

Ethnic identity 1: Weinreich

Peter Weinreich has designed a metatheoretical framework which builds on numerous influential psychoanalytical, sociological and psychological theories of identity: the social identity theory of H. Tajfel and J. Turner, symbolic interactionism of G.H. Mead and E. Goffman, psychodynamic approach of E. Eriksen and J. Marcia, and personal construct theory of M. Mair and D. Bannister. Weinreich argues that a universal grand theory of ethnic identity which would explain all forms of individual and collective identification is not possible, and he thus proposes the use of this 'open meta-theoretical framework' which in his view is able to provide 'an empirically grounded particular theory' for the study of ethnic identity (Weinreich 1986: 315). Such a theoretical framework provides for the operationalisation and development of a concrete set of research instruments, termed as Weinreich Identity Structure Analysis, designed to measure the salience and strength of individual and group attachments[3]. In Weinreich's (1983: 151) theoretical framework the concept of identity stands for 'the totality of one's self-construal, in which how one construes oneself in the present expresses the continuity between how one construes oneself as one was in the past and how one construes oneself as one aspires to be in the future'. Furthermore, drawing on Tajfel and Turner's (1979) social identity theory he sees individuals as always attempting to develop a positive sense of self-identity by seeing their in-groups more favourably than the out-groups. He also accepts social identity theory's understanding of ethnic identity as an element of a broader social identity that every individual possesses. Thus, Weinreich (1986: 308) defines ethnic identity in direct relation to general social identity arguing that ethnic identity is 'that part of the totality of one's self-construal made up of those dimensions that express the continuity between one's construal of past ancestry and one's future aspirations in relation to ethnicity'. In this approach there is a clear accent placed on the temporal dimension of one's self-conception of ethnic identity. This is visible from the definition's stress on both past (the construal of ethnic ancestry) and future (the construal of one's aspirations).

With the application of this model and especially with the operationalisation of Weinreich's definition of ethnic identity I have aimed to ascertain the possible links between an individual's awareness of their ethnic ancestry and their individual aspirations. Analysing the data gathered after conducting a survey on a representative sample of university students in Zagreb (Croatia) I have identified four distinct perceptions on respondent's ethnic ancestry ranging from strong affective identification with the ethnic ancestors to ignoring the links with ethnic ancestors (Malešević, 1993)[4] (see Table 2.1). The surveys also yielded six diverse orientations on respondents' individual aspirations/ life aims ranging from altruism as a main life goal to aspiration to consumerism and property ownership (see Table 2.2). However the statistically significant links between the two dimensions have proved to be fairly weak indicating the presence of a single type of 'ethnic identity' which was named descriptively as 'the identity of ethnic altruism', connecting together a factor of 'strong affective identification with the ethnic ancestors' on the one hand with a factor of 'altruism as a main life goal' on the other (see Table 2.3).

Table 2.1   Attitudes towards the ethnic ancestors (four orientations)

1. *Strong affective identification with the ethnic ancestors* – includes high support for statements that express the belief in strong links with ancestors on the basis of having common motherland, common blood and sacred territory; common spiritual unity of one's ethnic group, deep spiritual and cultural identity, the belief in the same god; common aims; common glorious history and tradition.

2. *Ignoring the links with ethnic ancestors* – includes high support for statements that express the belief in weak or non-existent links with ancestors with the only connection being speaking the same language and/or inhabiting the same territory, having no direct connection with ethnic ancestry, asserting more differences than similarities, having only accidental link with ancestors, or maintaining only a respect for ancestors and nothing more.

3. *Ritualistic identification with ethnic ancestors (non-affective identification)* – includes high support for statements that express the belief in moderate links with ancestors on the basis of having common customs, common tradition, culture and the same way of life and maintaining only a respect for ancestors and nothing more.

4. *Elements of the biological identification with ethnic ancestors* – includes high support for statements that express the belief in strong links with ancestors on the basis of having common genetic code, same way of life, common temperament, common blood and sacred territory, and the eternal motherland.

Table 2.2   Life aims/aspirations (six orientations)

1. *Altruism as a main life goal* – includes high support for values such as: to sacrifice for others, to help people when in trouble, to struggle for peace, justice and equality and to be honest.

2. *Aspiration to consumerism and property ownership* – includes high support for values such as: to be very rich, to spend a lot of money, to posses a car, villa and yacht, to be powerful, to drink fine and expensive drinks, to smoke high quality cigarettes, to be famous, to work as little as possible.

3. *An orientation to family values* – includes high support for values such as: to have children, to raise children so they would become responsible adults, to marry, to have good relations within the family, to be honest, to have clean consciousness.

4. *Knowledge and creativity oriented aspiration* – includes support for values such as: to persistently learn and acquire new knowledge; to leave something valuable to the future generations, to fight the problems and achieve successes in that way.

5. *Ecological-humanistic orientation* – includes high support for values such as: to care about nature, to fight for peace, justice and equality, to stay healthy, to be honest, to help people when in trouble, to have clean consciousness.

6. *Respect for the elementary ethical principles* – includes high support for values such as: to have clean consciousness, to be free and independent from others, to have strong life principles, to be honest, to raise children so they would become responsible adults, to have good relations within the family, and to help others.

Table 2.3   Types of 'ethnic identity' (one orientation)

1. *The identity of ethnic altruism* – includes strong positive correlation between 'altruism as a main life goal' and 'strong affective identification with the ethnic ancestors'.

Ethnic identity 2: Isajiw

The questionnaire used in the same set of surveys also included a research instrument derived from Wsevolod W. Isajiw's (1990) model of ethnic identity retention. Isajiw (1974:122) defines ethnic groups as involuntary associations 'who share the same culture or to descendants of such people who identify themselves and/or are identified by others as belonging to the same involuntary group'. In his model the emphasis is placed on two key determinants of individual and collective behaviour: identity and the social organisation of a particular group. While identity includes a subjective sense of historical importance and provides individuals with feelings of belonging to a particular community, social organisation establishes the concrete institutional frame for the existence of ethnic groups. In this functionalist model ethnic identity is related to the individuals' psychological self-conceptualisation relative to their ethnic origins and the range of social systems that constitute their social environment. This self-location also incorporates individuals' psychological relation to the other individuals including their locations and relations towards these social systems. In this sense an ethnic identity is understood as the degree of an individual's socialisation within the particular ethnic collective which is mostly dependent on the relative value attached to ethnic ancestries who are perceived as the real or symbolic members of that ethnic group.

For Isajiw ethnic identity comprises a number of internal and external segments. Whereas internally ethnic identities are supported by cognitive, ethical and affective attachments, external bonds can be inferred from socio-cultural behaviour. Thus cognitive aspects of ethnic identity include self-images, knowledge of one's own group, knowledge of the group's own heritage and historical past as well as the knowledge of group's common values. Ethical aspects relate to an individual's sense of group obligations such as passing on native language skills, ethnic endogamy or ethnic nepotism. Affective aspects include feelings of attachment to the group where the most important are the feeling of security and sympathy and the feeling of safety and comfort within the confines of one's own culture as well as the opposition to accepting the cultural traits of other groups or societies (Isajiw 1990: 36).

Unlike internal aspects of ethnic identity which are dependent on an individual's subjective sentiments, external features of ethnic identity are discernible in one's social behaviour. Thus, observation of whether an individual speaks a mother tongue, regularly practises cultural traditions, participates in ethnic group networks, more institutionalised ethnic associations, in voluntary ethnic organisations or other ethnic group sponsored activities is, according to Isajiw, a good indicator of the objective aspects of ethnic identity retention. Different combinations made up from a variety of these internal and external segments of identification are seen as constituents of different types of ethnic identity. For example 'negative images of one's own ethnic group, accompanied by a high degree of awareness of one's ethnic ancestry' are seen as an indicator of 'identity of resistance/revolt'. This ethnic identity type stands in stark contrast to the 'ritualistic ethnic identity' which is characterised by

Table 2.4   Types of 'ethnic identity' (three orientations)

1. Ritualistic-affective based ethnic identity – includes high support for values such as the practice of ethnic endogamy, adherence to ethnic traditions, sacrifice for the ethnic group, teaching one's children the customs and rites of the ethnic group, feeling safer and more protected within the limits of the ethnic community, the practice of ethnic rituals and rites, visits to the ethnic institutions, ethnic friendship, parading of ethnic flags and emblems and the active participation in ethnic events.

2. Identity of rebellion/non-ethnic identity – includes high support for values such as – showing no interest in the ethnic group's history, feeling no obligation towards own ethnic group, expressing no emotional attachment towards own ethnic community and trying to avoid contacts with own ethnic group.

3. Cognitive ethnic identity – includes high support for values such as to know common values that are part of the ethnic group's heritage, historical events, myths and stories related to the ethnic group's past as well as to teach children the customs and rites and sacrifice for the good of the ethnic group.

a high level of retention of particular ethnic traditions and a low level of feelings of collective obligation.

Just as with Weinreich's concept, Isajiw's model allows for the exploration of ethnic group identifications based on different aspects of group membership. Thus I have operationalised and employed this model on the same population to empirically identify the existence of distinct types of 'ethnic identity'. To my surprise the research generated three distinct dominant types of 'ethnic identity' named as: the ritualist-affective based ethnic identity, cognitive ethnic identity and identity of rebellion or non-ethnic identity (Malešević, 1994, Malešević and Malešević, 2001)[5] (see Table 2.4) which were very different to the results generated from Wienreich's model. Furthermore, the sum of arithmetic means for the first four variables in each factor also indicates that the dominant type of 'ethnic identity' for this particular population at the time of this survey was cognitive ethnic identity (Malešević, 1994:48). This was a far cry from the results obtained using Weinreich's model.

Where is the problem?

As with most positivist oriented research, the two models presented here start from the premise that social reality is something objective and real, discernible through our senses and detectable through meticulous research. In other words they start from the assumption that 'ethnic identities' exist as such and what is needed is only to perfect our research tools so that one is able to single out the exact types of ethnic identity that exist within a particular population. Following core empiricist propositions they begin from the supposition that 'ethnic identity' represents a universal aspect of the human condition which nevertheless exhibits a possible variety of patterns. In this perspective 'ethnic identity' is taken for granted so that what needs to be studied is simply the structure of existing contents and the particular nature and direction of their patterning. That is, both of the models presented here start from exactly the same assumption – there is such a thing as 'ethnic identity' and to capture the exact form and content of existing ethnic identities one needs only to deductively formulate an adequate theoretical model which would provide for the conceptual mapping of the entire field of 'ethnic identities'. Thus both models in their conceptual and operational forms are devised to measure exactly the same thing and to answer exactly the same questions: How many types of ethnic identity are there in this particular population? What kind of ethnic identities exist in this population? Which is a dominant type of ethnic identity for this population?

The survey outcome indicates that although two relatively complex and thorough conceptual models were directed at the same object and applied to the same sample in the same questionnaire, they generated not only very different but also contradictory results on the nature of 'ethnic identity' (see Table 2.5). While Weinreich's model indicates that there is only one dominant type of ethnic identity expressed among Zagreb university students – the identity of ethnic altruism, Isajiw's model points to three very different types of ethnic identity for the same population – ritualistic-affective, cognitive and non-ethnic identity. Whereas the survey results from Isajiw's model suggest that cognitive 'ethnic identity' prevails among the Zagreb students (e.g. knowledge of the ethnic groups heritage, history, mythology and passing those values to posterity), Weinreich's model indicates something completely

Table 2.5 Types of 'ethnic identity'

Model 1 (one type)	Model 2 (three types)
The identity of ethnic altruism	Ritualistic-affective based ethnic identity.
	Identity of rebellion/non-ethnic identity.
	Cognitive ethnic identity.

different – that the dominant type of 'ethnic identity' for this population is 'identity of ethnic altruism' which is predominantly composed of
affective attachments (e.g. common blood, sacred territory, spiritual unity
with ethnic ancestry).

The outcome indicates that despite their own claims and intentions to
measure 'ethnic identity', the two models 'gauge' two fairly different
things. But more importantly this research outcome also exposes the
profoundly vague nature of the concept which allows for almost
anything to hide under the gigantic and porous conceptual umbrella
called 'identity', more specifically 'ethnic identity'. All the conceptual
problems that surround 'identity' and 'ethnic identity' explored in the
first chapter of this book find their full reflection in operational
attempts to use the concept in the empirical world. Since 'ethnic identity' is so conceptually ambiguous and plastic it allows for adaptation in
very diverse research models. Whereas this conceptual ambiguity could
perhaps be seen as an advantage in qualitative research, it is nothing less
than a catastrophe for the quantitative research tradition. Simple excuses
of a kind that allow for the coexistence of models that supposedly
measure different aspects of the 'identity' phenomenon could only
support the relativistic claim that truth is socially constructed and that
social reality is not so objective after all – the recognition of which is
anathema for this research tradition and would ring as utter defeat for
empiricism.

None of this is to say that Weinreich's and Isajiw's research models are
useless. On the contrary they help us generate a lot of indispensable
information on the individual and collective perceptions of ethnically
framed social reality. They tell us a great deal about the importance
people attach to certain practices, rituals, symbols and beliefs. They also
indicate how these practices and beliefs are related to individual or
collective aspirations or behaviour. Thus despite their imperfections
these models enhance our knowledge about ethnicity and ethnic relations in general. However these and similar models do not and cannot
possibly tell us much about the mystical entity called 'ethnic identity'.

Assessing 'national identity': limits of qualitative techniques

The fact that the inherent vagueness of 'identity' cannot be pinned
down in empiricist oriented research might not be much of a surprise to
those who concede that social world does not allow for the simple
adoption of formalist concepts from non-human environment. Thus if

'identity' cannot be analysed as originally conceptualised in terms of absolute or relative difference, and since the human world is less one of equivalence and substitution and more one of unpredictable flux and contingency, then we are left only with the interpretative/nomotethic tradition of research. While its scope and methodology confines empiricism largely to the micro level of analysis, as its studies focus mostly on the psychological or micro sociological workings of 'ethnic identity', interpretativists have less difficulty in dealing with the macro, that is national, level as well.

The centre of our attention here will be the ways 'national identity' is conceptualised, understood and analysed in qualitative oriented research. A great majority of studies on 'national identity' either rely on un-standardised interviewing, participant observation, discourse, content or other textual analyses and ethnographic field work, or else utilise materials from archival and secondary historical research. In this process many researchers often employ national identity as a synonym for nation, nationality, nationhood or nationalism (i.e. Williams 1999: 7 writes about nationality or national identity). Quite often it is simply and incorrectly assumed that individual human beings, by virtue of being categorised as members of certain institutionalised or state reinforced collectivities automatically express a strong sense of attachment to those collectivities or are otherwise somehow predetermined to act on the basis of that collective membership[6]. In other words using national identity as a semantic equivalent to nation, nationality or nationalism suggests incorrectly that group designation inevitably implies a personal sense of belonging or generates social action. Hence one can regularly read how 'Basques and Kurds seek to establish their own state' or how 'Serbs are responsible for ethnic cleansing' or how 'Pakistanis are proud people' as if millions of highly distinct individuals who are externally categorised as Pakistani, Serb, Basque or Kurd somehow all think and act in the same way just as packs of buffalos or honeybees and ants. Obviously it is the case that some individuals organised in some social movements, political parties, socio-cultural associations or armed groups that seek the establishment of a particular state, are engaged in ethnic cleansing or feel proud of their group membership. Moreover even these highly committed and action-oriented individuals think and behave in this way only at certain moments of time and are equally prone to change their actions and thinking, as the history of party factionalism teaches us so well. The existence of 'national identity' can never be assumed from group designation.

Apart from reading group action from its name some researchers of 'national identity' are also engaged in rigid forms of reification as they attribute individual human qualities to the chunks of territory, organisations or abstract entities. So one can regularly read how 'Galicia has scarcely been vociferous in its demands for home-rule' (Williams, 1999: 10) as if piece of land can make a political demand; how 'national identity makes people aware of themselves' (Gutierrez, 2001: 9); how Yugoslavia disintegrated in 'a violent clash of identities' (Guibernau, 2001: 89); how Welsh poses their 'own highly distinctive personality' or how 'many minority cultures have sought political power in order to protect or reconstruct identities under threat' (Williams, 1999: 12,15). It is as if dynamic quality of millions of individual human beings would allow for existence of a single personality (i.e. choleric Welsh versus sanguine Scots?) or abstract entities such as 'identities' and 'cultures', and not human beings, are capable of engaging in violence or seek power to protect themselves. This last sentence where 'culture seeks power to protect its identity' is paradigmatic of many studies on national identity where unbridled essentialism and reification go hand in hand with reading collective action from the group's name. This strategy is not just nebulous research-wise, establishing as it does a rigid, causal and unproblematic relationship between the three if not highly taxing then extremely complex and dynamic set of process (culture, power and identity), but as we will see later in the book (Chapters 7,8, and 9) it can also help institutionalise and justify the most extreme forms of political violence.

As with empiricism, the list of examples indicating problematic uses of 'national identity' in the interpretativist tradition can go on almost indefinitely. What is more fruitful is to focus in greater detail on two models of qualitative study of national identity that have acquired praise for their sophistication, ambition and scope of analysis. The two studies under scrutiny here are representative of two forms of interpretativism: comparative-historical sociology exemplified by Krishan Kumar's influential *The Making of English National Identity* (2003), and an in-depth investigation of everyday forms of national identity as articulated in Tim Edensor's enlightening *National Identity, Popular Culture and Everyday Life* (2002). Whereas both of these studies are very good in their careful and multilayered dissection of the reality and transformations of nationess in time and space, they are also both guilty of attributing too much explanatory power to a highly contentious idiom which is national identity.

National identity 1: Edensor

Tim Edensor provides a well researched and detailed analysis of popular representations of nationess in the practice of everyday life. His focal point is on 'the dense spatial, material, performative, embodied and representative expressions and experiences of national identity' (2002: vii) which are seen as deeply linked, providing a vast repertoire of resources from which individuals can draw to 'actualise a sense of national belonging'. The model adopted here is built on mapping out the continuous development, articulation, re-articulation and encoring of nationhood through daily routine. Edensor examines the processes of spatialisation of nation as they are reflected in both nationalised rural and urban landscapes (as depicted in popular magazines reinforcing a particular nostalgic images of the past) and everyday, quotidian landscapes characterised by ordinary functional objects such as telephone boxes, fire hydrants, street lighting, post-boxes and many other items which with their distinct 'national' shapes and colours underpin the sense of nationhood. On the basis of his numerous empirical illustrations Edensor argues that 'the nation remains the paramount space within which identity is located' as 'the national space provides a common-sense context for situating identity' (65).

While his detail empirical work does indeed suggest that nationess is still in many respects a dominant cognitive framework of daily, routine social action there is no evidence here that it is 'identity' that fills the 'national space', or anything else for that matter. Instead of providing empirical support for his strong claims that identities are capable of doing things (i.e. cultural symbols 'can be claimed by a multitude of different identities' or 'identities territorialise and assume recognisable characteristics, can establish consistencies through time' [26,34]), Edensor takes the existence of 'national identity' for granted. He starts his analysis with unquestioned proclamations such as: 'we distinguish between ourselves and others at a collective and individual level, and express, feel and embody a sense of national identity' (24). Such a rigid statement operates on the same level as for example Marx's 'all history hitherto is a history of class struggle'. Not only do such claims assume the existence of something in need of investigation, but they also engage in circular, tautological reasoning which can be a serious obstacle to further analysis. Obviously if one presumes the unproblematic existence of clearly demarcated and anthropomorphised 'classes' or 'identities' she is more likely to find them even when they do not exist. The fact that nationess is routinely reproduced through rural landscapes or red telephone boxes may tell us much more about the dominant ideological terrain of our modern age and much less about the 'national identity'.

In addition to space Edensor also looks at public ceremonies to demonstrate how national identity is not only spatialised but also performed through daily habit. Analysing sporting events, popular carnivals and tourism he points to popular perceptions of distinct 'national' styles of football, tennis or rugby, on a variety of 'national' dances such as tango or waltz which are seen both externally and internally as the embodiments of diverse national identities, and on deliberately constructed theme tourist sites 'where national identity is on display' (86). Drawing on these and many other examples Edensor argues that such events and occasions provide an environment 'where bodily expression and emotional participation manifest highly charged expressions of national identity' (78) and where participants 'imprint their identities ... in more emotional, convivial fashion (82).

Here again one can encounter illuminating and detailed analysis of how nationess operates in practice but one is also struck by the overextension of an argument to unsupported claims about the existence of 'national identity'. The fact that most individuals hold on to stereotypical images of others and themselves as in popular conceptions of 'Brazilian playful samba football' versus 'German indestructible football machine', or that they regularly make claims to possession of distinct national identities by drawing on these ingrained stereotypical images is not a proof, even in the softer interpretative sense of the word, that national identities exist. A widely shared belief that the Earth is flat or standing on hundreds of giant tortoises does not make it flat or tortoise propped.

It is not enough to continually reiterate the dynamic, multiple or reflexive quality of identities as Edensor and many other identitarians do if the researcher also regularly slips into attributing to identities human-like qualities. While this might be seen as shorthand or a rhetorical or stylistic device of the author, it also helps to cement the reified image of group difference that already dominates much of the public view. Daily ritualism as present in sport, carnivals and tourist sites certainly does work towards fortifying distinct and unambiguous images of nationhood, and no doubt many if not the majority of individuals feel a sincere attachment to these images as symbols of 'their nation', but this still does not imply a straightforward and unproblematic 'performance of national identity'. On the contrary such popular claims and their corresponding practices require careful unpacking as they contain multiplicity of individual and collective motives, thoughts and emotions. Instead of simply following the popular doxa of 'our national identity', a researcher's job is to dissect and analyse what is really hiding behind such blunt and sweeping popular claims.

Finally Edensor also studies the practices of (national) symbol commodification and representations of nation in popular culture. On top of its spatial, temporal or ritualistic dimensions 'national identity' is also located in its material forms: in commodified objects such as automobiles where the lavishness and spaciousness of American cars competes with the smoothness and elegance of Italian or the reliability and technical excellence of German cars, and where all three are popularly perceived as epitomising distinct national cultures. These diverse 'motorscapes' together with 'memoryscapes', that is national 'self-portraits' as depicted in large-scale exhibitions such as the Millennium Dome in London or mass media and film representations such as *Braveheart* in Scotland, are interpreted by Edensor as embodiments of reflexive as well as unreflexive routine enactions of 'national identities'. He argues that this is not an uncontested process as 'a range of identities merge, squabble and ignore each other' (169). Once more what begins as an illuminative analysis of the rhetoric and practice of nationess is enveloped in the problematic language of 'identity'. Although Edensor is nominally non-essentialist and very aware of the dynamic nature of cultural practices his discourse of 'national identity' forces him into making reificatory statements where 'identities' and not human beings become subjects of action (as they 'squabble and ignore' each other). However this is not just a nonchalant slip, it is a very much a deliberate research strategy as Edensor (24) argues that identity is a powerful 'mediating concept' and a convenient and 'potent tool through which to explore diverse social and cultural transformations'. Unfortunately this pragmatic justification is futile as 'identity' cannot simultaneously be a 'potent' conceptual research device in the hands of a social analyst as well as a populist umbrella term through which political and other claims are made by political entrepreneurs or representatives of various social movements. As Brubaker (2004: 33) rightly emphasises one cannot concurrently operate as a political activist and social analyst as there is an irresolvable tension between the language of analysis and the discourses of foundationalism inherent in the process of political mobilisation.

To sum up Endensor provides a fine analysis of the process and rhetoric involved in the popular construction of everyday, habitual nationess, but he tells us very little about 'national identity'. Not only is it that no evidence is supplied on the subjective individual or group sense of belonging as this is simply assumed, but perhaps more importantly there is no empirical support for the sweeping claims that 'national identity' inevitably exists, or is present in popular practices. The only area where this is substantiated is the field of popular representation where the discourse of national identity is invoked externally by political entrepreneurs, mass media or films. Obviously this is far from being enough to demonstrate the reality of 'national identity'. Taking into account that Edensor's focus is on the almost exclusively popular, public, everyday forms of groupness he is in much better position to demonstrate this reality than researchers who study elite or state sponsored discourses of national identity. The fact that his attempt was not a success in this respect might be a good indicator not of the researcher's fault but of the porous and problematic nature of the subject itself. 'Identity' is an operational phantom that cannot be caught regardless of how tight our methodological nets are.

National identity 2: Kumar

If Edensor's is an attempt of horizontal analysis of 'national identity' as it operates through space, Krishan Kumar offers a vertical study of nation formation as it gradually emerges in time. His object of examination is the historical construction of 'English national identity' which was traditionally perceived either as one of the oldest and most ingrained national identities stretching back to the eighth, fourteenth or sixteenth century (as claimed by Hastings 1997, Elton 1992 and Greenfeld 1992 respectively), or was seen as something dormant, almost nonexistent and subsumed under wider imperial British identity. In contrast to these claims Kumar aims to show that there is a distinctive sense of Englishness as separate from Britishness but that this 'clear concern with questions of Englishness and English national identity' did not develop 'until the late nineteenth century' (Kumar 2003: xi). Kumar argumentatively demonstrates the unbridgeable discrepancy that existed between various social strata until the nineteenth century that allowed for the emergence of a commonly shared sense of nationhood. Although his study is compelling in successfully debunking the claim regarding the existence of national identity before the age of modernity, his argument is much weaker when attempting to prove the reality of English national identity since the late nineteenth century. While he acknowledges that all claims for 'national identity rest on shaky and questionable evidence' as 'there simply is no way of showing incontrovertibly that such a thing exists', he still maintains the view that this is no reason to discard this concept as it 'allows us to deal with certain questions and to describe certain attitudes and behaviour which cannot readily be comprehended in any other way' (Kumar 2003: 173). Here again, as with Edensor, one encounters a pragmatic justification for the conceptual use of 'identity'. However unlike Edensor's offensive ('a potent research tool') this is rather defensive and hence an even weaker justification ('nothing else is available'). Kumar is well aware not only that the concept of 'national identity' is problematic but also that its existence cannot be, to use a legislative phrase, substantiated without reasonable doubt. The argument that a concept should be used because nothing else is available is faulty on two accounts: it is based on poor logic (i.e. analogous to a claim that one should use hands to fly as no wings are available) and more importantly it ignores alternative concepts such as ideology, group categorisation or self-perception, to name a few, all of which are much more capable of dealing with this phenomenon than 'national identity' (see Chapters 3 and 4). Finally, it is very far from clear what is meant by 'certain questions' or 'certain attitudes and behaviour' that cannot be understood 'in any other way'.

Another important problem in Kumar's approach is his conceptual and terminological imprecision as he constantly shifts between terms such as national character, national consciousness, national psyche or nationalism and uses them as synonyms with national identity (i.e. Kumar, 2003: 173, 185, 194, 278). A typical example is: 'one kind of national identity is the imperial type I called imperial nationalism' (34). A great deal of his study is really about nationess and nationalism, that is about macro ideological projects and historical ideological transformations and much less about an individual or collective sense of self or personhood. His two key arguments and documented findings are both about political projects and ideologies – the articulations of imperial, missionary nationalism as a driving force that underpinned and was sustained by the expansions of British Empire, and the emergence of Englishness as a softer version of cultural nationalism at the end of nineteenth century. Whereas he is able to attest well both of his cases by pinpointing to works and actions of artists, thinkers, scientists, statesmen and other ideologues, and occasionally by illustrating this with the popular reception of these ideas, there is still little evidence that one can talk about 'strong and still developing British identity' (199) or how 'England got its identity by asserting its primacy, first in Britain, later in the world' (63). The fact that some or even most individuals start sharing particular sets of values and practices at a specific historical moment in time, even when empirically corroborated (which is not the case here), is not an undisputed indicator that they all embrace the same 'national identity'. As Kumar is aware, even at the end of the nineteenth century this sense of distinctive and shared collective beliefs and practices still does not have a clearly articulated political form, and so he prefers to speak of 'moment of Englishness' rather then clearly defined English national identity. Although this particular construction is a bit metaphoric it nevertheless is much more contingent, open ended and processual than most other categories he relies on. However the 'moment of Englishness', as Kumar (2003: 196) later acknowledges, is nothing else but a culturally enhanced 'substitute for nationalism'. That is, something much more akin to ideology than to identity. This is even more the case with imperial missionary nationalism, a doctrine initiated and entirely dependent on the externalised political and ideological project that is empire-building. While obviously both of these proto-nationalisms, the cultural Englishness and the imperial Britishness, require a degree of popular support and sincere expression of human emotions, they can never be equivalent to the almost unconditional and overpowering sense of in-group sameness and out-group difference that national identities seem to imply.

Finally, as a work of historical sociology *The Making of English National Identity* is even more riddled with essentialist, groupist and reificatory language than *National Identity, Popular Culture and Everyday Life*. Unlike anthropologists and sociologists of culture such as Edensor, historians and historical sociologists seem to be even less sensitive towards the concepts they use. In most historical studies, and Kumar's is no exception, the central narrative is couched in the language of what Billig (1995) and Brubaker (2004) call 'groupism' meaning a propensity to treat large groups of individuals as singular actors with a clearly defined will. Hence instead of writing about particular and concrete social movements, individual or collective political entrepreneurs, representatives of political parties, or cultural associations, there is a tendency to talk or write about 'Germans' or 'Danes' or 'Sunnis' and 'Shiias' as if all individuals categorised under these names pursue identical course of action. Kumar's study is heavily loaded with such sentences: 'It is *insecure nations*, such as Germany and Italy after First World War, who most stridently assert their nationalism' (37) or 'The English were an imperial nation ... *they* created a land empire ...' (35) or 'Even the French, who like the English might be thought to be sufficiently powerful and *self-confident* not to need nationalist solace ...' (185, all my italics) as if dozens of millions of people can all be insecure or self-confident in the same way as a single individual or have all been involved in the creation an empire. Obviously these are typical examples of attributing individual, often psychological, personality traits to highly dynamic mass collectivities.

Apart from strongly pronounced groupist discourse Kumar also regularly reifies and essentialises human behaviour by treating 'identities' as social actors or by inherently fixing groups of individuals to particular territories. For example he writes about Scottish and Irish identities as they constantly renew themselves (174), about how 'English identity had to find objects other than the English nation on which to fasten' (179), or about Ulster Protestant 'hostility to the Republic ... gave them a standing cause for holding to this identity' (246). Furthermore there are references to 'Scots, Welsh and Irish [who] submerged their identities' (200); 'the other British nations clung to their national identities' (187) or English who 'suppressed the assertion to their own separate identity' or 'could find a [new] identity' (188, 267). This is the language of essentialist and unreflective identitarianism.

It is important to note that this inclination towards groupism, essentialism and reification that one often encounters in macro historical studies of 'national identity' is not only a matter of the researcher's conceptual untidiness. More importantly the excessive reliance on non-sociological idiom which identity is, lends itself to the regular practice of psychologisation of social relations. While (self-) identity might be of some use in analysing the realities of individual personalities in a complex, mass, sociological terrain, one can gain little by simply borrowing from clinical analysis. Psychologising large-scale human collectivities and talking about 'insecure Germans' or 'self-confident French' is not particularly helpful in attempting to explain radical social transformations. Relying on the methodological whim of 'identity' cannot take us far in this process.

The two cases of qualitative/interpretative analysis of national identity briefly scrutinised here are symptomatic of the problems one faces when attempting to operationalise the concept of identity. Despite their highly sophisticated and valuable research both Edensor and Kumar are unable to substantiate their claims about national identity. Although we can learn a great deal about the processes of spatialisation, temporalisation, ritualisation, commodification or representation of nations and nationhood, there is very little evidence concerning the existence of clearly defined or clearly demarcated 'national identities'. Both studies have much more to say about the institutionalisation of particular nation-centric discourses, about transformations of distinctive nationalist ideologies, or about rhetoric and the routinisation of nationess than about 'national identities'. Even though they cover different areas in time and space, and in great detail, neither one is able to capture the chimera of 'national identity'. Just as with the two quantitative examples of Weinreich and Isajiw this is much more an indication of the problematic nature of the topic itself than of the competence of individual research designs. The lessons from the quantitative tradition are that 'identity' does not easily lend itself to operationalisation and even when one manages to perfect the research tools it turns out they measure a very diverse phenomena all of which are categorised as problems of 'identity'. Qualitative research supports this conclusion, with the porous umbrella term of 'identity' showing itself for what it is – an analytically hollow concept that cannot advance our research.

Conclusion: no proof of identity

Although 'identity' remains a highly popular concept, both in academic and everyday discourse, it is a conceptually, operationally and politically seriously troubled idiom. As I have argued in this and Chapter 1 the concept is so aloof and vague that it leads either to radically soft and loose uses where 'identity' stands for anything and everything, or it is articulated in a hard essentialist way so that through reified group membership the concept acquires features and attributes of individual human beings. Furthermore since the concept of 'identity' is relatively novel and historically and geographically exclusive, so its use also remains limited to a specific moment in time (the era of modernity/post-modernity) and to a specific location in space (a realm of the western and westernising world). Nevertheless, even in this relatively narrow temporal, social and cultural environment 'identity' is confined to a very restricted research use. Since its conceptual ambiguity prevents transparent operationalisation this has deep methodological implications: any somber attempt at the in-depth study of ethnic and national identities is nearly impossible within either quantitative or qualitative research design. All four of our sophisticated models, the empiricism of Weinreich and Isajiw as much as the interpretativism of Edensor and Kumar, have proved unable not only to measure, typify or investigate, but even to empirically locate existence of ethnic and national identities. However, as argued here, this has less to do with the strength of their individual theoretical models and a great deal to do with the chimerical quality of the concept of 'identity'. Ethnic and national identities cannot be simply assumed or taken for granted. Any accurate research practice has to be premised on decoupling the phenomena of ethnicity and nationess from the operational phantom which is 'identity'. The formalistic origin and nature of 'identity' leads researchers regularly into a tautological trap where, as Gödel and after him Harris (1995: 48) show, 'truth for any formal system cannot be defined within the system itself'. Despite all the talk about the variability, plasticity and multiplicity of identity, this was and remains a profoundly formalist concept, part of a rigid formalist system through which little can be explained. Instead of being an explanatory solution 'identity' is a more of an ideological symptom of a problem in need of explanation. Any serious attempt to come with grips of that explanation entails engaging with a more potent heuristic device – the concept of ideology.

3
Rehabilitating Ideology

Introduction

Until very recently, until the 1990s in fact, the concept of ideology was considered indispensable to the study of social and political life. Sociologists, political scientists, social and political theorists, anthropologists, social psychologists as well as those researching cultural studies all relied on this concept, the only real point of divergence and disagreement being, predictably, different conceptual understandings of what ideology is. For some, mostly political scientists and political theorists, ideologies were discussed in the plural, meaning different set of ideas and principles concerning the possible or desirable organisation of a particular society, as in liberalism, conservatism, socialism or environmentalism. Others, notably sociologists, have tended to speak of ideology in the singular, viewing it as a set of ideas or practices related to the specific structural organisation of a society – as in Marx's 'fetishism of commodities', Mannheim's distinction between ideology and utopia, Geertz's ideology as a cultural system, or Žižek's 'fantasy of enjoyment'. Although significantly different neither one of these traditions and approaches questioned the relevance of the concept of ideology. Post-structuralism was the first theoretically sustained movement to reject the notion of ideology, viewing it as totalistic, essentialist and methodologically and theoretically obsolete. Post-structuralism has been particularly critical of the way ideology was used in the writings of its direct predecessors – that is the structuralists. The apparent success of these criticisms has had a profound impact on the social sciences and humanities far beyond the relatively narrow confines of poststructuralist social theory. Coupled with the collapse of communism, delegitimisation of Marxism and the proliferation of non-class based social movements worldwide, 'ideology' has given way to 'identity' and 'discourse' the former concept a synonym for the old, and the outmoded, whereas the latter signalled the new, heuristically promising future.

This chapter aims to critically review and analyse the way the concept of ideology was and is used in structuralism and post-structuralism. Moreover my goal here is to try to defend and rehabilitate the concept of ideology not only from poststructuralist and postmodernist attacks but also from wider miscomprehension that surrenders this concept, a miscomprehension brought about in no small measure by the legacy of poststructuralist critique. I argue in this chapter that the theory and concept of ideology can be rescued as a valuable research tool by recognising and accommodating some of the pitfalls identified by poststructuralist approaches without accepting the radical relativism espoused in more extreme poststructuralist positions. The chapter is divided into three sections. In the first section structuralist approaches to ideology are briefly discussed and critically elaborated. In the second section a variety of poststructuralist criticisms of ideology are presented and criticised. The last section maps an outline for a new understanding of ideology which is elaborated in Chapter 4.

Structuralist approaches to ideology

In order to deal properly with the poststructuralist approaches to ideology it is necessary to examine briefly their epistemological ancestors, that is the structuralist views on ideology. There are basically three different and mutually opposing structuralist traditions – Marxist, functionalist and anthropological structuralism.

Marxist structuralism is usually associated with the work of Althusser but the early works of Hirst (critical structuralism), Goldmann (genetic structuralism), or Godelier (economic structuralism) are also representative examples. The common characteristic of Marxist structuralism is its emphasis on the state and economy. The state is seen as the principal agent of action and the concept of ideology is employed exclusively in reference to state power. Structuralist Marxists follow classical Marxism in their perception of the state as an instrument of repression, but they differ from agency-centred Marxism in downplaying the role of class struggle at the expense of structural determinants (i.e. capitalism) which are found to be central for the analysis of ideology.

For Althusser class hegemony is achieved not solely through Repressive State Apparatuses such as the military, police, and courts but also through Ideological State Apparatuses – the education system, mass media, family and church. He argues that 'no class can hold State power over a long period of time without at the same time exercising its hegemony over and in the State Ideological Apparatuses' (Althusser, 1994: 112).

Furthermore, ideology is seen as built into the material apparatuses that are determined by the relations of production – that is, capitalist economy. For structural Marxists ideology has a tangible, material form which is not only completely independent of individual subjectivity but is also able to create and mould subjects. As Althusser (1994: 125) puts it, ideology is 'not the system of the real relations which govern the existence of individuals, but the imaginary relation of those individuals to the real relations in which they live'. For structuralist Marxists human beings are constituted by ideology while ideology itself originates from the particular type of production in society – capitalism. In other words, the capitalist state hegemony is maintained through ideological state apparatuses, which are themselves tied to the dominant modes of production in a particular (capitalist) society. Structuralist Marxists also strongly oppose ideology and science. For Althusser, for example, ideology is abstract while science is concrete; ideology is historically contingent while science is ahistoric; ideology is only raw material while science is exact and accurate. Althusser sees his structuralist Marxism as a form of science *par excellence* and claims that the role of science is to creatively use and criticise the products of ideology.

Functionalist structuralism shares with its Marxist counterpart the emphasis on the collective roots of ideology as well as the perception of ideology as something that stands in opposition to science. Malinowski, Shils, Parsons and Sartori all define ideology in reference to dominant social institutions – the school, the family, the state. They all also make a strong distinction between closed, dogmatic and stable concepts associated with ideology and open, flexible values, which are and prone to change and seen as non-ideological.

However, unlike Marxism, structuralist functionalism ignores the economy and materialist explanations of ideology. In this tradition ideology is seen as a normative value system necessary for social cohesion and the proper functioning of societies. For Malinowski (1926) ideology/ myth is a sacred tale that functions as a practical justification of relationships and practices existing in the particular society. For Shils (1968) ideologies are no more than normative belief systems that are founded on 'systematic intellectual constructs' that command the total commitment of their followers. For Parsons (1991: 39) ideology is 'an evaluative, i.e. value-loaded existential statement about the actual or prospective state of a given social system or type or category of social system'. In Sartori's (1969) theory ideology is more precisely identified with the 'political part of a belief system' and is tied to strong affects and closed cognitive structure.

Although functionalist structuralism relates ideology strongly to society by looking at its collectivist origins, unlike Marxism it does not perceive of this relationship as being conflictual. Ideology is not viewed as something imposed upon human beings, but rather as a functional necessity without which society cannot exist. Ideologies do not shape, structure or *interpellate* and thus manipulate individuals, as in Althusser, but are rather seen as 'building blocks' for the integration of societies.

The anthropological structuralism of Levi-Strauss and Barthes shares with Marxists and functionalists their understanding of ideology as a macro structural phenomenon. As with Marxism, anthropological structuralists aim at discovering 'hidden' structures behind more manifest actions and similar to functionalists their goal is to demonstrate the necessity of ideology in every society. However, unlike Marxists they are only sporadically (Barthes) or not at all (Levi-Strauss) interested in the modes of production and the role that capitalism plays in the formation of ideologies and, unlike functionalists, are not concerned with the integrative role of ideology in society. Their main aim is to apply the methods of linguistics (i.e. structural analysis) to social relations. For anthropological structuralists myths and ideologies are no more than logical models that aim at overcoming a contradiction between nature and culture and as such function independently of individual consciousness. In the words of Levi-Strauss (1975: 12) the aim of structural analysis is not 'to show how men think in myths, but how myths operate in men's minds without them being aware of the fact'.

For Barthes (1993) and Levi-Strauss there is no significant difference between ideological/mythical contents and other contents; they all operate in a similar way, have a similar patterned structure and apply identical logical principles. Anthropological structuralists aim to use structural analysis with the simple aim of identifying the elementary logical structure on which message, myth, ritual or any other meaningful content is based. Levi-Strauss aims to discover the common structural forms and common logical patterns behind arbitrary symbols and randomness present in myths and ideologies. He looks for, what he calls, *mythemes*, which are the elementary units of myth, with the aim of identifying the logical order behind myth's formal structure. Levi-Strauss has little interest in the actual contents of the particular myths and ideologies. What is important to demonstrate and explain is the similarity between the structure of different myths and ideologies.

Although different these three structuralist approaches to ideology share several important common features. All three assign the overwhelming primacy to structure over agency in the explanation of ideology. All three perceive human will and individual consciousness as largely irrelevant in the explanation of ideology. All three argue for an ahistorical theory of ideology. All three share the view that with the right methodology one can successfully and precisely differentiate between ideological and non-ideological forms of knowledge.

The classical criticisms of structuralism have successfully challenged all of these claims. It has been convincingly argued that human beings are more than simply bearers of social roles and, regardless of how powerful ideologies are, there is always room for autonomous individual action. As Pareto (1966) argued ideologies cannot run against existing human sentiments, so that derivations (Pareto's term) can intensify residues but cannot manufacture them. The residues have to be there in the first place in order to be instrumentalised. Ideologies cannot work *ex nihilo*. In addition, as Gouldner (1970) and more recently Giddens (1991), Beck (1991) and Jenkins (2004) have convincingly argued, human beings are also self-reflexive creatures. It is very often the case that people are aware of the entire process of ideological interpolation and are still taking part in it, possibly adjusting this in accordance with their own interests, values and emotions.

Critics have also pointed out that ideologies always originate within a particular geographical and historical environment. Although all communist states derived their official ideologies from Lenin's interpretations of Marx and Engels, each society had a unique brand of state sponsored communist ideology which took into consideration the particularities of national history, the history of its own communist movement, differences in the economic, cultural and political development of the particular society, and so on. It was also often the case that these differences (perceived by outsiders as rather trivial) were central for the legitimisation of the particular regime, as was the case with Yugoslav self-management socialism, Polish nationalist communism, Maoism in China or *Juche* ideology in North Korea. The structuralist preference for 'synchronic' over 'diachronic' analysis omits these substantial and often crucial differences from its explanation.

However the most damning criticism was against the structuralist claim to scientific, meaning non-ideological, tools for the study of ideology. Although structuralism opposes the positivist ambition to explain phenomena only in terms of immediately observable entities, thus abandoning the search for laws of causality, it too is the victim of an over optimistic scientism. Its aim, to uncover the latent structures of manifest phenomena with the help of structural analysis, is even more arbitrary than the methods of positivist social science. If one cannot rely on the strict procedures of laboratory experimentation, sampling, surveying, factor or regression analysis, why would one trust the extreme arbitrariness of 'synchronic analysis'? In addition, as many critics have emphasised, the linguistic methods employed are hardly applicable to the study of the complexities and contingencies of social life. As Giddens (1987: 200) convincingly argues, 'linguistics cannot provide a model for analysing the nature of either agency or social institutions, because it is in a basic sense only explicable through an understanding of these'.

Other types of criticism such as those coming from the Frankfurt School sociologists show that even when knowledge is completely reduced to its technical forms, it is still far from being non-ideological or value free. As Marcuse (1964: 130) points out 'domination perpetuates and extends itself not only through technology but as technology, and the latter provides the great legitimisation of the expanding political power, which absorbs all spheres of culture'.

However, the most severe criticism of the structuralist approaches to ideology is to be found in the writings of poststructuralist authors, some of which emerged from the intellectual tradition of Marxist or anthropological structuralism. Let us take a brief look at how post structuralism views the concept of ideology.

Post structuralism and ideology

Although leading poststructuralist approaches differ on many points they agree on one thing – they all firmly reject the concept of ideology.[7] For Foucault (1980: 118) the concept of ideology cannot have any analytical relevance because it is (a) based on positivist true/false criteria; (b) it overemphasises the role of conscious subjects; and (c) it is overly economistic as it posits a rigid dichotomy between secondary reality (superstructure) that is perceived to be determined by the primary, economic base. According to Foucault knowledge and power are deeply related, since power always produces new information and novel types of knowledge. He argues that since 'no power can be exercised without extraction, appropriation, distribution or retention of knowledge' therefore 'power and knowledge imply one another' (Foucault, 1977: 27).

Because of this peculiar power–knowledge relationship ideology cannot be, as in the Marxist tradition, opposed to science. Ideology and science cannot be analysed and assessed in the light of a true/false criterion. As 'truth' in itself is situational and historically and geographically contingent and at the same time always tied to power, there are no universally accepted rationalist parameters to distinguish 'truth' from 'non-truth'. These parameters lay at all times in the realm of a particular concrete community. In place of ideology Foucault offers the concept of discourse. In his view discourses are much less totalistic and universalistic than the concept of ideology as used in structuralism. Discourses operate on a much lower level of generality and are not evaluated using true/false dichotomy. Unlike ideology, this concept is used in order to understand and explain how particular ideas and practices relate to the context which has 'its own history and conditions of existence'. What is crucial for Foucault is not whether the ideas and practices expressed within a particular normative discourse are provable but rather how they operate in relation to power.

Baudrillard (1988) and Lyotard (1984) follow similar lines of argument. They both oppose the analytical relevance of the concept of ideology. For Baudrillard we live in a post-modern world of isolated individual actions devolved of any intrinsic meaning, incoherent and incomprehensible social events and fragmented and fractured realities. This post-modern world does not depend on modes of production, industrial growth and economics, but predominantly on the production, use and exchange of images, signs, and information. However, these images, signs and information are not produced, exchanged and consumed as before, with material goods, to secure a new and better reality. They are rather seen by Baudrillard as simulations which have lost their original meanings and no longer reveal anything beyond the 'real'. In his view there is no reality anymore, everything has become an extensive simulation. Instead of reality we live in hyper reality which is continually falsified by different and often opposing representations.

Just like Foucault, Baudrillard does not believe in the autonomy of conscious subjects and prefers the idea of discourse to that of ideology. However, discourses in Baudrillard have little analytical strength, they are only empty images – simulacra. The problem of ideology critique for Baudrillard is that its aim is always the same – 'to restore the objective process' and he argues that 'it is always a false problem to want to restore the truth beneath the simulacrum. This is ultimately why power is so in accord with ideological discourses and discourses on ideology, for these are all discourses of truth – always good' (Baudrillard, 1988: 182).

Lyotard also thinks that in the post-modern world there is no place for individual subjects. Following Wittgenstein he views society as a sequence of language games where one can see only dissolved social subjects. According to Lyotard in the post-modern world there is no place for the single universalist Enlightenment concept of Reason, only many different, mutually incommensurable unprivileged reasons. He opposes any form of totality and ridicules universalist rationalist conceptions that promise comprehensive positive explanation and hold out the promise of emancipation and salvation. Theories and explanations which focus on and privilege a singular 'essential' mode of existence such as nation, gender, race or class are described as 'totalitarian meta-narratives' and are resolutely rejected. Consequently, there is no place for ideology critique in his position: all language games are equal and legitimate. Instead of hegemonic meta-narratives and the project of 'ideology critique' the focus is on the multiplicity of identity formations.

The post-Marxism of Laclau and Mouffe (1985) also shares many similarities with Foucault's, Baudrillard's or Lyotard's criticism of ideology. They too identify the concept of ideology with its Marxist derivative and intend to show the weaknesses of this position. They agree with poststructuralists that classical Marxist analyses reduce plurality and difference by attributing a privileged role to the proletariat and treat group memberships as stable and fixed. Laclau and Mouffe argue that social identities are fundamentally relational and situational. Adopting a post-essentialist position they argue that there are no privileged historical subjects be they classes, nations or something else. Accordingly no social relations between individuals or between groups are necessarily of a permanent, universal or continuous nature. As a result they also favour the concepts of discourse and multiple identities over that of ideology although, unlike other poststructuralists, they attempt to integrate a subordinated concept of ideology into discourse theory.

Nevertheless, their concept of discourse differs significantly from those of Foucault, Lyotard or Baudrillard. They define discourse as a 'structured totality resulting from the articulatory practice', where an articulatory practice is 'any practice establishing a relation among elements such that their identity is modified as a result of the articulatory practice' (Laclau and Mouffe, 1985: 105). Their understanding of discourse is thus much broader and more totalising than in earlier poststructuralist works.

For Laclau and Mouffe all social actions are discursively constructed. Discourses just like identities are also relational. They argue that individuals are dispersed by and within different discursive formations.

Since individual subjects change their social positions and relations to discourse so formations are never eternally fixed. For Laclau and Mouffe they are only 'partial fixations'. In their view 'any discourse is constituted as an attempt to dominate the field of discursivity, to arrest the flow of differences, to construct a centre' (Laclau and Mouffe, 1985: 112). Furthermore, they argue that as objects are always constituted as objects of – and in – a particular discourse, so one cannot distinguish between discursive and non-discursive practices. Following Gramsci and Foucault they also ascribe to discourses a value of materiality. In other words the practices of articulation have their material dimension: institutions, organisations, ritualistic practices, techniques and so on. However this materiality of discourses is not in any significant way connected to the consciousness of the subjects. Positions of the subjects are rather dispersed within a discursive formation. In the eyes of Laclau and Mouffe, society, as a stable articulated entity, does not exist. What one can observe are only perpetual attempts of discursive articulation.

The common features of poststructuralist approaches can be summarised in the following three points: (a) with the partial exception of Laclau and Mouffe they all renounce the entire concept of ideology and operate with alternative concepts such as 'discourses', 'identities', 'simulacras', 'language games' or 'meta-narratives'; (b) they all rebuff true/false or science/non-science criteria in distinguishing between different social actions viewing all knowledge claims as discursive, relative, situational and therefore implicitly equal; and (c) they all stand firmly against essentialism, positivism and universalism.

However, although post structuralism appears to be extremely critical of the structuralist concepts of ideology, it is still unable to overcome many of its shortcomings. First, even though post structuralism launches fierce criticism of the concept of ideology, as some have already observed (i.e. Larrain, 1994: 292), it re-introduces this concept through the back door thus contradicting itself. As Larrain (1994: 292) rightly states 'while they [poststructuralists] doubt the validity of total discourses and of their ideological critique they must assume the validity of their own critique of total discourses'. This criticism is of course derived from the much wider problem that concerns poststructuralist understanding of knowledge and truth. As Habermas (1987: 247), Taylor (1984: 175–7), Bevir (1999: 70) and others have pointed out in rejecting the possibility of individual freedom and reason poststructuralists cut the ground from under their feet. In other words the ethical criticisms of meta-narratives, language games and discourses are undermined when there is no epistemological or normative 'axis' to build upon.

This radical epistemological relativism is not only ethically problematic because it does not (want to) differentiate between different types of power thus (unintentionally) equalising for example the right to alternative sexual preferences and genocide, but more importantly for this study, it is analytically insufficient. Its methodology applies no appropriate criteria in distinguishing between different 'regimes of truth'. How can one distinguish between 'meta-narrative' and non-'meta narrative'? In order to move from the metaphoric level of analysis towards a useful empirical analysis of 'regimes of truth' one has to offer better criteria on how one is to decide on the incommensurability of particular discourses. Post structuralism does not offer us an adequate conceptual apparatus that could be used in empirical research. Instead it relies on vague and epistemologically porous concepts such as 'identity' or 'simulacrum'. Paradoxically while it denies human agency by attributing omnipotent powers to discourses it simultaneously operates with very voluntaristic notion of identity: while human sociability is moulded by discourses, identities are perceived as always being no more than 'partial fixations' or 'positions of temporary attachment'. As a result most poststructuralist analyses remain on the level of statement, metaphor or allegory. The main question here is certainly how to overcome the arbitrariness of poststructuralist methodology?

This arbitrariness is perhaps most visible in the way concepts such as 'power' are used in Foucault's writings. The statement that power is everywhere is analytically flawed. In social sciences when attempting to explain a particular social phenomenon we introduce concepts in order to organise our information in a meaningful way with an aim to differentiate between those events and actions that we find somehow more relevant from the rest. When it is said that power is everywhere in analytical terms this automatically means that power is nowhere. By relativising our concepts we are unable to provide explanations. One can agree with Foucault that micro or local dimensions of power are exceptionally important for understanding of social life, but this should not prevent us from differentiating, studying or finding that the macro state power can have wider and deeper impact on human condition. Furthermore, as argued and documented by Fox (1998: 424) while post structuralism may be able to provide research tools for the analysis of 'relatively unresisting subjectivities' (such as in Foucault's analysis of prisoners and patients in mental hospitals), this approach lacks conceptual tools for analysis of 'the conditions under which resistance to power becomes possible, why some people resist and others do not, and how resistance may be successful'.

There is also another problem with the poststructuralist position that has both ethical and analytical implications. By stating that every society or group has its own regime of truth we deny the possibility of individual choice within a group. The problem of cultural relativism is its insensitivity towards particularities within the particular. In other words, by assuming that a certain group of people or society share the same 'regime of truth' one remains totalist on the level of the particular. Is a macro 'meta-narrative' any less 'totalitarian' than a micro 'meta-narrative'?

Second, the preference for the concepts of 'discourse', 'identity', 'language games', simulacra or 'meta-narratives' over that of ideology does not solve the problem that exists in structuralist writings. On the one hand, it makes little difference whether we use concepts such as 'ideology', 'myth' or 'discourses' if our aims remain the same – to show that somebody else's views are less (or at least no more) true than ours. Although poststructuralists distance themselves from such an aim they too are engaged in the activity of delegitimising other perspectives describing them as a 'meta-narratives' or 'discourses'. On the other hand, the concepts of 'discourse' and 'identity' are very often used in an extremely imprecise and vague sense meaning everything and nothing.[8] As for example, Laclau and Mouffe (1985) recognise it is impossible to make a distinction between discursive and non-discursive practices. Similarly identity becomes a buzzword for the variety of forms of social action. Sometimes these two concepts are used only to refer to a particular set of ideas, views or values (i.e. in Baudrillard and Lyotard) while on other occasions as in the later Foucault or Laclau and Mouffe they include almost everything (i.e. practices and actions). Hence, when they refer only to ideas, values and meanings then we end up with a classical idealism that argues that human action is governed and shaped primarily by identities and discourses and only secondary by political or economic interests. When they include practices, actions, rituals, and so on (i.e. body instead of consciousness) we end up with a more materialist theory of 'discourses' that in the long run does not differ much from the Althusserian project. In other words, although poststructuralists prefer identity and discourse over ideology, when they are forced to specify the meaning of discourse and identity through concrete analysis then these two as well as other concepts (i.e. meta-narrative, simulacra or language games) differ little from that of ideology.

As in structuralism, we can read in Foucault or Laclau and Mouffe that 'discourses constitute the subject', that 'subjects are not the producers of discourse but rather "positions" in discourse which can be occupied by any individual' (Foucault 1977: 115), that 'every object is constituted as an object of discourse', or that 'every social identity becomes the meeting point for a multiplicity of articulatory practices (Laclau and Mouffe, 1985: 107, 138). If we replace the word 'discourse' or 'identity' with 'ideology' or 'myth' these sentences may well have been taken from Althusser's or Levi-Strauss's works.

To conclude, poststructuralist attempts to overcome the deficiencies of the structuralist concept of ideology are far from being successful. Even though post structuralism rightly challenges the totalist ambitions, hard essentialism and scientism of structuralist approaches, it fails to provide a better theoretical and methodological apparatus for the study of social life. It is very far from clear what is analytically gained if the concept of 'ideology' is replaced with 'discourse' 'identity' or 'language games'.

Ideology after post structuralism

In an article published in 1987 Giddens launched a sharp criticism of both structuralism and post structuralism, his first line reading: 'Structuralism, and post-structuralism also, are dead traditions of thought' (Giddens, 1987: 195). In the last two decades it has become apparent that the opposite is in fact the case – the late 1980s, 1990s as well as the beginning of this century have witnessed an unprecedented proliferation of books, studies and journal articles written from the poststructuralist or post-modernist perspective. Even structuralism has enjoyed a revival. The end of the Cold War and the total collapse of the communist world further rejuvenated poststructuralist thought, demonstrating the death of another great meta-narrative of the Enlightenment project (i.e. Marxism-Leninism). If post structuralism was a marginal movement in the 1980s, it has certainly become mainstream now. Today no serious academic can simply dismiss poststructuralist or post-modernist ideas. In fact, even Giddens's (1991, 1992) own work on reflexive modernisation and the transformation of intimacy incorporates many poststructuralist ideas, perhaps without being aware of this fact.

Hence, poststructuralist criticisms of scientism, universalism and hard essentialism as developed in various 'modernist' approaches (including their criticism of the concept of ideology) cannot be easily dismissed. Post structuralism rightly challenges the totalising ambitions of ideology critique. There really is no analytical ground to attribute a special and privileged role to one single social actor, be it class, nation, gender, or ethnicity, or to singular 'meta-narrative'. For example, a Marxist concept of ideology with its focus on economy, capitalism and the modes of production can hardly operate in societies where the economy does not exist as an independent realm, as was the case with communist and other centrally planned and state regulated economies. Furthermore, by locating the origins of ideology solely in the development of modes of production and class struggle, Marxist explanations ignore the evidence of sociological, historical and political research that relates the birth of ideology to the emergence of modernity, the development of modern bureaucratic nation-states or geopolitical transformations. Similarly, the rigid opposition of science and ideology as maintained in anthropological and functionalist structuralism cannot stand the scrutiny of empirical research, and it looks rather archaic in this day and age when the exactness of the natural sciences themselves have also become questionable. Post structuralism is convincing in demonstrating that the basis for having narratives with privileged agents of social change are quite weak, while reality itself is both multiple and discursive.

However, recognising that there are no universally privileged social agents does not mean accepting the view that all 'language games' are equal and that the social actions of all actors have equivalent impact on human relations. On the contrary, by acknowledging the idea that there are no general and omnipresent social agents one can better focus on how asymmetrical relations of power are produced and shaped in particular contexts. One can then concentrate on questions as to when, why and how interpretations and articulations of social reality by social agents become hegemonic, shared or trusted by many. In other words, although 'meta-naratives', 'discourses', 'simulacras' or 'language games' might be ontologically or even epistemologically of equal worth, their structural position (i.e. whether any particular discourse or meta-narrative is dominant and institutionalised or not) makes them structurally and ontologically very different and unequal. While many poststructuralists may nominally share this view of inherent political asymmetry (i.e. Torfing, 2005) their own epistemological position does not allow for such a conclusion: if there is no private language and we are all chained in self-containing and self-validating cultural worlds this necessarily implies a substantial degree of equivalence and symmetry.

And precisely because of this ingrained structural inequality and existing asymmetrical relations of power in everyday life one should not so easily abandon the concept of ideology in the social sciences and humanities. The concept of ideology still has many heuristic advantages over its direct competitors – 'discourse' 'identity' or 'meta-narrative'. Nevertheless, in order to accommodate criticism put forward by poststructuralists it is important to specify what the concept of ideology should stand for.

First of all, it is necessary to point out that poststructuralist criticism operates for the most part with the concept of ideology inherited from the Marxist structuralism. In their view ideology, as Barrett (1991) puts it, focuses on the 'economics of un-truth' whereas 'discourse analysis' deals with the 'politics of truth'. Foucault (1980:118) and Baudrillard (1988:182) have both explicitly stated that they are against 'ideological analysis' because 'it always stands in virtual opposition to something else which is supposed to count as truth' or 'it is always a false problem to want to restore the truth beneath the simulacrum'. However by reducing the concept of ideology to its Marxist variant, they have failed to account properly for the contributions of other theoretical traditions.

The concept of ideology cannot be equated with its structuralist and Marxist versions because there are many other traditions of inquiry that have developed and successfully implemented this concept in their works. These include diversity of approaches from the psychoanalytic tradition (Freud's 'illusion', 'delusion' and 'justification', Reich's 'political rationalisation of sadism', Žižek's 'enjoyment and lack'), to the classical elite theory of Pareto ('derivations'), Mosca ('political formulae'), Sorel's political myth, the cultural approach of Geertz ('ideology as a cultural system') and Mannheim ('ideology and utopia'), the neo-Weberianism of Boudon ('rationality of ideology') and Mann ('ideological power of the state'), Critical Theory ('science and technology as ideology') or more recently Freeden's morphology of ideology. Drawing on some of these approaches, particularly neo-Weberianism and classical elite theory, one is able to articulate a model of ideology that can build on or incorporate some features of poststructuralist criticism such as a rejection of the application of the crude true/ false and science/non-science dichotomies to the study of ideology, as well as poststructuralist criticism of meta-narratives without reinstating radical relativism (Malešević, 2002).

Such an approach to the study of ideology should be capable of reconciling the explanatory merits of ideology theories with the ideas and critique of post structuralism. However, this attempt raises a number of problems out of which the most important is the question: Is it possible to renounce positivism, universalism and attempts to build a grand meta theory while at the same time maintaining an explanatory oriented concept of ideology?

My argument is that this can be achieved if the concept of ideology is reformulated and removed from its Marxist obsession with the 'economics of untruth', its structuralist obsession with the latent and manifest patterns, its poststructuralist radical relativism obsessed with the 'celebration of differences', and the obsession of all three with the structure and the macro level of analysis. In order to rehabilitate the concept of ideology one needs to do three things: (1) to move the theory of ideology from structure centred approaches towards more agency oriented theories of ideology; (2) to shift the emphasis from the function to the form and content of ideology and in this way to develop better research tools for the analysis of ideology; and (3) to apply these research tools to the study of the different articulations of ideology among which the most important is the distinction between normative (i.e. official) and operative ideology (that is ideology as an institutionalised narrative).

As we have seen both structuralism and post-structuralism operate with a similar concept of the social giving it an extremely strong, and in the case of structuralism a deterministic tone, in favour of structure over agency. Individual consciousness, autonomous will and an actor's rationality are not simply negated, they are consciously expelled from the analysis. Structuralism and post structuralism differ little in their rejection of the subject. Although this strategy of removing the subject from the analysis can produce neat historical and cultural essays, as in Baudrillard or Foucault, analyses that exclude agency from their analyses certainly cannot properly explain the role of politically motivated ideas and practices in social life. In their rejection of the subject and ideology poststructuralists treat this relationship as if it is circular and one-dimensional. The concept of ideology is rejected because it is perceived in its narrow Marxist sense as a consciously employed device of manipulation of one class over another. On the other hand individual autonomy is rejected because it is understood as being historically determined and socially constructed. In other words, if there are no individual free wills there can be no ideology, whereas if there is no ideology there can be no subject.

This line of thinking is problematic for at least two reasons. First, as structuralists and especially Althusser show there is no necessary relationship between the two, a theory of ideology is possible without the subject. Second and more importantly for us, agency and ideology can and do have many different forms of relationship. Ideologies certainly can and do incorporate a level of manipulation though this is not necessarily tied to class relations or one social, economic or political order and they can include any form of group membership (gender, nation, ethnicity, age, and so on) as well as being oriented to society as a whole. The simple fact that every modern nation-state controls or has a decisive say on the shape of its educational system is a good indicator of potential ideological influence beyond social class. Compelling its young audience to use state approved textbooks of history or social science, often filled with soft or hard nationalistic interpretations of 'our' past and present, is a powerful ideological tool in communist Laos, Islamist Saudi Arabia, as much as in the liberal-democratic United States. As Billig (1995) has nicely shown 'banal nationalism' is a constantly reinforced and often unnoticeable feature of everyday life – in the newspapers we read, in the TV news we watch, in routine symbols and habits of language, practices such as saluting the flag, wearing particular colours, and even observing nation-centric weather reports.

Next, as we have learned from Weber (1968), individuals are attracted to a particular set of ideas, values and practices in at least four ways. First, this could be achieved through the form of instrumental rationality, meaning that individuals can be motivated in maximising their advantages that are in line with the teaching of the particular ideology. The familiar and more extreme examples (see Chapter 9) include support for an ideology that promotes ethnic cleansing or genocide and results in acquiring houses, banks, land and other material goods from the expelled group, as was the case with the ideology of Nazism and the attitude of ordinary Germans to Jews in Nazi Germany (Browning, 1992, Goldhagen, 1996). Or again, as with the Serbian ethno-nationalism and Serbian popular perceptions of the Bosnian Muslims or Albanians in the recent wars on the territory of former Yugoslavia (Silber and Little, 1995, Ron, 2003).

Second, individual actors as well as groups can act on the basis of personal or group value-rationality, or what Boudon (1989) calls axiological rationality, meaning that individuals uphold a particular set of beliefs because they consider these values as promoting certain symbolic benefits for them. In Weber's words (1968: 25) actors believe 'in the value for its own sake of some ethical, aesthetic, religious, or other form of behaviour, independently of its prospects of success'. Hence, most citizens of the United States will support the values of liberal democracy without extensive knowledge of political theory of liberalism, predominantly because they associate these values with symbolic (and, of course, material) rewards generated within the framework of the American nation-state. Similarly, many Hamas suicide bombers and jihad warriors are motivated by the belief in a symbolic reward – the increase of individual or family social status or religious fulfilment with all sins forgiven and a secured place in heaven.

Third, ideologies can work through an emotional appeal where, unlike the other two, there is no clearly defined ideal of action. Individuals can act out of fear, hatred, love, the need for security, serenity or any other affect. This type of social action is more likely to take place in relatively short periods of time during or immediately after some dramatic social change (i.e. revolutions, wars, break-up of the state structure, natural disasters, pandemic diseases and so on). The emotional appeal is most visible in the language of ideologies. Typical examples are the images associated with close family and kinship ties ('our sons die for our motherland', 'our proletarian sisters', 'diseased foreigners' 'Muslim brotherhood', and so on).

Finally, actors can also maintain the traditional course of action, meaning that an individual will behave in accordance with habit and custom. As Weber (1968), Elias (1983) and Billig (1995) have convincingly argued, commonly shared values, principles and ideas as well as collective action based on these values, are very often reproduced and maintained almost exclusively through the habits of everyday life. By taking for granted symbols and practices around us we maintain and reproduce many ideological constructs.

The answer to the question, 'Why are individuals and groups receptive to certain ideologies?' is not only to be found at the top of the social pyramid in structural manipulation (such as the 'fetishism' of commodities or logical structural patterns) or agency manipulation (the ruling class, the power-elite, the charismatic leader) but also at the bottom of the pyramid. Ideologies are not necessarily manipulative. Popular support for particular systematic beliefs and practices is often deeply grounded in the social or individual functions they fulfil. Their success is rooted in the promise of providing concrete symbolic or material rewards; they appeal to particular interests and affects; or they are simply seen as a part of traditional habitual action. The agency-oriented approach to ideology needs to analyse in particular this relationship between the reception and receptors of ideology. The main questions here should be: What do ideologies offer to individuals? Why and how can individual and collective agents be motivated or persuaded to believe in particular value systems? Why do individuals subscribe to one and not to another ideology? When, why and under which conditions is one articulation of an ideology preferred over another? and Why and when are some interpreters ('articulators') more trusted than others?

It is important to emphasise here that this agency-oriented model of ideology does not neglect the role the institutions of state play in the formation and dissemination of ideology, which are often important if not crucial. However unlike structuralism and poststructuralism it does not give primacy to institutions and structure. The institutions are often no more than means and objective obstacles of and for individual and group action. The institutional structure sets the parameters and imposes the limits on agency but does not determine human action. As I argue later in the book (Chapter 4) the historically built confines of the modern nation-state set an objective ceiling on what individual or collective actors can achieve but nevertheless do not completely mould the actor's behaviour. As Rex (1980: 119) rightly emphasises social structures are to be seen as 'arising from the continuity in time of interlocking patterns of interaction'.

The next element involves shifting the emphasis from the function to the form and content of ideology. As Lewins (1989: 680) and others have recognised most approaches to ideology are focused on the functionality of ideology (examining what ideologies do), while there are very few approaches that are focused on the content of particular ideologies (examining what ideologies are, how are they composed, what are their dominant themes and so on). Among the few theories that nominally concentrate on the content of ideology such as those of Pareto (1966) or Geertz (1964), there is very little serious analysis of ideology structure and content. Most of these approaches remain rather at the level of metaphoric description. In order to spot the similarities and differences between ideologies it is necessary to move our attention to the form and content of ideological narratives. The various action-oriented systems of beliefs, ideas and practices would hence be analysed and categorised by breaking them down into their constitutive elements in order to show similarities and differences between them. In this way we can secure a relatively simple but effective mechanism for the analysis of ideology. Thus, we need to identify and specify in detail conceptual segments of ideology. As a starting point I recommend seven such elements the analysis of which can help us to distinguish between different ways a given ideology may be structured. These include economy, politics, culture, the nation, dominant actors, type of language used and the depiction of principal counter-ideologies.

First, ideology is related to the conceptual organisation of society. Therefore, the analysis would concentrate on statements and practices related to the four central categories vital to the functioning of any society:

(a) *economy* (production, distribution, consumption and exchange of goods and services);
(b) *politics* (political systems, dominant socio-political beliefs, leadership, power distribution and party structure);

(c) *culture* (articulation and dissemination of culture products, shared cultural values, popular religious and secular beliefs, stated directions of cultural policies, popular perceptions of culture); and

(d) *the nation* (who counts among the nation, the intensity and direction of nationalist feelings, minority rights, the question of ethno-national homogeneity and the relationship between the nation and the state).

Second, every ideological narrative operates with a set of individual and group *actors*. The narratives depend on formulating and depicting the relationships between individuals and groups. They also portray social actors in different lights attributing them different human or non-human characteristics. Hence, the analysis would look at how these individual and group actors have been described, and what kind of names, descriptions and images are associated with them.

Third, the research would also concentrate on the detailed analysis of the *language* used and other images present in the statements and practices. One should be able to assess the emotional, rational and other types of appeal in the particular ideological texts. This would also include the analysis of particular symbols, metaphors, the dynamics of their ambiguity and the intensity of their appeal.

Fourth, one needs also to study the way *counter-ideologies* are depicted and presented. This analysis would especially focus on the categorisation and descriptions of various counter-ideologies, from those that are perceived as directly threatening to those that are seen as potentially 'friendly'. One would in particular look here at the delegitimising strategies and tactics used.

This research strategy can be applied to a number of ideological texts, and where possible ritualistic practices, regardless of their historical or geographical origins and location. The aim of such an analysis would be to single out similarities and differences between diverse ideological narratives and actions without treating any particular set of ideas and practices as being intrinsically privileged and hence accepting criticism put forward by poststructuralists. In parallel with this activity, by identifying common features of nominally different ideological stories, one would be in position to make some theoretically interesting generalisations about the nature of ideology. In this way if the model employed gives sufficient interpretation for the phenomena under study then it would achieve its main aim. It would provide the interpretation for the case studies under question and at the same time would demonstrate that the concept of ideology is still theoretically and methodologically viable. It would give an interpretation of ideology structure of particular societies or groups and would tell us at the same time something sociologically interesting about the concept of ideology. By focusing on identifiable patterns of ideologies as they have been developed and articulated in the ritual practices, educational system, mass media and any other social events and institutions one is in a position to find out what is common to many apparently diverse social and political orders. Studying the form and content of the language used, the character of symbols and metaphors, the portrayal of the main enemies and their ideas, the depiction of distinctive individual or collective agents as well as the general perceptions of social reality as they are tightly interwoven in the dominant texts and rituals can tell us a great deal about the human condition. Instead of the unproductive fixation on the 'economics of untruth' and 'politics of truth' it is more fruitful to dispense with the search for 'truth claims' altogether and focus our attention on the form and content of particular statements and practices. Rather than attempting to reveal the true hidden meanings behind veiled reality, either through structural analysis, dialectics, archaeology, genealogy or deconstruction, as advocated by structuralists, Marxists and poststructuralists, we can gain much more analytically when we focus our attention on the form and contents of nominally highly diverse ideologies. What matters in such an analysis is not whether a particular statement or practice is false, deceiving, manipulative or instrumental but rather what does it tell us about the particular understanding of social world – what type of language it relies on, who is the targeted recipient of its message, what kind of popular appeal it makes, what kind of image of the world it espouses and so on. The point of a successful ideology analysis is not to demonstrate that somebody else's views are wrong or dishonest – this is often no more than simple daily politics – but rather to identify some relatively universal forms of collective thinking and acting.

However, in order not to reduce ideologies to party politics, worldviews, incomparable discourses or language games that have equal structural or ontological standings and thus lose the analytical strength of this concept it is also necessary to distinguish between the two layers at which most ideologies operate – that is normative (or official) and operative levels. Although this distinction will receive detailed elaboration and empirical application in Chapter 4 it requires a summary description here. Thus, normative ideology largely refers to what Seliger would call 'fundamental principles which determine the final goals and the grand vistas in which they will be realised' (Seliger, 1976: 109). This layer of ideology contains all the central pillars of any particular value system including views and ideas on the complete organisation and structure of past, present and future for the particular society. It spells out in a relatively clear and coherent way what relationships between individuals and groups are taking place and what ought to be in order to change or preserve them. It gives a relatively consistent set of moral prescriptions often based on a particular set of knowledge claims and presents these prescriptions and claims as if addressing entire human kind. Unlike its normative counterpart the operative layer of ideology is one that is encountered in the features and patterns of everyday life in any given society. This type of ideology can consist of different conceptual elements and principles, some of which can serve to justify actual or potential social action. This is the form of ideology that penetrates and fills out social life through institutional and non-institutional channels. It consists of commonly (but not universally) shared patterns of belief and practice among the particular group of individuals. It is the way ideology functions and operates in the circumstances of daily routine.

The relationship between the normative and operative layers of ideology tends to be fairly complex and very much a matter of empirical evidence relating to individual case studies. The two can be composed of the same elements but they can also integrate entirely different ideas, values and practices. The cases of the Soviet Union and al-Qaeda's network provide very good examples. As evident from the analysis of their official documents, including the Soviet constitution and numerous communist party resolutions for the Soviet case, and the Quran, Sharia and Sunnah for Bin Laden's network, their normative ideologies were Marxism-Leninism and Islamism respectively. However, by analysing the patterns of their operative ideologies as they have been developed and have operated in the educational system, mass media, websites, recruiting videos or institutionalised rituals and other mass events, one could conclude that their operative ideologies were rather different – that is imperialist and traditionalist (Lane, 1984) in the case of the Soviet Union or nationalist and tribalist in the case of Bin Laden's group (McAuley, 2005).[9]

These and similar studies have also demonstrated that the most useful research tool in the analysis of ideologies tends to be a comparative method, because by using this technique one is able to produce more generalised findings concerning the nature of ideology. Comparative analysis also allows for the examination of differently articulated ideologies without the need for the crude true–false criteria. The emphasis then is not on whether particular ideas, beliefs, values and practices are true or not but rather what they consist of, what kind of feelings and emotions they provoke, what they offer to their followers, what kind of action they mobilise, or how they operate on normative and operative levels. In this way we will not focus exclusively on the modes of production, on logical patterning or on deconstruction or discursive framing, as with structuralism and post structuralism, in order to demonstrate how social structures create alienating human beings or coercively condition our bodies and hence produce iniquitous social relations. Instead our attention shifts to the form and contents of differently structured and articulated ideologies in order to pinpoint their similarities and differences. The findings that this type of research could yield, for example, that Syria and the United States have much in common at the level of operative ideology, despite their contrasting and mutually exclusive normative ideologies, would be politically provocative, theoretically interesting and sociologically important.

By applying this analytic approach and comparative method we are in position to overcome both unreflective and 'totalitarian' hard essentialism as well as the radical relativism and nihilism of poststructuralist critique. In other words, the theory and concept of ideology can be preserved by accepting and integrating some of poststructuralist ideas without the automatic incorporation of its relativist epistemology and its unsatisfactory research strategy.

Conclusion

In this chapter I have critically reviewed and analysed the main structuralist and poststructuralist approaches to the concept of ideology. I have tried to show that despite some positive criticism of poststructuralist approaches such as their critique of the totalistic ambitions and hard essentialist methodology of structuralism, their complete rejection of the concept of the ideology is unfounded. Concepts such as 'discourse', 'identity', 'language games', 'simulacras' or 'meta-narratives' recommended by poststructuralists in place of ideology have been criticised as adding very little to structuralist notion of ideology. It is thus argued that with the exception of clear and radical anti-scientism, poststructuralist approaches differ little from structuralism in their understanding of ideology. It is claimed that the concept and theory of ideology can be rehabilitated by removing it from its structuralist and Marxist emphasis on truth, science and macro structure. Instead, a new, more agency and content oriented model of ideology has been proposed. The next step is to explore whether this approach to the study of ideology has a secure empirical foundation. However before one embarks on empirical exploration it is necessary to provide adequate theoretical elaboration of this position. To do so it is essential to critically engage with the prevailing orthodoxy in contemporary sociology which denies the importance of ideology for the smooth operation of modern societies.

Part II
Theories

4
The Dominant Ideology of Modernity

Introduction

Although the poststructuralist critique of ideology has had a significant impact, a more devastating criticism has come from within sociology itself. The epistemologically external critique mounted by the anti-essentialist camp is thus reinforced by the internal, modernist and empirically grounded arguments of historical and political sociology, together nailing the coffin shut on both Marxist and functionalist concepts and theories of ideology. In a series of studies published between the late 1970s and early 1990s, Abercrombie, *et al.* (1978, 1980, 1983, 1986, 1990) made a decisive impact on the sociological understanding of ideology. In these works they provided a coherent theoretical, and a meticulous empirical, mostly historical, debunking of the so-called dominant ideology thesis (DIT). By challenging the two leading paradigms of their day, namely structuralist Marxism and structural functionalism, they attempted to demonstrate the analytical limitations of the dominant ideology concept in both of its uses: when linked to class structure as in Marxism, and in the notion of common culture apropos of the Parsonian functionalist tradition. Their argument was essentially that there is no, and never has been, such a thing as 'dominant ideology', in the sense of intra- and inter-group value unity, and that both functionalism and Marxism overstate the importance of shared values as generators of social action. Their research found that in pre-modern historical epochs there was little actual ideological amalgamation of subordinate social groups, and that the dominant ideas of the ruling groups had much more to do with the rulers themselves (providing a necessary sense of unity) than with the ruled masses. Furthermore they argued that this is even more pronounced in the context of modernity since the fragmented nature of advanced capitalism does not require ideological conformity for its smooth operation. In other words the notion of dominant ideology, as formulated both by Marxists and functionalists, never existed in the past and is unnecessary to the effective functioning of modern societies in the present.

This chapter challenges this view. While accepting many of the criticisms levelled against Marxist and functionalist accounts of the DIT, I argue that the concept remains sociologically indispensable when attempting to deal with the dominant ideological narrative of modernity – nationalism. In other words, the 'dominant ideology thesis' retains its theoretical and empirical value when re-conceptualised in broader and more subtler terms so to avoid the pitfalls of norm-centred functionalism and class-centred Marxism. The chapter is organised around the argument that nationalism, in all its diverse forms, remains an essential source and the principal glue of state legitimacy. However to fully comprehend its ideological power one needs to dissect a given society's ideological makeup at the two levels sketched in the last chapter – normative and operative. The potency of nationalism comes from its ability to adapt and metamorphose so as to dovetail with distinct and often contradictory official doctrines. In other words while normative ideologies may be transient and ephemeral, and may change or proliferate in different directions, operative ideologies, in the age of modernity, tend to remain stable and endure couched in the dominant narrative of nationalism. To substantiate this argument the chapter conducts a comparative analysis of three very diverse cases – post revolutionary Iran, Cold War Yugoslavia and contemporary Britain. By looking at the form and content of dominant ideologies in these three societies it aims to demonstrate that despite their mutually exclusive official doctrines all three cases show a great deal of similarity at the operative level where differently articulated nationalism remains a dominant ideology.

Dominant ideology thesis: the critique and after

Although the concept of dominant ideology is generally traced back to the famous statement from *The German Ideology* – 'the ideas of the ruling class are in every epoch the ruling ideas' (Marx and Engels, 1982: 64) – most commentators agree that Marx did not subscribe to a simple and a crude version of the DIT. Rather he developed a multi-layered theory of ideology that oscillates between functionalist and structuralist arguments

in its interpretation of social action as linked to the relations of production (Boudon, 1989, Markus, 1991, Malešević, 2002: 12–13). In fact
Abercrombie, *et al.* (1980: 8–9) explicitly argue that Marx did not adopt
the view of ideological incorporation of one class by the other. The
stronger versions of this thesis are far more discernible in the works of
structural Marxists such as Althusser, Poulantzas, Miliband, but also some
Frankfurt School theorists such as Marcuse and early Habermas.
According to Abercrombie *et al.* (1980: 29) despite minor conceptual
differences, all of these authors espouse a version of the DIT. The thesis is
constructed around four central propositions: (a) there is a dominant
ideology in capitalist society; (b) the existence of dominant ideology is
beneficial to the ruling classes; (c) through the dominant ideology subordinated classes are ideologically assimilated and made politically inert;
and (d) the apparatus of ideology dissemination has to be strong enough
to conceal the inherent contradictions of capitalism.

While originating in a completely different theoretical tradition and
developing on interpretation of social reality which is distinct from
Marxism, functionalism also operates with a notion analogous to that of
dominant ideology – 'common culture'. Although rejecting an instrumentalist view of ideological incorporation as articulated in materialist
perspectives, functionalists such as Parsons, Shils, and to a certain extent
Merton, also work with the view that societies require and are able to
achieve a substantial degree of ideological unity. Parsons's general theory
of social action (1937), and even more so his later work on the social
systems (1951), interpret social relations in a norm-centred way. For
Parsons 'the stability of the social system arises from the fact that the cultural patterns which are part of the general symbolic apparatus of society
are also embedded in people's minds' (Abercrombie *et al.*, 1980: 47–8). In
other words sharing common values, meanings and norms and passing
them onto young members of society through socialisation are essential
prerequisites for the existence of a meaningful social order. Despite the
inevitable individual differences all actors internalise dominant ideas of
their own society and adopt the 'central value system'. Thus just as in
Marxism here one finds a depiction of society as an entity which is more
or less culturally unified. Marxism sees this as a product of structural
manipulation originating in the exploitative nature of the capitalist economy, and aims to radically transform it, while functionalism sees it as an
inescapable law-like necessity of social life, yet both perspectives subscribe
to the view that there is a value unity at work in contemporary societies.

Abercrombie *et al.* (1980: 58, 1990) strongly oppose the existence of
such ideological unity. By examining pre-modern social orders in detail

as well as studying the contemporary capitalist world, they argue that 'ideology generally plays a secondary, partial and insignificant role in social order'. While they recognise that feudalism and early capitalism had more ideological coherency, the feudal order being infused with a Christian ethos and early capitalism with the doctrine of individualism, even here the sense of common values was more espoused and more important as a source of unity at the level of ruling groups. The near absence of state apparatuses of ideology dissemination as well as the strong cultural polarisation between peasants and aristocracy prevented the incorporation of one class by another. Although modernity has provided mechanisms of value transmission such as mass media and educational systems, the radically novel political and economic structure that emerged with the Enlightenment has, according to Abercrombie *et al.* (1980: 157–9), prevented the materialisation of ideological unity. In their view late capitalism is characterised by the existence of more diverse values, less normative coherence and less value incorporation of the dominant classes. The main mechanisms of social integration are material and coercive rather than normative: 'social classes do have different and conflicting ideologies but are, nevertheless, bound together by the network of objective social relations' (Abercrombie *et al.*, 1980: 168). Thus modernity does not require an ideological underpinning since 'there is no economic requirement for it' and 'late capitalism can function perfectly without it' (Abercrombie *et al.*, 1980: 185).

Similarly the functionalist argument regarding the necessity of cultural accord is also dismissed on the grounds that modernity, far from requiring cultural uniformity, as Durkheim (contra Parsons) was already well aware in his elaboration of mechanical and organic solidarity, is largely dependent on the proliferation of distinct ways of living. In this respect Parsonians make the error of minimising structural differences between traditional and modern social orders, portraying them all as exhibiting similar principles of value consensus and ritualistic re-affirmation. However as Abercrombie *et al.* demonstrate, neither modern nor traditional orders depend on common culture: while late capitalism thrives on cultural diversity, the pre-modern world lacked the means of cultural transmission (thus preventing successful socialisation beyond the small in-groups) and it was coercion rather than its normative counterpart that was the more important mechanism of social control.

Although Abercrombie *et al.* provide a powerful and historically well-documented critique of the DIT, the inherent economism of their approach prevents them from appreciating the more subtle impact ideas and values have on social action. Whereas one can find partial recognition of the shortcomings of this view, acknowledging for example that their argument is 'production' oriented and focuses predominantly on work and class structure (Abercrombie, 1990: 199), or that their analysis 'implies an economistic theory of social and cultural relations' where 'social solidarity is explained by economic constraint' (Turner, 1990: 231), or that their original position was indeed economistic but it 'put forward a distinctive twist to existing Marxist theory' (Hill, 1990: 1), there is little to suggest that they have attempted to surmount this economism. On the contrary, their later work aims to justify earlier arguments by depicting them as pioneering criticisms of unreflexive Marxism which anticipated contemporary developments in social thought such the cultural turn, neo-functionalism and postmodernism (Turner, 1990).

However their persistence with hard economistic and structuralist argument prevents them from understanding or accounting for the impact that values and action oriented ideas have on social groups. This is particularly relevant when one attempts to go beyond their (almost exclusive) focus on a single politico-economic order (capitalism) and a single geographical location (Europe). This stubborn adherence to economistic structuralism evokes at least three fundamental criticisms: (a) an inadequate understanding of culture; (b) a profound neglect of politics; and (c) macro-structural determinism.

First, the authors of the DIT operate with a somewhat paradoxical understanding of culture which is both too wide and too narrow. Their conceptualisation of ideology tends to allow only for two possible versions of 'culture' – the functionalist norm-centred view and the materialist interest-centred perspective (Abercrombie *et al.*, 1980: 252). In neither case is culture analysed on its own terms as a partially sui generis phenomena and thus remains a second order reality whose substance is derived either from the system's inherent need for the existence of normative social order, or from the necessity of a particular mode of production. On the one hand the latter understanding is very narrow, linked primarily to socio-economic structure of Europe and beyond this to the Western or semi-Westernised world. On the other hand the former view is absurdly wide and conflates culture and ideology. The problem here is that neither position allows for a non-instrumentalist or non-normativist concepts of culture such as those developed in neo-Weberian (Collins, 1986), neo-Simmelian (Bauman, 1997), interactionist (Jenkins, 2002) or poststructuralist perspectives (Bhaba, 1994).

Second, the argument against DIT avoids the role of political institutions and tends to assimilate politics to economics. This is partially recognised by Turner (1990: 251) who acknowledges that arguments in the DIT 'may be criticized for failing to analyse ideology in relation to politics' and in particular the role of citizenship. While they do provide some interesting analysis of the role, function and organisation of political and other elites in various historical periods, most of this analysis remains embedded in the language of political economy, and leaves little or no room for the autonomy of the state. Most problematic here is their explicit dismissal[10] of the main political institutions of ideology transmission such as mass media and educational system, but also their explanatory neglect of the role of military apparatus, political parties or scientific institutions and authorities in the articulation and dissemination of ideology. This is a grave omission since as most empirical research shows (Apple and Wies, 1983, GUMG, 1985, MacKenzie, 1989, Miller, 1991, Herman and Chomsky, 1994) these state institutions are clearly influential in the formulation and transmission of ideological messages.

Finally, despite their declared commitment to agency-centred analyses their approach to the study of ideology is a profoundly macro-structural enterprise. They conceptualise DIT in a very hard way which requires every ideological narrative to have internal coherency, thus foreclosing on the kinds of subtleties, inconsistencies and tensions which are intrinsic to ideological thought and which tend to help rather than hinder the dissemination of successful ideologies. As Billig *et al.* (1988) rightly point out, the power of ideologies is built into their conflicting and partially incoherent messages – that is their dilemmatic structure. Furthermore, a fully elaborated ideological narrative demands high levels of discursive literacy, which automatically excludes a great majority of the population from 'absorbing' the concepts of dominant ideology. If dominant ideologies exhibited the coherent and fully articulated form presupposed by Abercrombie, Hill and Turner, then obviously ideologies would have no resonance outside the narrow group of ideologues and their disciples. However this is not how ideologies operate. Instead of crude macro-structural narratives mediated by particular modes of production, what takes place is a subtle 'translation' of semi-coherent dominant normative doctrines into a set of micro stories, with recognisable discourses, events and actors which are available and accessible to the general population (Malešević, 2002). Ideology is not a 'thing' as Abercrombie, Hill and Turner seem to suggest, but rather a complex, multi-faceted and messy *process*. It is also not merely a sphere of ideas and values which are disconnected or opposed to 'material constraints'. On the contrary ideology is best conceived, as Michael Freeden (1996: 43–6, 2003: 71–2) proposes, a 'thought–action', or in more precise terms 'a form of thought–behaviour that penetrates all [social and] political practice'. Sociologically speaking ideology is to be understood as thought–action related to the conceptual organisation of a particular social order. Its contents often surpass experience and are largely non-testable as they offer 'a transcendent vision of social authority' (Mann, 2005: 30, 1986: 519). Ideologies make an appeal to moral norms, individual or collective interests or to superior knowledge with the purpose of justifying potential or actual social action. As I have argued elsewhere (Malešević, 2002) little is gained when ideologies are evaluated in terms of true/false and science/non-science criteria. Ideology is best conceptualised as a relatively universal phenomenon, potentially present in all social action. Thus, as I have argued in the Chapter 3, the traditional sociological pre-occupation with the (macro-structural) *function* of ideology should give a way to the (agency-oriented) analysis of its *form and content*.

While Abercrombie *et al.* provide a useful and pointed criticism of the traditional Marxist/functionalist comprehension of ideology, the three shortcomings discussed above prevent them from engaging with and understanding the dominant ideology of modernity: nationalism.

Nationalism as a dominant (operative) ideology of modernity

As most macro-sociologists and socially minded historians now agree, nationalism is a modern phenomenon (Gellner, 1983, Smith, 1991, Breuilly, 1993, Hobsbawm, 1992). The pre-modern world was too politically, economically and especially socially hierarchical and stratified to allow for any significant degree of congruence between polity and culture. Before the era of Enlightenment and the French Revolution the social realm was clearly divided between small nobility concerned with status and prone to warfare, and the masses of illiterate agricultural producers who were both socially and geographically immobile. This separated the world of 'high' Latin speaking culture, concerned with recovering the glory of the Roman Empire under the guise of Christianity, from the ocean of 'low' oral cultures of the peasant populations, who communicated through a multitude of unstandardised and often mutually incomprehensible vernaculars. This was also the world of empires, fiefdoms and city-states, all underpinned by a shared belief in the monarch's right to rule on the basis of blood and 'divine origins'. Although there existed notions of France, England or Russia, very few among the general population would conceive of themselves as Russian, English or French, identifying instead with a particular family, clan, religious group or village. In other words, for nations to happen it was necessary that an overwhelming majority of the population were transformed 'from peasants into Frenchmen' (Weber, 1976). So the individual sense of nationhood goes hand in hand with dramatic structural transformations – the birth of the modern bureaucratic rationalistic state, the introduction and expansion of mass public education conducted through a single standardised vernacular, the corresponding growth of literacy, and the democratisation and secularisation of public space. Nationalism is born in and expands with modernity: initially the preserve of political and cultural elites, the excluded intelligentsia, disappointed revolutionaries and a few literate others, through the nineteenth century it gradually captured the hearts and minds of the middle classes in Europe and America (Mann, 1988). With the extension of the franchise and other citizenship rights to manual workers, peasants, and later women and minorities, nationalism cemented itself as the dominant ideology in the northern hemisphere. The steady erosion of colonial rule from the 1950s and the establishment of new independent states worldwide further extended nationalism, from a largely European or Northern phenomenon into a truly global and dominant ideology of modernity.

Since its power and mass appeal expanded simultaneously with the proliferation of modern bureaucratic state structures and corresponding mechanisms of integration such as civil, political and social rights (Marshal, 1948, Mann, 1988), welfare provisions, economic growth and coercive apparatuses, the development of nationalism and the modern state is a deeply intertwined process.

Breuilly (1993) and Mann (1995) have both argued convincingly, and demonstrated empirically, that one of the key reasons why nationalism and the modern state became so entangled lies in the big rupture caused by modernity, meaning in this case the relation between the newly emerging arenas of the civil society and the sovereign state. The expansion of capitalism, the development of a centralising administrative apparatus under the authority of a territorially bound, and often war-prone state, the secularisation of society and increasing literacy rates among the general population all created a fundamental tension between the public, rational and often absolutist state on the one hand and the expanding private sphere of civil society on the other. All modern ideologies such as liberalism, socialism and conservatism emerged in this period; all offered a coherent, plausible and relatively certain answer on how to reconcile the conflict between the (often dehumanising) realm of the public, and the (emotional) realm of the private.

However, despite the obvious successes of socialism, conservatism and liberalism it is nationalism in its many guises that proved to be the most potent and popular ideology of modernity. Both historically and geographically one finds nationalist movements and doctrines spreading with equal vigour on the right, center and left of the political spectrum – from the Flemish Block and Bharatiya Janata Party (BJP), to Kuomintang and Peronism, to Sinn Feinn or the Socialist Party of Serbia. Nationalism comes to prominence in times of economic crisis just as in times of unprecedented economic boom (Connor, 1994). The ascendancy and vigour of nationalist discourse is to be found today in the most globalised areas of the world such as North America or Europe as much as in the most isolated and sanction ridden states such as North Korea or Myanmar. Whether acute or dormant, or to use Billig's (1995) terminology, whether hot or cold/banal, nationalism remains the most potent ideology of modernity. More than any other ideology nationalism was able to articulate narratives that promised to reconcile the tension between the public and the private, the institutional and the communal, the political and the cultural, utilising the most egalitarian and democratic expression – 'we the nation'. As Gellner (1997: 74) succinctly phrases it: 'nationalism is a phenomenon of *Gesellschaft* using the idiom of *Gemeinschaft*: a mobile anonymous society simulating a closed cosy community'.

The success of nationalist narrativity has a lot to do with its ability to offer a solution to the problem of personal oblivion in a secular age, thus providing a modern equivalent of religious belief (Kedourie, 1960, Smith, 2003a). It also owes much to the ability of political elites to 'invent traditions' in times of dramatic social change (Hobsbawm, 1992) which also facilitates the changing nature of geopolitics and war in the post-feudal period (Giddens, 1985, Mann, 1988). We now have some answers as to why nationalism has become such a prevalent discourse in modern times but we still know very little about the workings of nationalist ideology. We know that in the modern age the two main pillars of political legitimacy are the ability to generate economic growth and nationalism (Gellner, 1997: 25), but we lack a coherent account of the machinery of nationalism – its inner workings and logics. To do that one has to look more closely at the structure, form and content of the various modalities that nationalist ideology can take. As I have argued elsewhere (Malešević, 2002) it is fruitful to analyse conceptual segments of ideological narratives such as the statements and practices relating to the prospective organisation of a particular society (economy, politics, culture and the image of the nation), the dominant actors depicted in the narratives, the type of language used, as well as the portrayal of principal counter-ideologies. But to understand the potency of ideological appeal it is essential to dissect the two principal layers through which political ideologies operate, that is, the realm of the normative and that of the operative.

The domain of the normative is articulated in ideal typical terms. It is built around principles outlining fundamental goals and values as well as providing a blueprint for the realisation of these goals. The normative realm contains a strong kernel of utopian thinking as conceptualised by Mannheim (1936), a set of ideas that 'transcend the present' and are geared towards the future. This realm is formulated to espouse key tenets of a particular *weltanschauung*, providing well-elaborated statements and diagnoses regarding the structure and organisation of the past, the present and the future of an entire society. It is in the normative domain where ideas concerning actual and possible relationships between individuals and groups are clearly spelled out and the assessment of their present or future direction is provided. More than anything, the normative realm presents a relatively clear and uncompromising set of ethical prescriptions which are in large part derived from concrete knowledge claims or 'given' moral absolutes. In this respect the normative realm is articulated in a way which is profoundly universalist. It may explicitly or implicitly address humanity as a whole by speaking with the voice of moral or cognitive (or both) authority. Its focus can be on individuals or a specific group (i.e. workers, women, citizens, etc.) but its message generally remains within the confines of rationality, ethical universality, or the combination of both. Even when aimed at a very particular collectivity it still operates through a logic and language that resonates beyond the borders of that particular community. The realm of the normative defines itself through reason and ethics and is most likely to challenge other *weltanschauungen* by pinpointing faults in their ethics and reasoning. The normative layer of ideology is most often deduced from authoritative texts and scriptures such as religious 'holy books' (Bible, Quran, Talmud, Vedas, etc.), the influential publications of mystics, philosophers, prophets, scientists, or documents with powerful legal, ethical or semi-sacred status (Bill of Rights, Declarations of Independence, Magna Carta, Geneva Convention etc.), the constitutions of sovereign states, political and party manifestos, and so on.

The operative realm functions rather differently. It is an arena of everyday life with all its complexities, contingencies and ideational flux. The concepts, ideas, values and practices present in this realm can never be ultimate, final or uncompromising. This is a domain of existential ambiguity and a constant value dynamism where different images of the world and different diagnoses of reality compete for the 'souls' of each and all. The operative realm is expressed in institutional as well as extra-institutional arenas of individual and social life. It is the way that ideas and values, often evident in socio-cultural practices and rituals, operate in the routine circumstances of daily life in any given society. The dominant beliefs and values in this domain can be composed of different concepts and ideas, some of which can be intentionally formulated with the aim of justifying a particular course of action (or inaction), or to legitimise or de-legitimise particular policies. The realm of the operative is the realm of the mundane. However, unlike Durkheim's (1915) understanding, the mundane does not always equal the profane. On the contrary the operative realm can be articulated and visualised by majorities as the arena of the sacred, just as much, if not more, as the normative realm can be. Since the operative realm has to address, in one or another way the majority of the population in any given society, it is bound to rely on simplified concepts, language and images with popular appeal. It is also more likely to use emotional and instrumental discourse when making an appeal to the public. The general message, and in particular the key principles and ideas employed in this realm are more likely to be personalised in the image of concrete individuals so as to be recognisable and acceptable to the mass public. Most of all, the operative layer of ideology is more likely to address individuals and groups as members of a very specific interest and emotion bound groups using a narrow particularist discourse. The language of the operative realm is most often the language of affect and individual or collective self-interest. To dissect the dominant operative ideas and values of a particular collectivity or society one can analyse such sources as school textbooks, tabloid newspapers, mainstream news programmes on the TV, specific internet web-sites, political or commercial adverts, speeches of political leaders, and so on.

The relationship between the normative and operative realms, that is, between the two layers of ideology is always a question of empirical evidence. They may overlap, express similar or even identical values and ideas, but more often than not tend to be composed of differently articulated concepts. For example, analysing the dominant normative and operative layers of ideology in the cases of communist Yugoslavia and post-communist Serbia and Croatia, I have attempted to demonstrate how, despite sharp differences on the normative level, all three cases exhibit a great deal of similarity on the level of operative ideology. Whereas normative ideology may be as different as 'self-management' and 'reformed democratic socialism' or 'Christian democracy', in all three cases the operative ideology was found to be staunchly nationalist (Malešević, 2002). Careful analysis of the inner workings of normative and operative layers of ideology can bring us much closer to understanding the complexities of nationalist appeal. To achieve this it is essential to recognise that nationalism is not only a dominant ideology of modernity (as seen from the West or North), as argued by Gellner, Mann, Smith and other leading historical sociologists, but more precisely that it is a dominant *operative* ideology of modern times. Whether democratic or authoritarian, left wing or right wing, religious or secularist, radical or moderate, at the end of the day modern political orders tend predominantly to legitimise their rule or to delegitimise the rule of others in nationalist terms. In other words the rulers of any modern nation-state may formulate their official doctrine or normative ideology as liberal, socialist, Islamist, or environmentalist, but their operative ideologies are more likely to supplement those normative ideals with an extensive dose of nationalism. Regardless of the official pronouncements made by various governments and oppositional groups representing or attempting to represent a particular nation-state, and these are invariably couched in universalist terms, it is nationalism, in all its forms, which remains the dominant operative ideology of the modern age. To demonstrate this I provide a brief analysis of three diverse case studies generally considered to be the epitome of ideological difference: Islamic Iran, communist Yugoslavia and liberal-democratic United Kingdom. The argument is that despite sharp and irreconcilable differences in their normative ideologies there is a great deal of congruence between their respective operative ideologies, with all three articulated in strict nationalist terms. The analysis of the normative level of ideology will focus on the State Constitutions as they most succinctly articulate the dominant official doctrine of any modern nation-state. The operative ideology will be decoded from key speeches of the respective leaders, as well as from school textbooks as they most effectively reflect the dominant values of the operative realm.

The two layers of ideology

The focus of the analysis is the differences and similarities between the two layers of ideology and not on the popular reception of normative or operative layers, as this would require a more thorough and complex study. Unfortunately there is little trustworthy research on the social effects of ideology 'translation' in general and none that I am aware of for the three case studies analysed here. Furthermore in two of my case studies there is a profound lack of reliable information regarding the popular response to ruling ideas and practices, not least because of the non-democratic nature of two societies under study (Iran and Yugoslavia). As Shlapentokh (1982) both argues and demonstrates, in such socio-political orders the sincerity of the answers given by respondents in public polls and surveys, under implicit or explicit political duress, cannot be trusted. This is especially so with a sensitive issue like ideology which potentially challenges or threatens the ideas and practices of the rulers. Similarly, as no genuine democratic elections were held in either of these two cases one cannot make inference about the popularity of particular ideas and practices from the results. However, as Beetham (1991) and Huntington (1968) argue, in authoritarian systems of rule one can infer the popularity of the ruling doctrine indirectly from mass mobilisation. Since in both of these two cases the ruling doctrine was sustained by pervasive mass mobilisation including intensive leader adulation (Tito and Khomeini), widespread and regular street gatherings, as well as the unprecedented mass participation at the post-revolutionary plebiscites in support of the new socio-political order, there is substantial ground to argue the case of widespread support for the ruling doctrine. The third case (United Kingdom) is more complicated as it involves a democratic political order characterised by regular elections, freedom of information and assembly, together with vibrant public debates on key ideational constituents of the social order. However despite pronounced opposition from some quarters concerning core values of the normative doctrine (liberal democracy and state nationalism), all available surveys suggest intensive popular support for the dominant values of both the normative (liberal democracy) and operative (state nationalism) layers of ideology. So for example as Eurobarometer surveys consistently show the population of the United Kingdom expresses by far the strongest sense of belonging to their nation-state. In the most recent survey when asked whether they feel European only, European and national, or national only, 67 per cent of respondents express the attitude that they feel strong attachment only to their nation (Eurobarometer, 2000: 11). Similarly, as the recent Rowentree Fund Survey on the state of British Democracy indicates, an overwhelming majority of UK citizens support a liberal democratic political order, including over 80 per cent support for the Bill of Rights (with 93 per cent support for the inclusion of the right to a fair trial, 85 per cent for privacy in personal communication, and 78 per cent for the right to free assembly for peaceful demonstrations) while 90 per cent express the view that ordinary voters should have a great deal of influence over state policy (JRRT, 2004: 4).

Islamic Iran

The contours of the dominant normative ideology in the Iranian case can be extracted from the 1979 Constitution of the Islamic Republic of Iran (CIRI). This document states that Shia Islam of the Twelver Ja'fari sect is the State's official religion and ideology. According to the Constitution this view is sanctioned 'by the people of Iran on the basis of their longstanding belief in the sovereignty of truth and Qur'anic justice' (CIRI, 1979: Article 1). This revolutionary republican Shia doctrine is grounded in a belief' 'in One God (as stated in the phrase "There is no god except Allah"), His exclusive sovereignty and the right to legislate, and the necessity of submission to His commands' (CIRI, 1979: Article 2.1). In other words, absolute sovereignty over the world and man belongs to God and not to the people. The Constitution stipulates that all laws in the State (e.g. civil, military, economic, cultural etc.) have to be 'based on Islamic criteria' (CIRI, 1979: Article 4). One of the central ethical goals of the Republic is fostering the conditions 'for the growth of moral virtues based on faith and piety and the struggle against all forms of vice and corruption' (CIRI, 1979: Article 3.1). This is clearly a normative realm formulated as a set of uncompromising and universalistic moral prescriptions.

The Constitution also explains that the economic system is divided between the State, co-operative and private sectors, but all three are 'to be based on systematic and sound planning'. The system has to be 'self-sufficient', 'correct and just', can not go 'beyond the bounds of Islamic law', while the State itself reserves the right to administer and control 'all large-scale and mother industries' (e.g. banking, foreign trade, power generation, radio and television, postal services, railroads, etc.) (CIRI, 1979: Articles 3, 43, 44). The family is seen as 'the fundamental unit of Islamic society' (CIRI, 1979: Article 10) and it is stated that 'government must ensure the rights of women in all respects, in conformity with Islamic criteria' (CIRI, 1979: Article 21). Following specific verses from the Qur'an the constitution specifies that 'all Muslims form a single nation' which implies that the State 'has the duty of formulating its general policies with a view to cultivating the friendship and unity of all Muslim peoples'; is committed to 'the defence of the rights of all Muslims'; and 'must constantly strive to bring about the political, economic, and cultural unity of the Islamic world' (CIRI, 1979: Articles 3.16, 11, 152).

The message given in the normative ideology is clearly a universalist one making an appeal to the superior knowledge and the moral absolutes as formulated in a specific literary source – Qur'an. The focus is on universal principles and ideas which go beyond the particularity of any single state, nation or political order. When the concept of nation is invoked it does not refer so much to Iran but rather to 'all Muslims' which potentially include all human beings. The normative ideology legitimises itself by invoking the discourse of morality and reason. It calls upon what is considered to be the ultimate form of ethics (Quranic justice) and the most rational and advanced form of social organisation (Islamic republic).

The operative level of ideology as discernible from school textbooks published in the post-revolutionary period, and key speeches of the 'founding father of the Republic', Ayatolah Khomeini,[11] give us a very different picture of reality. While here too Islamic principles are empha- sised in culture, politics, economy and the social sphere, there is a particular twist to it, that is they are largely couched in nationalist terms.

While reading Khomeini's speeches one encounters numerous references to the 'the noble Iranian nation', 'our beloved country', 'dear nation', 'beloved Iran' and so on (Khomeini, 1985: 243–4). Instead of deriving legitimacy from the unquestionable doctrines of Qur'an and the clergy's exclusive ability to access these ultimate truths as stated in the Constitution, in the speeches their superiority comes principally from loyalty to the nation. Hence one can read how – 'the noble Iranian nation, by supporting the genuine and committed Iranian clergy, who have always been the guardians and protectors of this country, will remit their debts to Islam and will cut off the hands of all of history's oppressors of their country' (Khomeini, 1985: 247). The speaker rarely discusses the complexity of theological arguments but instead refers to the need to 'defend your dignity and honour' and since 'our dignity has been trampled underfoot; the dignity of Iran has been destroyed' (Khomeini, 1985: 243, 181). Instead of a universalistic appeal to broth- erhood among all underprivileged people, and especially the unity of all Muslims throughout the world, the speeches devote far more attention to the glorification of the Iranian nation. Thus one finds references to the 'noble Iranian Armed Forces' as Khomeini (1985: 244, 176) explains that 'we know that the commanders of the great Iranian army ... share our aims and are ready to sacrifice themselves for the sake of the dignity of Iran'. One also learns how corrupt and servile rulers 'have reduced the Iranian people to a level lower than that of an American dog', how 'gov- ernment has sold our independence, reduced us to the level of a colony'

(Khomeini, 1985: 182). Again, the focus of the speeches is less on the universal moral message of Islam than on the particularist values of nationhood couched in terms of collective self-interest and emotions.

Thus the problem with the enemy is not so much that they stray from the true religion, but rather that the enemy constitutes a physical and tangible threat: Israel is 'assaulting us, and assaulting you, the nation; it wishes to seize your economy, to destroy your trade and agriculture, to appropriate your wealth' (Khomeini, 1985: 177). The enemy is not only threatening in a material sense it also assaults the nation's dignity:

> Iranian nation! Those among you who are thirty or forty years of age or more will remember how three foreign countries attacked us during WWII. The Soviet Union, Britain, and America invaded Iran and occupied our country. The property of the people was exposed to danger and their honour was imperiled. (Khomeini, 1985: 179)

Those who do not oppose foreign influence are not only branded un-Islamic, as in the constitution, but as un-Iranian and treacherous. So Iran under the despised Shah regime 'has sold itself to obtain dollars' since when 'you take the dollars and use them and we become slaves', and in this way the former leaders are said to have 'have committed treason against this country' (Khomeini, 1985: 187). Intellectuals are also warned to give up their fascination with Westernization and Easternization and 'follow the straight path of Islam and nationalism' (Khomeini, 1985: 243).

School textbooks give us a very similar picture. Here too Islamic principles are regularly couched in nationalist terms. The Iranian nation is depicted in a primordialist sense as an ancient phenomenon emanating a sense of eternity, existing before and often beyond Islam. So one can read how 'the people of our country ... have been involved in sports since times immemorial. At the very same time the Greeks inaugurated the Olympic games, the ancient Iranians taught their children horse-riding, archery and the game of polo' (Ram, 2000: 79). Similar to Khomeini's speeches the Iranian nation is glorified by the heroes and martyrs who regularly made sacrifices for their country. The Mongol invasion was stopped only because Iranians were in possession of these noble qualities: 'in this barbarous attack the valiant people of Iran did not disdain from any display of manliness and sacrifice. Men, women, the old and the young ... excelled in the defence of the country, not accepting the disgrace of foreign rule' (Ram, 2000: 81). It is Iran and not Islam that elicits the special emotions of devotion and uniqueness, as in the following excerpt from a poem which is given prominence in the school textbooks:

> O Iran, O my splendours house! I love you. The laughter of your children, the clamour of your youth, the [battle] cries of your men, I love them all. O splendours house. I hold dear your pure soil, which is coloured with the blood of the martyrs. (Ram, 2000: 85)

Unlike the normative level of ideology which speaks in the voice of universality, rationality, and superior ethics, that is in the name of Universal Islam, the operative layer of ideology is profoundly particularistic and appeals to affect and group self-interest among a specific and exceptional social entity – the Iranian nation.

Communist Yugoslavia

The 1974 Constitution of the Socialist Federative Republic of Yugoslavia (CSFRY) provides the skeleton of a dominant normative ideology often referred to as 'socialist self-management'. Its first Article defines the State as a federal voluntary association of 'nations and their Socialist Republics' which is 'based on the power of and self-management by the working class and all working people' (CSFRY, 1974: Article 1). The central focus of the Constitution are work relations, workers and the economic system and it is emphasised that the 'socialist socio-economic system' of the State is based 'on freely associated labour and socially-owned means of production, and on self-management by the working people' (CSFRY, 1974: Article 10). In such a system the means of production are the property of the society and 'no one may gain any material or other benefits, directly or indirectly, by exploiting the labour of others' (CSFRY, 1974: Article 11). The document also refers to the authority of science (including economics) in planning the social development of society as a whole. So one is informed that 'workers in basic and other organisations of associated labour … shall have the right and duty, by relying on scientific achievements … and by taking into account economic laws, independently to adopt working and development plans and programmes for their organisations and communities …' (CSFRY, 1974: Article 69). Social planning is seen as an essential normative principle both in the economic and the social spheres: 'workers in organisations of associated labour and working people in other self-managing organisations and communities … shall be responsible for the fulfilment of the working and development plans of their organisations and communities' (CSFRY, 1974: Article 74). Hence, as with Iranian normative ideology, the central principles are derived from a realm of superior knowledge (Marxist science with rational social planning) and universal ethics (the equality of all working people and the gradual disappearance of classes).

The political system is also founded on the principle of devolving a decisive role to workers: 'power and management of social affairs shall be vested in the working class and all working people' (CSFRY, 1974: Article 88). To fully participate in decision making 'working people' were to organise themselves 'on a self-management basis in organisations of associated labour, local communities, [and] self-managing communities of interest' (CSFRY, 1974: Article 90). The rights of 'working people' are also linked to their duties and sense of responsibility relating to the dominant ideology of socialist self-management: 'every worker shall be personally responsible for the conscientious exercise of his self-management functions' (CSFRY, 1974: Article 108). As a multi-ethnic federal state Yugoslavia was devised as a state where all its 'nations and nationalities ... shall have equal rights' (CSFRY, 1974: Article 245). These rights are defined in terms of 'the freedoms, rights and duties of man and the citizen' which are to be 'realised through solidarity among people and through the fulfilment of duties and responsibilities of everyone towards all and of all towards everyone' (CSFRY, 1974: Article 153). In addition to standard citizenship rights (freedom of thought and opinion, freedom of press, profession of religion, freedom of movement, etc.), the Constitution also invokes the right to self-management where 'each individual shall be responsible for self-management decision-making and the implementation of decisions' (CSFRY, 1974: Article 155).

All the ideas expressed in the normative realm either refer to the authority of science (as the most efficient and most rational course of action), or to the authority of universal ethical principles (invoking a sense of justice for all). Again, similar to the Iranian case, though this time cast in the image of the socialist worker rather than the pious universal Muslim, normative ideology appeals to general values of relevance to humanity as a whole. Socialism is presented as the most progressive and most virtuous doctrine which is open to all open human beings. There is no reference to particularistic identities or closed group memberships. This is a transcendental realm of fundamental values and ethical absolutes.

However when one examines the articulation of this at the level of operative ideology it is possible to see, as with the Iranian case, a certain synergy of socialist self-management rhetoric with explicit reliance on nationalist discourse. One can discern this by examining excerpts from the Yugoslav leader Tito's speeches and the content of school textbooks. Tito, echoing Khomeini, addresses his public in nationalist (albeit state nationalist) rather than socialist terms. The authority of scientific central planning and ethical universality is displaced by the argument that 'We have spilt an ocean of blood for fraternity and unity of our peoples – and we shall not allow anyone to touch this or destroy it from inside, to break this fraternity and unity ...' (Tito, 1975: 2). There is less by way of reference to proletarians and workers of the world than to our 'Croatian mothers', 'brothers and sisters', to Croatian 'sons and sisters who fought together with Serbs, Slovenes, Bosnians, Montenegrins and Macedonians to clear your Croatian name', or to injustices that 'were washed with the blood of the best sons of all peoples of Yugoslavia' (Tito, 1945a: 1). Instead of socialist self-management of the workers the speaker invokes the idea of 'brotherhood and unity of peoples of Yugoslavia who fought against superior enemy force in terrible conditions and won' (Tito, 1945a: 1). Instead of appealing to the Soviet Union as a fellow socialist state sharing the goal of emancipating labour and establishing proletarian internationalism, one encounters reference to 'our big Slavic brother' whose cooperation with 'us' was 'signed by blood of our best sons' (Tito, 1945b: 1). Even the defeated enemy is not delegitimised on the grounds of inferior or unethical political ideology (i.e. Nazism) but rather by reference to ethno-national origins: 'we are entering a historical moment of unification of Slavs in the Balkans and if internally divided by quarrels we can easily become a booty of the greatest enemy of all Slavs – German conquerors' (Tito, 1945a: 1). Thus what is emphasised as essential in the process of creating a new socialist Yugoslavia is less economic equality or worker solidarity, but rather the mythical and sacred experience of fighting and dying together for the new state:

> Have you ever seen in the entire human history until this very day [a case like this] where, in the process of struggle for life and death, [Yugoslav people] with their bare hands fought and defeated the powerful enemy and in that process built such an army that all peoples of Yugoslavia can be proud of. (Tito, 1945a: 1)

This precious state, argues Tito, 'was liberated with the blood and lives of the sons of all peoples of Yugoslavia' (Tito, 1945a: 1). That is why this new state is our 'shared house' built on the human sacrifices by 'spilling a sea of blood'. And most all it is made clear that 'these sacrifices are holy, they will be remembered by our descendants for thousands of years' (Tito, 1974: 2). As such 'they have to be preserved as a pupil of one's eye' (Tito, 1966: 1).

School textbooks exhibit a similar narrative. The focus is less on socio-economic issues than on the idea of Yugoslav 'brotherhood and unity' which is continually defined and legitimised in relation to a common struggle against a common enemy. So one is informed that 'the brother-hood and unity of Serbs and Croats has been built by the struggle' and that 'the struggle of our peoples against a superior enemy was difficult and bloody' (Teodosić, 1946: 97). Here again while making explicit reference to countries of the socialist block and to the USSR in particu-lar, there is an appeal to Slavic unity instead of universal socialism. So the Soviet Union is described as our Slavic brother, 'our hope and tower of light' and its army as a 'mighty brotherly Red Army' (Čulinović, 1959: 54, Teodosić, 1946: 62). The leadership of the Communist party of Yugoslavia is not legitimised through its capacity to bring about socialist revolution but almost exclusively as liberators of the nation:

> when fascist conquerors enslaved our country in 1941, they started to destroy, rob and kill our people. Peoples of Yugoslavia have raised the uprising under the leadership of the Communist party and its spear-head comrade Tito against German, Italian and Hungarian fascists and their collaborators. (Teodosić, 1946: 62)

The ideological enemies are rarely depicted as espousing different 'recipes' of social development (i.e. liberalism, monarchism, etc.) but again are delegitimised in nationalist terms as traitors who are 'rotten', who have 'openly collaborated with occupiers', and who have 'poured' poison and acid between the peoples of Yugoslavia' and are now 'whispering from [their] holes' (Čulinović, 1959: 57–81).

Thus, one finds here a very similar pattern to the one identified in the Iranian case. The lofty normative message of progress and justice for all, or the appeal to humanity as a whole, has been transformed into an emotional and ethnocentric battle cry within the operative realm, aimed not at the world proletariat and 'the wretched of the world', but at a very specific and ideologically privileged group of people – the Yugoslavs.

Liberal-democratic United Kingdom

Although the United Kingdom of Great Britain and Northern Ireland does not have a formal Constitution as such, it has a number of legal documents such as the Acts of Government, Bill of Rights, Common law, The Human Rights Act 1998 and so on which clearly codify key ideas and principles constituting the dominant normative ideology of the State. This social and political order is termed liberal democracy and is defined as 'a system of representative and responsible government in which voters elect the members of a representative institution, the House of Commons, and the government is accountable to the House and ultimately to the electorate' (Turpin, 2002: 20). The system is underpinned by the notion of parliamentary sovereignty, which establishes the legislative supremacy of the Parliament. This is historically 'assured by the Glorious Revolution of 1688 which established the primacy of statute over prerogative' so as that the 'statutes enacted by Parliament must be enforced, and must be given priority over rules of common law, [and] international law' (Turpin, 2002: 23). The State is built on the principle of a separation of powers, so that the relation between the legislative, executive and judiciary establishes a set of checks and balances that guarantee the rule of law. The rule of law is viewed as

> ... a political ideal or principle of governance comprising values that should be reflected in the rules of the legal system and be respected by those concerned in the making, development and enforcement of the law. (Turpin, 2002: 66)

Again, as with the other two cases the realm of normative ideology is articulated by principles that transcend the particular. In this case legitimacy comes from the legislative supremacy of a system of government which is founded on reason and grounded in the tripartite division of powers thus providing the most righteous system for the organisation of social life. The ultimate principle invoked is one of parliamentary sovereignty which codifies the universal principle that all individuals are of equal moral worth and equal before the law.

This is underlined in the Human Rights Act of 1998 which guarantees citizens the following rights: the right to life, freedom from torture and slavery (including the death penalty), right to liberty and security, fair trial, freedom of thought, conscience, religion, expression and information, assembly, association, freedom from discrimination, free elections, and the peaceful enjoyment of possessions (Turpin, 2002: 142). Although this particular document is recent, the idiom of universal human rights is understood as giving expression to the original Bill of Rights (1689), a document which not only established Parliament as the ultimate ruling body of the state by limiting royal powers, such as levying money from its subjects or keeping a standing army in time of peace, but it also asserted a number of mechanisms to secure democracy such as the freedom of speech and debate, a right to petition the sovereign, free parliamentary elections, the necessity of frequent parliaments, and the abolition of 'cruel and unusual punishments'. In other words the emphasis is on the universality of human rights, and justice and equality before the law. While these principles and statutes make special provisions for the royal family, for example that it be referred to as the 'Crown' instead of the state, and that the members of government are nominally 'servants of the Crown', the powers of the monarch are nonetheless limited to the symbolic realm. The monarch has 'the right to be consulted, the right to encourage, and the right to warn' the government, but in practice has no actual power to interfere in the process of governing (Turpin, 2002: 198).

Although clearly different in terms of content, the form which normative ideology takes in the British case corresponds to the Yugoslav and Iranian cases in the sense that it too speaks through the voice of higher reason and superior ethics. While it discusses ideal-typical conditions in one concrete society, it also addresses humanity in its entirety by relying on a single and uncompromising value – the principle of human rights.

When turning to the level of operative ideology as formulated in school textbooks and speeches of leaders one again finds a shift from the universal message of liberal democratic values to the more restricted and particularist expressions of dominant values grounded in the discourse of state-centred nationalism. Hence Tony Blair regularly addresses the public in state nationalist and even ethnocentric terms rather than in the language of liberal-democratic universality, declaring himself to be a British patriot who is 'proud of my country and proud of the British people' (Blair, 1999a: 1). According to the British Prime Minister one has to be proud of being British because Britain has produced, and continues to produce 'some of the world's finest scientists, authors, composers, artists, sports people, designers'. But more than this is the unique British national character which constitutes a horizon of pride – 'what makes us different is our character: hard working, tolerant, understated, creative, courageous, generous' (Blair, 1999a: 1). And this is complemented by 'our humour, our integrity, or what people know as basic British decency' (Blair, 1999a: 1). These unique British characteristics are 'deep in the British character' and are something that one should be 'immensely proud' of because 'so much that is good in the world bears the stamp of Britain' (Blair, 1999a: 2).

Blair's speeches often make reference to historical events such as wars and other collective tragedies where Britain and the British people are depicted as heroic martyrs who sacrifice themselves for the greater cause of the nation. So he argues: 'I don't believe there was a finer episode in this often glorious history than in the Second World War when Britain led the world in a crusade against dictatorship and barbarity' (Blair, 2000: 1). This was seen as a magnificent 'victory over tyranny' and again the people are instructed to 'take pride' in such emblems of 'our country's remarkable history and achievements' (Blair, 2000: 2). There is also a need for solemn reflection given that such victories were built on enormous 'sacrifice and selflessness' on the part of ordinary British men and women, and according to the prime minister, there is a moral obligation to 'properly remember the efforts of all who ensured freedom and decency triumphed more than fifty years ago' since 'we have reaped the full rewards of this selfless sacrifice' (Blair, 2000: 2). In linking the experience of the Second World War to the more recent Kosovo war, Blair appeals to the uniqueness of British qualities: 'the poor defenceless people [of Kosovo] are begging us to show strength and determination; we would have shown unpardonable weakness and dereliction. This is not the tradition of Britain' (Blair, 1999b: 2). For Blair the unity of British people is essential and he envisages 'a one nation Britain coming together' as people continue a 'patriotic alliance that puts country before Party' (Blair, 1999a: 2, 1999c: 1).

A similar nation-centred discourse is also evident in school textbooks. As many analysts of British history and geography textbooks have documented (Crawford, 2000, Hopkin, 2001, Doyle, 2002) most textbooks espouse direct or indirect ethnocentrism which conflicts with the official commitment to pluralism, cosmopolitanism and multiculturalism. The contents of a great majority of textbooks are focused on the positive portrayal of 'British people' and Britain (Robson, 1993), glorifying its imperial past and overlooking the contributions of others. When discussing wars and other major historical events the narrative tends to represent the British nation as a unified actor standing alone against impossible odds, and achieving glorious victory through heroic sacrifice (Kallis, 1999, Crawford, 2000, 2001). For example the events of the Second World War and especially the 1941 blitz and the withdrawal of British troops from Dunkirk are discussed in many history textbooks in terms of the unique sacrifice and bravery of 'the British people': 'by June [1940] Britain stood completely alone' and the blitz 'brought out the best in people' (Lancaster and Lancaster, 1995: 560, 67). The textbooks invoke and construct a 'Dunkirk Spirit' – 'the feeling that even though Britain was alone, it would fight on until victory was done' (Gray and Little, 1997: 69). The unwavering unity and commitment to the national cause is self-evident given the fact that German air raids killed tens of thousands and destroyed millions of homes but 'did not break the will of the people' (Lancaster and Lancaster, 1995: 83). What was essential in achieving such a glorious victory was the sense of national equality: 'during the war, everyone was equal and there was a community spirit' (Lancaster and Lancaster, 1995: 69).

The layer of operative ideology again differs sharply from its normative counterpart. Instead of universal human rights, the impartial rule of the law and other liberal democratic values articulated at the normative level, operative ideology resembles the other two cases. Again one notices a dramatic slip into particularism expressed in self-adoration, the instrumentality of collective egoism and an intense emotional appeal. In place of the liberal, democratic, and cosmopolitan *citoyen* one finds a chosen people with a unique and exceptional character – the British.

Ideological power of nationalism

The argument that nationalism is the dominant operative ideology of modernity does not imply some unquestionable and uniform sense of societal cohesion as the functionalists would have it. Ideological unity is never fully accomplished. Rather it is a messy, contested, and unending struggle – a process which is shaped by social, political and historical contingencies. While this process is highly dependent on asymmetrical power relations, these are not reducible to the capitalist mode of production; they do not necessarily entail the ideological assimilation of one strata by another, and nor are they always beneficial to the rulers. This much is true of Abercrombie, Turner and Hill's criticism of the dominant ideology thesis.

However one cannot underestimate the simple fact that nearly all contemporary socio-political orders, whether described as liberal-democratic, state socialist, Islamist, Buddhist, authoritarian or bureaucratic, have one thing in common – they all tend to legitimise their existence in nationalist terms. This is not to say that nationalist discourse is the only one present in the rhetoric of state leaders, school textbooks or tabloid newspapers. That is clearly not the case. What is argued here is that for normative principles to be acceptable and to resonate with the desires, projects, aspirations of the general public, it is necessary that they be articulated in a nation-centric way. The success of a particular normative doctrine is in the process of its 'translation' into its operative counterpart. The world of abstract principles, complex and distant ideas, and grand vistas have to be transformed and concretised into accessible images, familiar personality traits, stark metaphors and the general language of everyday life. This can entail a conscious attempt at manipulation on the part of political entrepreneurs, always happy to aid such an endeavour, but in most cases it is more a matter of habit and daily routine, as certain practices, beliefs, values and modes of conduct are simply taken for granted and often reproduced in an almost mechanical way. As Billig (1995: 37) argues, it is not easy to pinpoint and analyse these discursive practices because they seem so obvious, normal and natural: 'One cannot step outside the world of nations, nor rid oneself of the assumptions and common-sense habits which come from living within that world'. And this is precisely how every successful ideological project operates. It does not lie, for that would be amateurish and in the long term counterproductive. Instead, as Barthes (1993: 143) explains, it makes things seem innocent, natural, clear and apparent. The modern nation-state as a 'bordered power-container' (Giddens, 1985) by its very design, largely created and institutionalised in the last two hundred years, provides clearly demarcated and delineated contours within which any successful attempt at self-legitimisation has to be made. No serious power seeker can dramatically amend these rules. Even a potential revolutionary cannot build the world from scratch, and every successful revolution since Second World War 'has defined itself in *national* terms' (Anderson, 1983: 12). Hence the dominance of the nationalist content of operative ideology may have less to do with the aims and actions of concrete individual power holders but much more with the existing mechanisms, institutionalised routines and geopolitical arrangements which are already in place. One does not have to be particularly nationalistic when in power, one just has to implicitly or explicitly draw on and reproduce what is already there. In this sense the modern state is like a game of chess: there are thousands of combinations one can play (as a ruler), one can even at some point exchange a pawn for a queen, but one is extremely limited in altering the existing moves of the figures on the chessboard, or in changing the structure of the board.

The striking similarities between the three operative ideologies in the case studies discussed here underlines this point. In the case of Iran, the former Yugoslavia and the United Kingdom, one encounters three extremely different and in many respects incommensurable normative ideologies, which is perhaps unsurprising given that they are drawn from three radically different cultural and geographical environments. Yet on the level of operative ideology all three cases exhibit a remarkable degree of similarity, invoking nearly identical images and metaphors of kinship and group solidarity. Unlike its normative counterpart, the operative domain is predominantly instrumental and emotional in its appeal, but more importantly the central principles of normative ideology are also transformed. Thus in all three cases the central values of Islam, socialism or human rights and democracy do not stand on their own in operative ideology, meaning the key principles around which society is to be built, but rather become submerged and deduced from the central idea of the operative ideology which is the nation. In other words while at the normative level all particularistic attachments are downplayed or subordinated to grand ethical or epistemic vistas, on the operative level it is the other way around so that where human rights and democracy, Islam and socialism are seen as valuable only insofar as they help to con-solidate or contribute to the cause of the particular nation. So despite Abercrombie *et al.*'s authoritative attempt to demonstrate otherwise, there is a process (and not a thing) called dominant ideology. For the last two hundred years nationalism has been and continues to be the domi-nant operative ideology of the modern age.

5
Divine *Ethnies* and Sacred Nations

Introduction

The failure of nationalism to abate during the twentieth century came largely as a surprise to many social and political thinkers. The ideological power of nationalism was such that it continued to penetrate nearly all spheres of social and individual life, to such an extent that it seemed to become the normal and natural condition of humanity. Most modern human beings are socialised in such a way the existence of ethnic and national identity is taken as a given and unproblematic feature of lived life. As Gellner (1983: 6) put it, today it is commonly assumed that 'a man must have a nationality as he must have a nose and two ears', a potent indicator of the enormously successful ideological penetration of nationalism. It is also worth citing Barthes (1993) again, who long ago noted that the success of a particular ideological practice is best gauged by the degree of its naturalisation – the fact that something is generally understood as normal and natural. Moreover the intensity of this widespread and universally shared feeling hides its profoundly contingent character and its historical novelty. The fact that 'methodological nationalism' (Wimmer and Glick-Schiller, 2002) is so ingrained in everything we do could not escape social and political thought, and it was not until late into the second half of the twentieth century that sociology took the study of nations and nationalism seriously. The true pioneers of this study, those whose works have shaped the direction of contemporary analyses and debates, are without doubt Ernest Gellner and Anthony D. Smith. These two authors are often seen as representing two distinct and mutually exclusive positions of analysis – modernist versus ethno-symbolist, clashing over the questions of whether nations and nationalism are exclusively modern, as claimed by modernists such as

Gellner, or whether contemporary nations have been built on the pre-existing cultural cores as argued by ethno-symbolists such as Smith.

Although this particular historical debate is important and illuminating, the commentary has tended to diminish the complexity of the arguments posed by both thinkers. In this chapter and the Chapter 6 my aim is to go beyond the narrow representations of the Smith–Gellner debate by exploring the epistemological foundations of their sociological accounts of social change. To paraphrase, in a different context, Billig's (2005: 4) use of Kippling's phrase.[12] What do they know of nations and nationalism who nations and nationalism only know? In other words nationalism cannot be explained or analysed by looking exclusively at the processes of nation-formation. Any substantial account of ethnicity and nationess requires a deeper engagement with the broader social reality in which these concepts and categories operate. To understand the explanatory implications of Smith's and Gellner's accounts of nationalism we have to dig deeper into the epistemological base of their theories of modernity.

Smith as a theorist of nationalism

Anthony D. Smith's theory of nationalism is thematically, conceptually and historically specific. He largely focuses on the origins of *ethnies* and nations, their interrelations, the emergence of nationalism, ethnic survival, myths and memories of the nation and similar themes. However despite the specificity of his analyses and models they necessarily presuppose a particular view of the social world, that is, they operate within a universalist framework. In order to say something meaningful about nationalist doctrine, its roots and its popular appeal, about the relevance of the myths of ethnic descent or about *ethnoscapes*, one has to start from particular premises about human beings, social action, group solidarity and so on. In other words one cannot make specific claims about the nature of ethnic and national identity and nationalism without simultaneously saying or implying something about the social world and the individual human beings inhabiting that world. Eventually such claims lead us back to specific conceptual, epistemological and even ontological understandings of the social world. My contention in this chapter is that Smith's work on nationalism is one of the most clearly articulated identitarian approaches to the study of nationess which can be understood only when one fully engages with the sociological *weltanschauung* that his project is part of, that is, with the Durkhemian view of the social world. More specifically the chapter is built around an interesting paradox: As it is commonly acknowledged that Durkheim wrote very little on nations and nationalism (Llobera, 1994, Guibernau, 1996), while Smith only rarely and sporadically makes explicit reference to Durkheim's works, Smith's sociological arguments on the rationale behind the rise and development of nationalism as a paramount ideology of modernity cannot be properly understood without first engaging analytically with Durkheim. While Smith's work is predominantly focused on the study of the socio-historical origins of nations and nationalism, the sociological and epistemological underpinnings of his position can only be grasped if one understands it as a part of the larger Durkheimian project. In other words, to fully comprehend Smith's theories of nations and nationalism one has to deal with Durkheim's general theory of society.

This chapter focuses in particular on the three conceptual cornerstones that link Durkheim's and Smith's work: the nature of (inter- and intra-) group solidarity, the perception of social groups as moral communities, and the crucial distinction that separates sacred from profane forms of sociability. First I explore the analytical parallels between Durkheim's notion of transition from mechanical and organic solidarity and Smith's evolutionary understanding of the genealogy of nationhood as a process that starts with ethnies and moves towards fully fledged nations. Second the emphasis is placed on the interpretation and understanding of ethnies and nations as distinct forms of collectivity created, re-created and maintained through articulation of the communal borders defining the parameters of individual and group morality. In particular the focus is on the collective mechanisms of moral responsibility that sustain groups as groups by invoking shared mythologies (i.e. the myth of common descent) as decisive for the creation of a meaningful moral universe. Finally, I aim to pinpoint the analytical links between Durkheim's concepts of sacred and profane and Smith's emphasis on the notion of a chosen people, the importance of collective memories and the symbolic underpinnings of group ontologies. The chapter finishes with a brief critique of the neo-Durkhemian position indicating some of its loopholes and analytical deficiencies that prevents a comprehensive explanation of nations and nationalism in their totality.

Neo-Durkheimian theory of nationalism?

Given his prolific body of writings, it is perhaps unsurprising that one can find many points of contact between Smith and Weber, Marx and Simmel, although ultimately it must be said that Smith is an intellectual heir of Durkheim. While he undoubtedly shares Weber's views on the importance of legitimacy and religious beliefs as generators of social action and social change, evident for example in his early works on the emergence of the 'rational scientific state' and the problem of 'dual legitimation' that arise with modernity (Smith, 1983a), he openly departs from contemporary Weberian understandings of nations and nationalism which he finds overly instrumentalist, individualist, rationalist and materialist (Smith, 1998). Similarly, Smith is sympathetic to Marxist inspired anti-colonial and anti-imperialist conceptions of the world which posit nationalism as a powerful force of social development (i.e. Smith 1995: 16–19; 147–160). However the staunch economistic explanations of social change that are at the heart of Marxism, as well as its fundamental understanding of nationalist doctrine as useful, but ultimately a form of false consciousness, have very little in common with Smith's culture centred position. Finally, among the classics, we might expect Smith to have the most affinity with Simmel, as both scholars place a strong emphasis on the role of ideas, values and culture in motivating human action. Indeed Smith recognises the importance of Simmel's work, and in particular his illuminating analyses of conflict and the role of the stranger (Smith, 1983b, 1998). Nevertheless here too Simmel's preoccupation with individual and group interaction at the micro level (the theory of sociation) and Smith's focus on the more macro structural and historical events (the *longue duree* perspective) means that their respective scope of study and corresponding perspective proceed in different directions. Thus, out of the four founding fathers of sociology it is the legacy of Durkheim that informs Smith's theories of nations and nationalism.[13]

However, since Durkheim himself had very little to say about nations and nationalism the link between his and Smith's work tends to be implicit. The main argument of this chapter is that despite this shadowy presence of Durkheim in Smith's opus, his theories of nations and nationalism are built on an understanding of the social world which is fundamentally Durkheimian and can only be fully comprehended when one engages with the core concepts of Durkheim's theory. However, given that Smith awards primacy to a topic which is largely neglected in Durkheim's work, it is to be expected that he went much further than his predecessor. Grounded in a Durkhemian ontology of the social world on one hand, and having to respond to non- and anti- Durkhemian developments in contemporary sociology on the other hand (i.e. neo-Marxist, neo-Weberian and neo-Simmelian interpretations of nationalism), Smith had no choice but to go beyond the mere application of Durkheim's ideas to the study of nation formation. Instead his work is best read not merely as an attempt to take the Durkheimian position to its logical conclusion in the area of nations and nationalism, but to go beyond this through a creative and comprehensive exploration of this particular *weltanschauung*. This is most pronounced in Smith's articulation of the ethnic origins of nations, his vision of nations as moral communities, and the notion of ethnic sacredness, all of which find their epistemological parallels in Durkheim's theories of solidarity, morality, religion and collective consciousness. Let us explore each of these explanatory connections in greater detail.

From mechanical solidarity of ethnies to organic solidarity of nations

Smith's ethno-symbolism in general and his theory of ethnic origins of nations in particular is an attempt to transcend modernist interpretations of the formation of nations. While agreeing in large part with the contention that nationalism is a modern phenomenon linked to the emergence of Enlightenment and the ideas and practices of the French Revolution, he disputes the modernist insistence on the complete novelty of nations themselves. Instead of conceptualising nations in terms of a structural rupture that occurred between the seventeenth and eighteenth centuries, which for the first time in human history provided the institutional, political and socio-cultural environment for increased social and spatial mobility, in turn facilitating the emergence of trans-class cultural identities, Smith argues for an essential element of continuity between earlier forms of cultural identity and newly emerging nations. In other words nations are not to be conceived in modernist terms as collectivities that emerge *ex nihilo*, but rather as social entities that have grown out of pre-modern ethnic cores, that is *ethnies*. According to Smith (1986: 22–31, 1991: 21) an *ethnie* is a community characterised by a common collective name, shared myth of common descent, shared historical memories, one or more elements of common culture, an association with a specific territory, and a sense of solidarity. By 'sense of solidarity' Smith means deep feelings of group commitment expressed in altruistic values and actions. This includes a sense of belonging to a common ethnic group, which is conceptualised as active and in times of crises as superior to other forms of collective identification. In other words ethnic solidarity is a *sine qua non* of ethnic group membership which overrides all other types of individual and collective attachments such as those based on class, religion, politics or regional affiliations. Although group solidarity can vary and change in time to include one or more strata of society, as Smith (1986: 30) points out, 'to speak of a genuine ethnie, this sense of solidarity and community must animate at least the educated upper strata, who can, if need be, communicate it to other strata and regions in the community'. Such groups have been in his view 'widespread in all eras of history' and although not necessarily universal they are 'chronic' and 'persistent'. Ethnies are most commonly formed through two processes: division – the fission of a larger group, and coalescence – the fusion via processes of amalgamation or assimilation of smaller cultural units (Smith, 1991: 24). Although ethnies are prone to change due to conquest, protracted warfare, immigration, religious conversion and other traumatic events, once formed they are essentially extremely sturdy and enduring communities.

The central argument in Smith's theory is that despite the uniqueness and unprecedented character of modernity, creating as it did the structural conditions for the emergence of nationalism as a fully fledged ideology, and thus also helping to create nations and nation-states as we now know them, the process of modern nation-formation is ultimately dependent on pre-existing forms of communal identities – ethnies. In other words, the continuity and stability of 'ethnic cores' and their distinct patterns of articulation have played a crucial role in the processes of nation-formation. Moreover they have determined the direction in which social mobilisation was to proceed – as ethnic (demotic) or civic (territorial) forms of nationalism.

Smith's position is thus rooted in a conviction that for the most part nations have gradually evolved from ethnies. In this sense Smith (1986: 153) explicitly accepts that the process is an evolutionary one where the transformation from ethnie to nation, in many ways, corresponds to a broader socio-historical transition from 'tradition' to 'modernity'. In the modern, dynamic, instrumentally driven world, ethnic communities have been forced towards politicisation and as such are likely to become nations. In Smith's (1986: 157) own words: 'a transition from *Gemeinschaft* to *Gesellschaft* finds confirmation in the more limited but vital sphere of ethnicity: in the modern era, ethnie must become politicised ... and must begin to move towards nationhood ... [and] take on some of the attributes of *Gesellschaft*, with its features of rational political centralisation, mass literacy, and social mobilisation'. So nations are modern, dynamic, complex, heterogeneous and in some ways impersonal collectivities developed in the context of dramatic social change but built on the contours of pre-modern, largely static, close, homogenous, and immobile, often kin-related *ethnies*. Since nations are formed around ethnic cores they share some key features such as common names, common myths and memories and a shared sense of territoriality. However, they also differ in vital respects such as the level and nature of group solidarity, the existence of public culture, common legal system and a single economy. So unlike an ethnie whose essential component is a myth of common descent, a nation is defined as 'a named human community occupying a homeland, and having common myths and a shared history, a common public culture, a single economy and common rights and duties for all members' (Smith, 2001a: 13).

This conceptualisation of ethnies as traditional communities, and nations as their modern equivalents, as well as their genealogical ties and the changing nature of solidarity exhibits a strong imprint of the Durkhemian worldview. It is Durkheim (1933) who differentiates between traditional communities, characterised by lack of diversity, simplicity and low levels of interaction, and modern societies articulated through the interdependence of its autonomous and heterogeneous parts. The process of modernisation is conceived in terms of complex differentiation, which is rooted in a comprehensive division of labour that secures operational and functional superiority to modern societies over traditional communities. However at the heart of both forms of collectivity is a *conscience collective*, which Durkheim defines as 'the totality of beliefs and sentiments common to average citizens of the same society [that] forms a determinate system which has its own life' (Durkheim, 1933: 79). Although the *conscience collective* is a much stronger force in the traditional world where community in every sense overpowers the individual conscience of its members, its influence is also significant in modern societies. While with modernity the *conscience collective* becomes less intense and rigid as it encounters other objective and subjective socio-cultural forces, such as the division of labour and individual conscience, it nevertheless persists and occasionally expands, even as it is transformed. Taking the example of religion Durkheim (1933: 172) argues: 'As all the other beliefs and all the other practices take on a character less and less religious, the individual becomes the object of a sort of religion. We erect a cult in belief of personal dignity which, as every strong cult, already has its superstitions'.

There is a clear overlap here between Smith's and Durkheim's concepts. This is most obvious in Smith's characterisation of ethnie in terms of dominant collective beliefs and sentiments. Although not explicitly acknowledged as such, ethnie is nonetheless a *conscience collective* in its purest form. On can read in Smith (1986: 97) that ethnie constitutes a 'cluster of populations with similar perceptions and sentiments generated by, and encoded in, specific beliefs, values and practices'. It is composed of 'symbolic, cognitive and normative elements common to a unit of population'; it is shaped by 'practices and mores that bind them together over generations'; and it is grounded in 'sentiments and attitudes that are held in common' that set it apart from other such collectivities. The popular belief in common descent, a key feature of ethnie, is also mirrored in Durkheim's (1933) characterisation of traditional communities as clan based segmental societies whose solidarity is largely based on simple resemblance. With the expansion of modernisation such collectivities transform into nations. Although built on the skeleton of ethnies, nations are qualitatively different forms of collective identity. Not only are nations much more dynamic, differentiated and complex, they are at the same time more stable and functionally superior entities underpinned by a common public culture, universal written laws and regulations, and a unitary economic structure which together create a profoundly distinct and much more cohesive sense of inter-reliance. In other words modernity creates conditions under which the kinship-like solidarity of resemblance is transformed into more complex and more diverse cultural units linked by much stronger ties where solidarity is based on mutual interdependence. And this is exactly how Durkheim (1933) explains changing patterns of group solidarity caused by the arrival of modernity and the ever increasing division of labour. Put bluntly traditional communities are held together by mechanical solidarity while modern societies are integrated through organic solidarity. Whereas the former implies only the sense of group similarity on the basis of extended family ties and virtual or real kinship, the latter involves a highly sophisticated social order of autonomous and diverse but at the same time mutually co-reliant individuals. For Durkheim organic forms of group solidarity are much more compelling since they are rooted in the mechanisms of a complex division of labour where every individual has a specific role and where the individual actions of one are intertwined and dependent on the actions of all the others. As he puts it: '... each one depends as much more strictly on society as labour is more divided ... [while] the activity of each is as much more personal as it is more specialised ... the individuality of all grows at the same time as that of its parts. Society becomes more capable of collective movement, at the same time that each of its elements has more freedom of movement ... the unity of the organism is as great as the individuation of the parts is more marked' (Durkheim, 1933: 131). From this it seems obvious that the mechanical solidarity of pre-modern ethnies is a significantly weaker force than the organic solidarity of modern day nations. The organic quality of nations provides a distinct and novel but more forceful sense of group cohesion. And Smith recognises this explicitly when he portrays the nation as a collectivity of individuals who are now 'generalised equals' linked by 'impersonal but fraternal' ties. As he (1986: 170) points out in one of the rare moments when he invokes Durkheim directly: 'individuals in a nation are essentially substitutable. Their links are certainly "organic" in Durkheim's sense of the term: that is they occupy complementary roles with mutual expectations based on a complex division of labour. At the same time, the incumbents of those roles are interchangeable and expendable *qua* individuals'. Unlike ethnies nations are defined by a more intensive division of labour, increasing social mobility and formal differentiation, while at the same time fostering a stronger sense of identity and interdependence. In other words the egalitarian ethos underpinned by a common 'high' culture, together with intensive developments in communication, transport and other technological developments, and the concurrent decline of religious beliefs as there are gradually displaced by a 'scientific bureaucratic state', provide a new form of modern organisation, a nation which is enclosed in a new and advanced form of collective unity – organic solidarity.

So far there is strong sense of compatibility between Smith's concepts and Durkheim's theory of modernisation. Smith shares with Durkheim an understanding of social life as it progresses from traditional ethnies held together by mechanical solidarity towards modern nations underpinned by a sense of organic comradeship. However Smith also goes a step further. Unlike Durkheim he argues that modernity does not emerge in a singular form but instead takes two principal and often incongruous routes – civic and ethnic types of nationhood. Smith (1991) traces the origins of the two back to the existence of the two dominant ideal-types of ethnies in history – lateral and vertical. While lateral ethnies tend to consist mostly of aristocracy and high ranking clergy and occasionally include a top military echelon, wealthy merchants and some civil servants, vertical ethnies are for most part constituted from the bottom up and include a variety of social strata. The inherent diversity of these social origins of ethnies are seen as important for their later day transformations into two diverse forms of nation-formation – territorial and ethnic. With the arrival of modernity they are both forced towards establishing the institutions of the nation-state compatible with the modern age (i.e. bound and compact territory, single economy, common public culture and common legal system). However their distinct roots set them in motion towards distinct developmental patterns of modern day nationhood: one achieved from above with the help of a bureaucratic state that effectively forges the nation, and the other formed from below as, through vernacular mobilisation, nations emerge before states (Smith, 1998: 194). These two divergent forms of nation formation are also two different articulations of modernity which create diverse forms of social conflict and a plurality of social being in general. They also offer different remedies to deal with the intractable problems of the contemporary world such as assimilation and acculturation versus unbridled cultural pluralism, state induced secularism versus religious forms of cultural essentialism and so on. The diverse attempts to resolve these dilemmas are often ingrained in different normative universes, which are likely to conflict whenever one endeavours to judge the other using one's own moral yardstick. In other words, in contrast to Durkheim, Smith operates with a pluralistic understanding of modernity, more akin to recent debates on 'multiple modernities' (Mouzelis, 1999, Eisenstadt, 2000, 2002). Smith introduces an important and relatively novel[14] intervention in the Durkheimian original position by identifying two quite diverse and often mutually opposing modalities of organic solidarity at the heart of modern day social conflicts – cultural and political forms of nationhood.

Ethnies and nations as moral communities

The fierce debate between modernists (Gellner, 1983, 1997, Breuilly, 1993, Mann, 1995) and ethno-symbolists such as Smith is not only about dating the emergence of the nation or its relationship to pre-modern ethnic communities. More importantly the two approaches clash over the question of whether – as ethno-symbolists argue – common values, ideas and beliefs or – as modernists claim – political and economic interests had the upper hand in shaping the direction and intensity of nationalism. While recognising the impact of political elites in swaying mass behaviour and the economic imbalances of capitalism as it produces regional disparities and culturally articulated inequalities in the local and global division of labour, Smith holds firm in his belief that ethnies and nations are defined as distinct and enduring forms of human collectivity by relatively unique sets of shared trans-generational values. These communally shared beliefs are for the most part expressed in rich mosaics of myths and memories that constitute ethnies and nations as meaningful moral universes. While they offer popular ad hoc accounts of assumed group similarity and unity their role is, as Smith argues (1986: 24), not only cognitive but also expressive and aesthetic. Collective mythologies provide road maps to decode a group's past, articulated in dramatic and poetic fashion as heroic morality tales which establish the parameters for individual and group action. In Smith's theory such constitutive myths, termed after Armstrong's (1982) *mythomoteurs*, have a central place in providing the meaning and 'essence' of group being, since without such foundational myths 'a group cannot define itself to itself or to others' (Smith, 1986: 25). For ethnies it is the myth of common descent that is decisive in constituting a group as such. By invoking the common ancestry these myths help to establish a direct link between present and past events which in turn impose a particular set of moral guidelines and obligations that project and direct collective action in the future. This array of myths furnishes a particular ethnie with a sense of meaning, which goes beyond the contours of an individual. By symbolically locating itself in space and time and linking present with the tangible past via putative kinship and a feeling of collective ascendancy, an ethnie provides a powerful mechanism of ontological security. However what is also important is that this sense of group attachment is predicated on the existence of communal borders that defines the dimensions and content of both group and individual morality. Ethnie does not only help sustain one's sense of identity, it also creates it. Morality is always defined in communal terms and being a moral person implies subscribing to a particular set of values shared by a group. Beyond the boundaries of the group is nothing but a moral wasteland.

This understanding of ethnie as a collectivity that supports a set of ethical parameters is profoundly Durkhemian. In Durkheim we encounter the view that posits collective life as a source of normative strength. As he puts it: 'man is a moral being only because he lives within established societies' (Durkheim, 1986: 202). In this perspective society is only possible when individuals fully subscribe to a particular normative order. However this can never be a question of individual free will, as in the Hobbesian and Lockeian understandings of a hypothetical social contract. Rather in the Durkheimain view society is 'the sum total of norms' (Poggi, 2000: 91) which precedes and regularly overpowers individual will. But more importantly, being a force beyond the individual, a society is able to transcend the diversity and particularity of its parts, providing a superior form of collective character while simultaneously establishing rules of ethical behaviour. That is 'if a morality exists, it can only have as its object the group formed by a plurality of individuals associating together, i.e. society, *on condition, however, that the society can be considered as a personality qualitatively different from the individual personalities that go to make it up*. Thus morality begins where there begins an attachment to a group of any kind' (Durkheim, 1986: 157 italics in original). In other words what makes a group or a society a distinctive entity is its propensity for morality. So morality is not only the product but also the substance of society: 'morals are what the society is' (Durkheim, 1986: 203).

Since in Smith's view nations are in large part a logical extension of ethnies, they too are constituted around a particular set of values and beliefs. Unlike ethnies which cling to a more or less loose myth of common descent, nations are characterised by well articulated and often fully institutionalised sets of collective beliefs expressed in common memories and in ethno-history. As Smith (1995: 63) explains, ethno-history 'represents an amalgam of selective historical truth and idealisation, with varying degrees of documented fact and political myth, stressing elements of romance, heroism and the unique, to present a stirring and emotionally intimate portrait of the community's history, constructed by, and seen from the standpoint of, successive generations of community members'. Standard history textbooks, regularly used in primary and secondary education, are a case in point here as they are often written from such an ethno-historical perspective which combines factual evidence (albeit in a selective manner) with poetic, heroic and dramatic narrative. Those master narratives often depict the nation as a coherent and self-conscious agent passing through and overcoming, in a mode of linear time, numerous Scylla and Charybdis of the past epochs to arrive at a victorious present or future. The fact that ethno-history and collective memories tend to have an institutional underpinning in modern nations makes them exceptionally powerful mechanisms of collective influence. Not only is it that they provide a seal of authentication regarding 'our true' traditions, they also impose moral requirements on the actions and behaviour of members of a particular nation. The great effort of nationalists to purge everything of what is not culturally 'ours' and authentic, and to clearly demarcate and delineate 'our' unique heritage and tradition from 'theirs' is not a simple sign of fear about the Other. Rather this attempt of collective purification rests on a specific moral principle – to remain true to oneself. Since an individual's morality is deduced from his group membership this principle implies that an individual's moral worth is determined by her stance towards that group. Being a moral person is first and foremost dependent on one's loyalty to a group. In this way passing on tradition, preserving the group's name, myths and memories indicates a sense of loyalty towards the ancestry – 'our' forefathers and foremothers. Any deviation from the purity of the original tradition is a sign of moral weakness on the part of the individual, which automatically dilutes the group's essence and makes it weaker. To uphold the sense of a communal past becomes the central preoccupation of nationhood since adopting or assimilating 'foreign' cultural traits becomes a question of moral capitulation and ultimately a sign of betrayal of one's (super) family. That is why ethnohistory and collective memories become a cornerstone of modern nations: their heroic and didactic narratives provide a role model, 'an inner standard for the community, an *exemplum virtutis* for subsequent emulation' (Smith, 1995: 63). However for the nation to be fully and constantly reproduced and recreated it is also necessary for it to rest on ritualistic practices – 'parades, remembrance ceremonies, anniversary celebrations, monuments to the fallen, oaths, coinage, flags, eulogies of heroes and memorials of heroic events' all of which remind co-nationals of what it is that makes them unique as a cultural group and a political community (Smith, 1991: 162).

Durkheim shares this perception of an individual's bond to a particular nation-state, which is expressed through unique feelings and group rituals. This sense of national attachment establishes clear moral parameters for the group and hence also the individual's behaviour, or as Durkheim puts it 'if we suppose it to have weakened or to have ceased to exist, where is an individual to find this moral authority, whose curb is to this extent salutary?' (Durkheim, 1915: 202–3). The nation is a superior moral community since it functions on the principles of organic solidarity, in itself the most advanced form of group unity, and 'everything which is a source of solidarity is moral ... and everything which forces man to regulate his conduct through something other than the striving of his ego is moral' (1933: 398). This moral unity of the nations is expressed in common values and sentiments that find their articulation in group rituals. As he puts it 'it is by virtue of screaming the same cry, pronouncing the same word, performing the same gesture concerning the same object that they achieve and experience an accord ... It is the homogeneity of these movements which imparts to the group the sense of identity and consequently makes it be' (Durkheim, 1915: 230). So a nation's existence is dependent on periodic and regular reaffirmation of its values and symbols and there is little difference here between explicitly religious values, symbols and rituals and those of a nominally secular character: commemorating the death of heroes fallen in a war of nations is equivalent to Jews commemorating the exodus from Egypt or Christians commemorating the crucifixion of Christ (Durkheim, 1915: 427). If not periodically reiterated through common rituals, then national identity disintegrates and with it crumbles the moral order of a society.

Thus Smith's understanding of ethnies and nations as moral regenerators is deeply Durkhemian. However, here too Smith goes beyond Durkheim. Although nations are moral collectivities and as such impinge themselves fully on their individual members, Smith allows more scope for individual action than Durkheim would. Although national identity is seen by Smith (1991: 175, 1995: 159) as the dominant form of collective identification which has no serious rivals today, he recognises flexibility and the situational context of personal identifications. More specifically he accepts that the human sense of attachment has multiple forms so that one goes through life with crosscutting allegiances such as those of class, gender, religion, region, profession and so on. In other words we all have multiple identities the strength of which is largely determined by the changing social context: when surrounded by male chauvinists a woman might more strongly stress her gender identity while an encounter with a group of upper class women may provoke an intensive feeling of class identity. However, Smith also differentiates between individual and collective identities arguing that whereas the former can regularly be situational and even optional the latter is much more stable and often resistant to even the most dramatic social changes. In his view this is especially evident in modern day national identities 'when the power of mass political fervour reinforces the technological instruments of mass political organisation, so that national identities can outlast the defection or apathy of quite large numbers of individual members' (Smith, 1999: 230). Thus Smith, as with Durkheim, gives primacy to the collective over the individual, and derives morality from group existence, yet he operates with a less deterministic concept of collective morality by permitting more scope for individual action and a multiplicity of personal identifications.

Ethnic and national sacredness

The intensity and strength of national attachments and the omnipotence of nationalist ideology have proved to be both a surprise within the context of, and a major challenge to modernity. The majority of classical social and political analysts subscribed to an Enlightenment- induced teleology of human development as an irreversible path of progress; a relentless movement towards a tolerant and rational world free of conflict wherein the growth of universalism and cosmopolitanism would leave the particularistic, provincial, and gregarious attachments of the past in its wake. This view saw the periodic outbursts of national/ist feelings as no more than a temporary glitch in the unstoppable advancement of humanity under the grindstone of reason and progress. However this view was as simplistic as it was naïve. Within the context of modernity nationalism actually intensified, spreading to the remotest corners of the globe, and most of all, as argued in Chapter 4, becoming fully institutionalised as the dominant operative ideology of modern states. Instead of its predicted decline, with the help of modernity and its direct offshoots such as democratisation and secularisation, nationalism captured the hearts and minds of nearly all social strata. Thus the central question now is: Why has nationalism proved to be such a stubborn force? A. Smith finds the answer in the ability of nationalist ideology to link past and present in a communally meaningful way, providing a stable sense of self-worth in an increasingly secularising and atomistic world of modernity. Modernity has brought upon us spectacular changes including the delegitimisation of the medieval doctrine of the divine origins of monarchs, the dramatic expansion of literacy rates, and the institutionalisation of state sponsored educational systems. All of these changes, coupled with the decline in religious practice and the demise of collective beliefs in the possibility of individual salvation through super-terrestrial intervention, have created an environment of collective and individual uncertainty. The spectre of personal annihilation is a daunting condition of existence. Thus nationalism emerges as a powerful and seductive force that seems able to overcome the problem of personal oblivion. As Smith (1991: 160) puts it: 'Identification with the "nation" in a secular era is the surest way to surmount the finality of death and ensure a measure of personal immortality'. By symbolically linking past, present and future generations the nation appears as a durable entity which provides a concrete substitute for everlasting life. In other words in the age of modernity nationalism arises as a secular equivalent to religious belief. Instead of supernatural divinity, it is nations themselves that become the object of collective self-adoration. Modernity helps to constitute a new object of collective worship – in place of a holy cow or Christian liturgy one glorifies a national flag, or a fallen hero, or shivers when the national anthem is sung. Instead of devotion and piety shown to saints and gods, modernity opens the way for unlimited and blatant forms of collective self-worship – nationalism. In this vision of nations and nationalism as a surrogate for religious beliefs one can find the most explicit connection to Durkheim's general theory of society. It is Durkheim who analysed religion as a force of moral integration through which society worships its own image. He found in totemism, which he regarded as the simplest form of religious belief, the key principles around which collective self-veneration is built. These very same principles persist in all other known forms of religious belief. A totem is simultaneously a symbol of divinity, the 'totemic principle or god' of the particular clan, and the clan itself. As Durkheim (1915: 206) puts it: 'It is its flag; it is the sign by which each clan distinguishes itself from the others, the visible mark of its personality ... it is at once the symbol of the god and of the society'. Thus, the devotion to the clan totem is nothing else than devotion to the clan itself, which is simply personified in the symbol of the totem. In other words divinity and society are one – in the guise and image of divinity the group in fact worships itself. Durkheim's understanding of clan is fully compatible with Smith's conceptualisation of ethnies and nations, which are far less bounded by 'blood connections' than by 'the mere fact that they have the same name' (Durkheim, 1915: 102). But sharing a name also implies something more profound – a sacred representation of the group itself. 'The crow' or 'the kangaroo' correspond to 'the Armenian' or 'the Serb' and their representations which are not merely names and emblems designating a particular collective, but also symbols that stand for and create a sacred image of the group itself. Both totemic and ethno-national imagery have a religious character which is a symbolic representation of a material force – the clan, ethnie or nation. Hence the collective adoration of these sacred representations are no more than collective self-adoration. Smith (1991: 77–8) recognises this explicitly when he argues that: 'much of what Durkheim attributes to the totemic rites and symbols of the Arunta and other Australian tribes applies with far greater force to nationalist rites and ceremonies'. With modernity the nation becomes the principal deity while nationalism becomes the dominant form of religious belief.

In his recent work Smith (2001a: 792, 2001: 35, 2003a) is even more explicit in this conceptualisation when he describes nations as 'sacred communions of citizens' and nationalism as 'a form of political religion'. Nations are defined through their sacred properties such as the notion of being a chosen people, group attachment to the sacred territory, collective memories of the nation's spiritual heights in the 'golden age', and the cults of the 'glorious dead' (Smith, 2001a: 144). The idea of 'chosen people' is crucial for understanding the sacred dimension of nationhood. This widely held myth of ethnic election has its roots in ancient religious notions of 'sacred covenant' which goes back to Sumerians and Akkadians, ancient Egyptians and Persians but is most coherently articulated in the Old Testament depicting Jews as the chosen ones. As Smith (1999b: 335) explains: 'According to this ideal, Israelites were chosen by God and freely entered into an agreement, by which the privilege of election was strictly conditional upon full and correct performance of all God's moral and ritual commandments.' The idea of a 'chosen people' was then adopted in different guises by ethnies and nations professing Christian beliefs (from Armenians and Copts to Orthodox Russians, New England Protestants or Afrikaners) and has survived well into the modern era where, coupled with nationalist ideology, it was transformed into contemporary concepts of national destiny and national mission. The myth of ethnic election is a powerful mechanism of social integration. It offers a sense of group superiority and promises collective and thus individual salvation. However the salvation is firmly couched in the individual's as well as the group's ability to unconditionally preserve the particular moral order, understood as given by supernatural authority. 'To be chosen is to be placed under moral obligations. One is chosen on condition that one observes certain moral, ritual, and legal codes, and only for as long as one continues to do so. The privilege of election is accorded only to those who are sanctified, whose life-style is an expression of sacred values' (Smith, 1999a: 130). The group's shared belief in ethnic election is seen as being essential for the long-term survival and it is in this belief that Smith finds the source of group durability which has been decisive for the preservation of ethnies over the *longue duree* and secures their successful transformation into modern nations. The powerful modern images of national destiny that nationalism espouses are, for Smith, deeply rooted in these ancient visions of ethnic election. This is most palpable in the four common functions that they serve: the sense of moral superiority over outsiders, spiritual liberation, firm group boundary maintenance and collective mobilisation (Smith, 1999b: 336–9). Nationalism builds on these visions of ethnic election by upholding a near universal ethnocentric image of the social world by placing one's own group at the pedestal of virtue and rightness which in itself helps sustain the group's existence over time. The notion of being chosen also offers a possibility of 'status reversal' and a potential return to a 'golden age' among those groups who find themselves in a state of technological, economic or political inferiority. Finally this group feeling of uniqueness helps large-scale mobilisation for the national cause and simultaneously establishes clear borderlines between Us and Them, segregating 'the chosen community from a profane and alien world' (Smith, 1999b: 336). It is perhaps in this understanding of nations as sacred communities and nationalism as a form of political religion that Smith makes his most explicit link to Durkheim. The idea of sacredness is a cornerstone of Durkheim's understanding of the social. As Nisbet (1976: v) rightly points out: 'the sacred and the social are for Durkheim two sides of the same coin'. The sacred is inconceivable without the social, while the long-term persistence of any communal order is dependent on its ability to maintain the separation between the sacred and profane realms. For Durkheim (1915) the distinction between scared and profane is the unique and ultimate form of separation which is beyond any other humanly created classification. The profane and the sacred are two polar and absolute opposites that can never have anything in common. That is, the existence of one can only be formulated in opposition to the other: 'The sacred thing is *par excellence* that which the profane should not touch, and cannot touch with impunity' (Durkheim, 1915: 40). The realm of the profane is characterised by routine, secular and mundane experience of everyday life governed by principles of utility, instrumental rationality and practicality. The realm of sacred is its exact opposite – it is a sphere of moral absolute which goes beyond the mundane, and which evokes veneration, awe and reverence. The sacred is non-utilitarian, non-empirical and can never be based on human knowledge. It involves a powerful system of beliefs which gives strength to individuals and groups. However this power is profoundly ambiguous since sacred things can be both positive and negative, dangerous and helpful or threatening and reassuring. Most of all the realm of the sacred implies a strict sense of moral obligation and collective adoration. The existence of coherent religious beliefs and practices requires a bipartite division of the universe and is premised on keeping the two mutually hostile domains apart. Durkheim (1915: 47) defines religion in terms of sacred beliefs and practices that unite and set apart a particular moral community of believers. It is in this view that one can find epistemological roots of Smith's understanding of nations and nationalism. In a strictly Durkhemian move, Smith posits sacredness at the heart of the nation-formation processes. Nations are constituted as sacred communities and are defined by their sacred properties while nationalism has all the attributes of a political religion. Nationalism is nothing else than a contemporary articulation of the 'old doctrine of chosen people' (Smith, 1991: 99) constituted in the context of the secularising world of modernity. A strong sense of attachment to the nation helps individuals keep separate the everyday reality of instrumental rationality, materiality and utility, which are indispensable in the highly complex, bureaucratic and chaotic world of modernity, from the sphere which houses one's emotional, ideational and non-instrumental needs. In other words nationalist ideology maintains and preserves the duality and mutual incompatibility of the sacred and profane realms by conceiving of nations as the ultimate domains of sacredness. In this way nationalism operates as a political religion which provides a collective sense of meaning in the ever changing, individualising world of restless modernity. Just as with Durkheim, Smith's image of a human being is that of *homo duplex*, a creature stretched between individually driven rationalities of profane life and collective effervescence built in the extraordinary realm of the sacred.

However here too Smith goes a bit further than Durkheim. The different focus and specificity of his research (i.e. the nation-formation processes) leads him to the recognition that these processes are not only a matter of collective self-understanding but are also highly dependent on mutual inter-group perceptions. That is, the sacred nature of the group is a social product of both collective self-perception as well as its positioning vis-à-vis other such groups. In contrast to Durkheim's concept of sacredness, which is inward looking and centred on demonstrating how the group and its totem are truly one, Smith adds an outward oriented concept of sacredness where the group's divinity is also premised on mutual denial of such status to other groups. Hence sacredness is not only rooted in the objects through which a particular collectivity worships itself, but also in the constant process of categorising others as impure, morally inferior, mundane, or in a word – profane. The notion of ethnic election has precisely this exclusionary function which is almost completely dependent on rejecting the status of others as chosen. Since 'the others' are conceived as part and parcel of the profane world any attempt on their part to claim its status of being among the elect can only be seen as symbolically or even physically threatening to the 'chosen people'. 'The effect of such a drive is to harden the boundary between 'us' and 'them' to an unprecedented degree, expelling all those who have no place in the nation's cultural mission or its heritage, and are likely to contaminate its pristine culture and prevent its true mission' (Smith, 1999b: 338). Thus sacredness is a process equally dependent on inter-group categorisation as much as on the intra-collective self-identification.

Unravelling the facets of the neo-Durkhemian view of nationalism

Anthony Smith provides us with a nuanced, coherent and persuasive theory of nations and nationalism, and one that seems able to explain the multifaceted nature of nation-formation processes. His theory offers strong accounts of the historical transformation of pre-modern forms of collectivity into modern day nations, the moral foundations of group action, and of the religious origins and nature of pervasive national identifications. The strength and coherence of his arguments about the development of nations and nationalism is rooted in the robust episte-mological bedrock the Durkhemian tradition supplies. The claims made about genealogy of ethnies or nations, myths and memories, chosen peoples, ethnoscapes, and so on, are, as I have tried to show, firmly embedded in a Durkhemian *weltanschauung* and so to fully understand Smith's contribution to the study of nations and nationalism one has to move below the surface and look at its epistemological roots. In other words to unravel the facets of Smith's position it is not enough to focus narrowly on the issues such as dating the emergence of nations and nationalism, counterpoising ethnic and civic forms of nationhood or reassessing the strength of popular mythologies in generating national-ist movements. Attempts to challenge Smith's arguments on this basis will always remain partial, and can be countered with relative ease. And this is exactly what Smith (1998, 2003b, 2004) does when attacked over his concepts and definitions (Connor, 2004, Guibernaou, 2004), his historical dating of nations (Özkirimli, 2003) or his underrating of struc-tural differences between pre-modern and modern forms of cultural identities (Breuilly, 1993). Any form of criticism which does not chal-lenge the epistemological roots of his argument, that is his Durkhemian foundations, is likely to be too weak to undermine his theory. Removing or attempting to rearrange a few pieces in a pre-formed jigsaw puzzle will not give us an entirely new or compelling image on the board; it will only impair or ruin the one we have. And indeed Smith does offer an elegant solution to the puzzle of nations and nationalism which seem to be missing few, if any, pieces. However the problem is not with the exist-ing or missing pieces, the problem is with the entire jigsaw itself: a model pretty and well composed but profoundly inaccurate. That is, a proper challenge of Smith's theory has simultaneously to be a challenge of the entire Durkhemian tradition and its peculiar conceptualisation of social life. Such an undertaking is a huge project in itself so I will con-fine myself here only to sketching some possible lines of criticism which would serve to undermine the neo-Durkhemian explanation of nations and nationalism. There are three principle epistemological weaknesses which can be highlighted: the evolutionist, collectivist and idealist nature of its arguments. Let us deal briefly with each of them in turn.

Evolutionary historicism

There is a certain irony in Smith's life-long project – while he started his academic career with fierce attacks on the structural-functionalist paradigm in general and neo-evolutionism in particular (i.e. Smith, 1973, 1976), the main predecessor of which is Durkheim himself, his mature work has largely, albeit in a nuanced way, embraced this very paradigm. One of the core explanatory principles of structural-functionalism is the evolutionary character of its argumentation which, bluntly put, views social units as gradually moving from simple towards complex forms of organisation. While there is more room for contingency and chance in Smith than in classical evolutionist approaches, which is exemplified in his preference for the historical concept of *longue duree* over that of evolution, his argument nevertheless remains staunchly evolutionist in a truly Durkhemian sense. While Smith invokes terms such as 'destiny', 'historical mission' or 'choseness' to understand the motives of social actors, his analysis tends to coalesce with the views of the subjects of his study so that it slips into advocacy for their cause. Not only do statements such as 'nations and nationalism remain the only realistic basis for a free society of states in the modern world', or 'only nationalism can secure the assent of the governed' (Smith, 1995: 147 and 154) read in an extremely deterministic way, as do Smith's essentialist links between ethnies and nations, but this position is also a clear example of what Popper (1957) has termed a 'historicist fallacy'. The evolutionary historicism that characterises Smith's neo-Durkhemian position has a great operational difficulty in moving away from the following three ontological assumptions: determinism (the existence of a predetermined path), fatalism (unalterable necessity of this process), and finalism (the existence of predetermined stages in history) (Sztompka, 1993: 181). In this perspective history is seen as having relatively clearly defined patterns or stages of development through which most if not all collectivities are ordained to pass. In other words, historical development is perceived as having a mission: ethnies are in one or another way destined to become nations, nations are the most functional vessels of modernity and their historical embeddedness puts them in this incontrovertible state of superiority (Smith, 1995). The result is that the principal actors in the drama of history ethnies (and after them nations) have a purpose and a functional role in the Great Chain of Being.[15] There is too much coherence and still too little contingency in this teleologically crafted narrative. Although he does offer us two possible ideal types of modernity (territorial/civic and genealogical/ethnic) Smith's argument remains chained to an understanding of historical change as a one-way process. Not only is it that nations do not have to have navels (Gellner, 1997) and can be created from individuals and groups with distinct cultural origins, but as Eriksen (2004: 53) rightly points out 'there is no logical reason why mythomoteur often referred by Smith that is the constititutive myth of the ethnic polity, should necessarily create an ethnic group rather than another kind of corporate entity'. The rigid historicist connection between an ethnie and a nation, underpinned in a Durkhemian sense by distinct forms of group solidarity, prevents any hypothetical possibility of different directions or reversibility of that process. As Tilly's (1984, 2002) historical research clearly demonstrates, instead of clear-cut transformation from one historical stage onto other (from *Gemeinschaft* of ethnie to *Gesselschaft* of nation) the historical record comprises 'numerous fragmentary processes of various levels of complexity, running parallel, or in opposite directions, separate or overlapping'. There are no clearly marked stages of historical development and any attempt to identify phases of such a development can only be provisional and arbitrary. Historical processes are for the most part neither linear nor continuous whereas social change is variable, uneven and situational. Not only is it that there is nothing inevitable in the process of nation-formation, the process itself is just one among many historical possibilities.

Collectivism/identitarianism

Unlike methodological individualism which is built on the premise that collective beliefs or collective desires do not exist (Elster, 1985), and that proper sociological analysis can yield meaningful results only if carried out solely in reference to concrete individual actors, the Durkhemian tradition holds the view that collective action generates a unique set of traits which can never be captured if one focuses on individual behaviour alone. In other words, when analysed at the level of the group the actions and behaviour of human beings assumes a qualitatively novel form of existence that goes beyond the characters of its individual constituent parts. For Smith ethnies and nations have this exceptional quality which in many ways has an aura of timelessness that is more durable and more powerful than the ethnic and national attachments of concrete individuals. By the mere fact of assuming a collective form ethnies and nations articulate moral universes of and for individuals. Morality, seen as a quintessential human quality, is in this perspective premised on the existence of collective life.

Although humans are indeed social beings whose actions are certainly governed by more than selfish gain-maximising – the error of radical methodological individualism – their sociability has different origins. Neo-Durkemian collectivism/identitarianism understates not only the fact that group formation and hence collective morality is often driven by self-interest or necessity, but also that this can be a profoundly asymmetrical process by which individuals can be ideologically manipulated or coerced into group action. The moral unity of nations is quite often created through violent processes, initiated and motivated by actions of powerful individual and social agents, and underpinned by complex structural forces. In this respect it is erroneous to look at communities and societies or at ethnies and nations as relatively homogeneous entities with clearly discernible borders; instead they must be studied as 'fluid, complex, overlapping, cross-cutting and superimposed networks of multiple relationships' (Sztompka, 1993: 187).[16] By attributing too much power to the collective force of group morality, holistic epistemologies of the neo-Durkhemian type are prone to the reification of group action. Hence instead of viewing inter-and intra-group relations as dynamic processes, through which groups emerge and change, collectivism often ends up ascribing individual qualities to entire groups. So in Smith (2003a: viii, 66, 95) we can read about 'continual source of inspiration ... among so many *Christian peoples* in Europe and America', about '*covenanted peoples*' or '*missionary peoples*' who become fully fledged actors of social change. In this way dynamic social processes and individual and collective action have been essentialised and reified to the extreme. Instead of providing an explanation as to why and how actors reify their group membership and perceive other actors as homogeneous entities (i.e. 'Christian peoples' and such), neo-Durkhemian identitarianists simply accept folk concepts and treat large-scale social actors as if they have singular and recognisable wills.[17] There are numerous essentialist and groupist references in Smith's work such as, 'Kievan Rus' [is] claimed by the Ukrainians as exclusively their golden age, but also by the Russians as the first of their golden ages'; 'the English, along with the Irish and Welsh, and not long afterwards the Scots, were both aware of themselves as separate peoples and saw themselves as standing under the sign of God as His elect'; 'Finns looked back to an age of wisdom and heroism ... the Slovaks returned to an early Moravian kingdom ... while Zimbabweans have found an ancestral age of greatness ...' (Smith, 2003: 190, 116; Smith, 2001a:141). How is it possible for Smith to know what 5,200 000 individual citizens of Finland think or have ever thought about the 'age of heroism'? How many individual Slovaks regularly and unconditionally 'return to an early Moravian kingdom'? Is 'Kievan Rus' claimed by every single individual who describes themselves as Ukrainian or Russian or is this claim made by some groups and individuals in the name of Ukrainians and Russians? Do these perceptions ever change? Are there any competing understandings of Slovakness,

Finishness or Zimbabweaness? Even if the particular view of what it means to be a Slovak or Finn is temporarily dominant throughout the population it surely is dependent on the particular social and historical context. Such a dominant interpretation of the reality of 'the national' is in itself a result of various more or less successful attempts at articulating the national idea on the part of social movements or various cultural or political elites. As Brubaker (2004: 167) rightly points out, social researchers should not think about ethnies and nations as tangible, bounded and substantial groups but rather as 'practical categories, cultural idioms, cognitive schemas, discursive frames, organisational routines, institutional forms, political projects and contingent events'. Even when sharing a particular moral ideal of the group, as Giddens (1978: 107) indicates in his critique of Durkheim, one can believe that this ideal is 'currently defined or interpreted in a degraded or mistaken way'. Although Smith allows much more scope for individual action than Durkheim ever would, there is still an overwhelming dominance of the collective over the individual in his theory.[18] On top of that there is also little room for individual or group resistance in Smith's account of the nation-formation processes: ethno-history and collective memories do perhaps serve as didactic devices but they are always re-interpreted and more importantly renegotiated or utterly transformed through violent and bloody experiences of everyday life. The relative hegemonic position of a particular form of ethno-historic narrative has less to do with its supposedly uninterrupted link with the pristine folk tales of pre-modern ethnies and much more to do with current and historical power struggles over the modes of ideological dissemination.

Idealism

What is perhaps most distinguishable in the neo-Durkhemian theory of nationalism is its explanatory idealism. While briefly acknowledging the importance of social institutions, political elites, bureaucracy, capitalism or war as relevant to the process of nation-formation, Smith gives an overwhelming weight to non-economic and non-political factors in his account of the genealogy of nations and nationalism. In his creative application of the notions of sacred and profane to the study of nations, as well as his analytical connection between social/national and sacred/religious one can detect the full force of the Durkhemian norm-centred legacy. For Smith nationalism is after all a political religion imbedded in the ancient mythology of chosen people, while nations represent a 'sacred communion of citizens', an oasis of divinity in a desert of restless and ever secularising modernity.

Although nationalism does often exhibit a quasi-religious appeal, building on deified rituals, borrowing from spiritual language and imagery, and portraying nations as semi-divine entities, this does not explain the large part of the story of its contemporary success. Moreover even the idealist argument itself is riddled with contradictions. First both Durkheim and Smith draw too tightly the relations between the social and the sacred. The sacred is deduced from the social whereas the social is held together by the sacred. The divinity of national being is traced back to the roots of communal life while the communal bonds are themselves explained by the sense of sacredness that individuals attribute to this collective relationship. This form of reasoning is not only tauto-logical since it uses a circular form of argumentation (i.e. religious/national is really social and social is really religious/national) but it also reduces the religious and the national to the social and vice versa. As Lukes (1973: 508) rightly indicates: 'the social was not *ipso facto* religious; there were many collective phenomena, such as feasts and assemblies, that were in no way religious'. Although the sacred is per-haps an important form of the social it is far from being the only form of the social. As Weber (1968) and Billig (2002) are well aware, and I argue this in Chapters 3 and 4, the social can take a plurality of forms: instrumental, value-rational, habitual, or emotional. Furthermore in their attempt to find a solution to the Hobbesian dilemma of how is social order possible, neo-Durkhemianism offers us a contradictory solution – their functionalist argument is built on the idea that the collective affirmation of the sacred helps establish group solidarity but for that to happen it is necessary to have a group in the first place. Do religion and nationalism, as a form of political religion, 'express the pre-given solidarity of the group, or bring it about?' (Hamnett, 2001: 55). Neo-Durkheimians cannot have it both ways.

Similarly as many critics of Durkheim have empirically demonstrated (Leach, 1961, Evans-Pritchard, 1965, Lukes, 1973, Giddens, 1978), although the sacred/profane dichotomy is a valuable research tool, it is far from being universal (it does not exist in all religions or all religious practices), it is not as rigid (i.e. a knife used in sacrifice on one occasion and for cleaning teeth after a meal on other), and it works better if con-ceptualised in relation to aspects of different events or things rather than as a description of the entire realm. There is also the problem in the conceptualisation of the sacred as eternal which is explicit in Durkheim (Pickering, 2001: 104) and implicit in Smith's (1995, 2003a) under-standing of the near universal durability of cultural identities. This is highly questionable since as anthropologists show (Douglas, 1970,

Pickering, 2001) there are many collectivities that have scant or near non-existent use of rituals and whose religious beliefs and practices do not include 'cosmic categories, acts of transgression or rules of purity' (i.e. the Basseri, Persian nomads, Itury pygmies). Although ethnies and nations can have a sacred dimension this is neither universal nor essential.

Second, to return to the overall criticism of the idealist epistemology: its overemphasis on normative integration over social conflict is misplaced. Even though ethnic identities and nationalism do often serve as sources of group integration, as Barth (1969) rightly emphasised, this only happens in a context when other groups are present. While Smith does acknowledge that the outer categorisation supplements the process of collective identification, his account, being couched solely in status terms, remains overly value centred and downplays political and economic sources of group competition. However what is essential for any sudden and intensive display of group membership is precisely the context of potential or actual social conflict. The fact that there might be a degree of continuity between some pre-modern ethnies and modern nations has less to do with shared narratives of mythical past and collective memories, since there is a huge and inexhaustible repertoire of those, and much more with the actual and contemporary social conflicts. It is for the most part in such situations that one needs to invoke a sense of unity and collective difference, to borrow from 'past experiences' and to demonstrate utter dissimilarity vis-à-vis the threatening neighbours. It is exactly via such portrayals of ethnic collectivities and nations as homogeneous, timeless cosy communities that political leaders, intellectuals, social movements and other ethno-national mobilisers brush over the existing social cleavages in their own society (e.g. class, gender, status or unequal access to political resources) and legitimise their own position of privilege. In other words idealist interpretations of nationalism downplay what is, as Simmel (1955) noted so long ago, a crucial and distinctive feature of social life – its conflictual and competitive dimension.

Conclusion

For more than thirty years Anthony D. Smith has been a leading theorist of nationalism as well as the most prominent representative of the so-called ethno-symbolist perspective. As such his work has been extensively analysed, appraised and criticised. However both critics and supporters alike have predominantly focused on the very specific, mostly historical, issues that his theory addresses: the origins of nations and nationalism, the importance of collective mythologies, the questions of ethnic election or ethnic survival. This chapter has challenged such partial understandings by exploring the epistemological and ontological roots of Smith's position which, as argued here, is part of the broader Durkhemian worldview. Although Smith rarely makes explicit reference to Durkheim his perception of the social world and the social actors inhabiting that world, and hence his theory of nationalism, is best described as neo-Durkhemian. This is most evident in his conceptualisation of ethnies and nations as historically evolving solidary groups, his view of such groups as moral communities underpinned by the shared sense of a collective past, and finally in his understanding of ethnic and national collectivities as sacred unions developing in the context of the profane nature of modernity. Although Smith's vision of the social world in general and nations and nationalism in particular goes a step beyond classical Durkhemianism, the evolutionist, collectivist and idealist nature of his argument is still chained to the Durkhemian legacy which prevents it from developing a fully fledged explanation of nation-formation processes.

Let us now turn to Gellner's account of nationalism. To do so it is essential, just as with Smith, to engage with the epistemological foundations of Gellner's theory of social change which means tackling head-on his theory of modernity.

6
Coercion, Nationalism and Popular Culture

Introduction

Nominally and officially, we moderns have no stomach for systematic mass violence. Inspired by the Enlightenment, the widely dispersed and institutionalised ideas of progress, humanism, rationality and moral equality of all human beings stand in stark contrast to feudal hierarchy, hereditary inequality and periodic butchery of 'inferior' others. Yet it is this historical epoch more than any other – and especially its most recent phase, the twentieth century – that witnessed systematic mass killings on an unprecedented scale. While coercion in all its forms is now utterly disdained, it nevertheless constitutes an essential ingredient of modernity as we know it. This is explicitly recognised by Gellner (1996: 31) when he states that 'there are fairly good reasons why only coercion can constitute the foundation of any social order'. More to the point, he concludes his most important work of historical sociology, *Plough, Sword and Book,* by emphasising the role of state coercion in late modernity:

> It is the sphere of coercion, of politics, which is now crucial. Contrary to the two main ideologies born of the age of transition, the political order can neither be diminished and consigned to the dog-house, nor will it wither away. A new kind of need for coercion or enforcement of decisions has arisen. (Gellner, 1988: 278)

However, in this book as well as in many others, Gellner's argument about the exceptional character of the transition from traditional to modern order is founded on a premise which tends to contradict the view expressed in the quote above. While recognising the importance of

136

force ('fear') and the necessity of shared values that sustain the social, political and economic inequalities ('falsehoods') throughout the most of human history, it is his view of late modernity that is epistemologically more troubling. Although the 'great miracle' of dramatic and unprecedented transition is undisputed in its uniqueness, Gellner's insistence on the economic foundations underpinning this transformation remain questionable.

In particular, this chapter challenges the view of modernity that prizes the plough over sword and book; that is, production over coercion and culture. I contend that Gellner underestimates the role of both violence (in its internal and external forms) and ideology in the modern, and particularly the late modern, era. I will argue that modernity was born not only through (and with) violence, but that violence has been dramatically intensified and transformed through modernity as it gave birth to much more potent and subtle sources of self-justification: the proliferation and development of powerful and pervasive ideological doctrines. In other words, 'fear' and 'falsehoods' do not disappear with modernity; nor does the economy subsume politics and culture. While the transition to modernity is truly an exceptional historical moment, its outcome does not obliterate but rather *transforms* the character of both coercion and ideology. Enlightenment-inspired modernity, more than any other historical epoch, requires and is constituted by both violence and ideological blueprints.

The Big Ditch theory

The core concern of Gellner's historical sociology is what is often referred to (Jones, 1981, Mann, 1986, Hall, 1988, 1989) as a 'great miracle' of modernity.[19] In this sense, Gellner is puzzled by the very same questions that troubled the great classical sociologists from Marx, Weber and Durkheim to de Tocqueville: How and why modernity came about? Why it took the form it did? And why 'the miracle occurred, not in the West as such, not even in Europe, but in one small part of Europe, and on one occasion only' (Gellner, 1989: 4).

However, while the classicists of sociology, (with the partial exception of Weber), viewed this seismic shift as an almost inevitable process, or a sort of historical 'master plan' – envisaged as a dialectic of historical laws of development (Marx), the inescapable transformations in the moral order and corresponding forms of group solidarity (Durkheim), or through the prism of ever increasing rationalisation (Weber) – Gellner's contention is that what happened in a relatively short period of time, in a very small part of the world, and 'on one occasion only', was purely coincidental, against all the odds and all of known historical experience. And it is this series of events that have changed the world forever.

So what are the general contours of his argument? According to Gellner (1988: 16, 1997: 14), humankind has passed through three principal stages, characterised by the three distinct types of social organisation: foraging, agrarian, and industrial/scientific. While these three stages of development differ in practically every respect – such as their diverse cultural and coercive organisation – what is essential for Gellner is their distinct nature of production. What sets hunter-gatherers apart from peasants, and peasants from industrial workers, is their reliance and dependence on utterly different modes of economic production. Gellner (1988: 19) recognises that his position clearly privileges economy over politics and culture as a master *explanandum*: 'The contention is that *the economic or productive base does indeed determine our problems, but that it does not determine our solutions*' [my italics].

Although he acknowledges the importance of Neolithic revolution and the extraordinary character of the first great transformation (from foraging to the agrarian world), the focus of his analysis is almost exclusively on the second and much more profound societal transformation – a dramatic and unprecedented transition from Agraria into Industria. It is here that the difference between the old and the new world is most striking. The agrarian world of yesteryear and the industrial world of today (and tomorrow) stand on opposite sides of the Big Ditch – one dominated by food production and storage (characterised by a stable and stagnant economy with 'a ceiling on possible production, though not on population growth' (Gellner, 1997: 17)), the other based on perpetual economic and scientific growth, innovation and change, extensive division of labour, and pervasive social mobility. In the deeply hierarchical, Malthusian, world of Agraria, people 'starve according to rank' while work is despised and honour valued. By contrast, Industria is a vibrant, egalitarian, dynamic place embodying an unstable occupation structure and meritocratic principles of organisation. The agrarian world is dominated by coercion and immensely asymmetrical power relations, with small castes of nobility and clergy exercising absolute control over vast peasant populations. The scientific/industrial world is one where, as Gellner (1988: 158) puts it, 'Production replaced Predation as a central theme and value of life' – one where the benefits of cognitive and economic growth translate directly into 'an expanding bribery fund', allowing society to satisfy the enormous appetite of the rulers by keeping them wealthy without the need to resort to mass scale violence, while curbing social aggression (in all social strata) with unprecedented material enhancement of their living conditions.

Finally, each side of the Big Ditch exhibits an exceptional degree of cultural difference. Whereas Agraria is culturally split between a small number of high cultures (the court, nobility and clergy), and numerous low vernacular folk cultures of the countryside, the industrial world requires a linguistically unified, literate, educationally transmitted medium of expression shared by all members of the society. The function of culture in the agrarian world is to 'reinforce, underwrite, and render visible and authoritative, the hierarchical status system of that social order' (Gellner, 1997: 20). By contrast, the semantic nature of work in the industrial world demands a universal, context-free literacy in an idiom that is functional for 'frequent and precise communication between strangers involving a sharing of explicit meanings'. However, what is most striking about the two worlds are their inversely proportional sociological foundations. Agraria prioritises social over logical coherence – or as Gellner (1988: 272) writes, 'social cohesion cannot be based on truth. Truth butters no parsnips and legitimises no social arrangements'. Industria is built on exactly the opposite principle – logical coherence and truth come before social cohesion. This implies that the transition from Agraria into Industria also involves a transformation from a Durkhemian world of deep communal bonds to a Weberian world of instrumental rationality, anonymity and atomistic individualism.

This rather sketchy snapshot of Gellner's theory of modernity certainly does not do justice to the many subtle points he makes. Nevertheless, it does spell out as clearly as possible his main argument – that modernity emerged as a set of utterly contingent, unique and unprecedented events, replacing an old, economically inert, coercive, brutal and profoundly unequal world with one distinguished by continuous economic and scientific progress, excessive social mobility, cultural uniformity, egalitarian principles, and a relatively peaceful social order. While I think Gellner's diagnosis of the great transformation (and particularly the exceptional character of this phenomenon) is in many respects correct, and his analysis of this event highly edifying, his understanding of the modern condition itself is much more problematic. By valuing production over coercion – that is, economy over politics – Gellner's account of modernity, particularly late modernity, fails to account for the persistence and constant intensification of violence in contemporary times. This shortcoming is also reflected in the way he minimises the role of ideology in an economically advanced social order. Let us explore both of these deficits in greater detail.

The modern sword

Despite his sharp, bickering rhetoric, his interests in clashing (and often incommensurable) worldviews, and the conflicted nature of social change, Gellner is predominantly a sociologist of consensus. In this regard he is not so different from his anti-materialist opponents, such as Geertz or Parsons.[20] They all share an analytical view of the world that prizes social accord and normative consensus over social conflict. This is even explicitly stated by Gellner himself (1996: 139–40): 'Men prefer to think themselves sinners, rather than to damn the system in which they live ... The dependence of the individual on the social consensus which surrounds him ... is the normal social condition of mankind'. However, Gellner's strong historicism makes his position more complex than the one developed in the structural-functionalist school. Although he meets the structural functionalists halfway in insisting on the consensual nature of modern society, the sharp break between the traditional and modern world in Gellner's thought posits pre-modern forms of social organisation as inherently conflictual. Hence one can read how 'agrarian society is doomed to violence' whereas in the industrial world, production replaces coercion (Gellner, 1988: 154, 145).

Epistemologically, this view is highly problematic – how can one view human beings as utterly conflictual creatures in one type of social order, and as almost exclusively norm-oriented in another? While one can readily agree with Gellner that social conditions have a tremendous impact on individual and group behaviour, and that one's environment helps mould one's human condition, there is no explanatory room for viewing human beings in such a historically particularistic and determinist manner. If the social environment can so dramatically change human beings that they now (in modernity) appear as an almost separate species, then we can assume Gellner operates with a very plastic (and hence weak) concept of human agency – which is in many ways contradictory to his oft-professed commitment to positivist/scientist methodology (which treats human action in universalist terms) and individualism (that has no patience for hard structuralist reasoning). It is this epistemological fallacy that drives Gellner's argument (1988: 179) towards the view that the traditional world was one of coercion while the modern world is one of production where 'the ultimate and underlying principle of coercion is yes/no, life or death; and the ultimate principle of the market is – a bit more or a bit less'. In other words, he staunchly argues that with the arrival of modernity, politics is transformed into economics: a calculable and negotiable reasoning of trade replaces the uncompromising and non-negotiable reasoning of force.

The alternative, and epistemologically more coherent view, would start with the proposition that human agents have some universal, trans-historical qualities which, though these may be re-articulated, transformed and greatly influenced by changing social conditions, can never be obliterated. Simply put, the intrinsically conflictual nature of human life does not – nor could it possibly – disappear with modernity, for this would imply a teleology of sorts. While one might agree with Gellner that modernity presupposes an utterly different attitude to violence than the one present in the traditional world, this does not suggest that conflict, coercion and violence evaporate.

On the contrary, as W. McNiell (1984), M. Mann (1993), A. Giddens (1985) and others convincingly argue and empirically demonstrate, it is only in modernity that conditions are created for the successful centralisation, bureaucratisation and monopolisation of power – where violence becomes not only concentrated and hegemonised in the institutions of the modern nation-state, but also becomes simultaneously externalised. While modernity leads to 'internal pacification' (Giddens, 1985: 181–97) within a nation-state with relatively little direct violence exercised, it nevertheless concurrently exports mass scale violence at its borders. This externalisation of violence is most often reflected in the practice of warfare which, with modernity, acquires a greater degree of scope and legitimacy. Not only does modernity impose a sharp distinction between external (legitimate) and internal (illegitimate) violence, it also sets the stage for an unimagined proliferation of mass murder. This fact leads us to the greatest paradox of both modernity and Gellner's theory: while the modern era deplores violence legally, morally and politically – and develops the most sophisticated ideological and technological mechanisms for its elimination – this very epoch is the epicentre of systematic killing on a mass scale. The twentieth century reached a pinnacle of great scientific discoveries and unprecedented development of the most elaborate ethical theories of humanity. But it was also the century of mass extermination. Up to 120 million people have been massacred through ethnic cleansing and genocide alone (Mann, 2001, 2005) and more than 400 million have died as a result of two world wars, revolutions, rebellions, local wars, political massacres or state terrorism (Holsti, 1991, Tilly, 2003: 55). Hence, violence does not vanish with modernity; rather, it intensifies at an unprecedented scale.

While the traditional world was nominally and ritualistically more violent, its killing ratio was almost negligible compared to what was to come in modernity. Compared with contemporary standards the feudal armies were tiny, while the numbers of people who died on the battlefield were relatively miniscule. For example the first known and celebrated imperial warlord in recorded history, Sargon the Great of Akkad, conquered and held Mesopotamia, Syria and Caanan with no more than 5,400 soldiers (Mann, 1986: 145). William of Normandy conquered England in 1066–70 with less than 7,000 soldiers, while the largest army ever gathered during the crusades in defence of Jerusalem (1183) had less than 15,000 soldiers (Beeler, 1971: 249–50).[21] All this is virtually incomparable to the modern war machine, where in just two battles of the First World War – Verdun and the Somme, in 1916 – more than two million soldiers perished over a period of several months (Keegan, 1999). The traditional world preached hatred and war, but was rather inefficient in implementing either. The modern world preaches peace and egalitarianism but practices mass scale killings, ethnic hatred, and global inequality. We moderns do not cut off fingers and hands or gouge the eyes of our thieves and enemies; but with relative ease, we give tacit approval for the surgical killing of thousands. What one can see in the pre-modern world is largely a theatrical, ritualistic, spectacular violence characterised by dramatic individual acts of a gruesome nature – whereas modernity minimises the macabre and replaces it with brutal efficiency. We are appalled by photographs depicting a soldier urinating on a prisoner in Abu Ghraib – but we simply pass by or ignore daily statistics on tens of thousands who die from malnutrition, disease, war, climatic changes and other modernity-induced causes.

The main problem with Gellner's argument is that it remains almost exclusively inward-oriented. He explores an ideal type of modern/ industrial society as if that entity develops and exists in a geopolitical vacuum. Such an inner centred analysis which confines itself within the borders of the nation-state is likely to minimise or ignore the reality of inter-state (or even intra-state-to-be) violence and warfare. Once a revolution is achieved, war is won, or ethnic minorities are cleansed, an efficient, socially mobile, egalitarian, peaceful and production-oriented society can and indeed often *does* emerge. But what is crucial here is that this outcome is much less determined by its internal economic structure or by its inherent 'incentives for economic accumulation' (its sophisticated division of labour, or its 'expanding bribery fund' which all play their part) than by the fact that internal pacification is achieved through conflict, coercion and war. The nation-state does not emerge and exist on its own; it can only appear as a segment of a larger (post-Westphalian) international system of many such nation-states which requires mutual recognition (Hirst, 2001: 56). As Carl Schmitt (1976) noticed a long time ago, states are created through friend versus foe relationships, where their unlimited sovereignty is achieved at the expense of the externalisation of domestic conflicts and the de-politicisation of the inner society. The story of modern development, as M. Howard (1976) and C. Dandeker (1990) demonstrate so well, is the story of the gradual expansion of coercion and warfare. In C. Tilly's (1995) famous phrase, 'states made war and war made states'. Modernity was born with and through violence – and as it grew, so did the violence. Ultimately, both of the leading intellectual movements of modernity – the Enlightenment and Romanticism – established their influence through coercive means (from the French and American revolutions to colonial expansion to bolshevism, Holocausts, or the two world wars, to name just a few of the more recognisable historical episodes that transformed the world).

Moreover, the two central organising principles of modernity identified by Weber (1968) – bureaucratic administration and rationalisation – were pioneered in a military environment, as are nearly all the major scientific and technological discoveries of modernity (Giddens, 1984, Dandeker, 1990). The sophisticated mechanisms of the division of labour so central to the functioning of any modern society (and so essential to Gellner's argument) originated not in the economy but in the military, modelled as it was on the efficiency of a tripartite division of the army into infantry, cavalry and artillery – or, more generally, the division of the modern military machine into what we know today as a universal separation between army, navy and air force.

What is most damaging for Gellner's argument, however, is the fact that coercion and violence have not only affected inter-state affairs. As a result of the intensification of war through the *reson d'etat*, they have also deeply penetrated both the state itself and civil society. The maturation of modernity from the French Revolution onwards created the conditions for the emergence of total war, where – for the first time – new rulers could rely on the total mobilisation of all available resources and people. Not only has the state's infrastructural powers (Mann, 1986) dramatically expanded with its ability to fully conscript, transport, tax, police, censor, communicate or monitor a great majority of its subjects but also by gradually extending citizenship rights and welfare provisions to many groups, the nation-state established fixed parameters of inclusion and exclusion. And, as Bauman (1991: 2) rightly argues, any attempt to institutionally classify individuals and groups along these lines requires coercion – and 'it can hold as long as the volume of applied coercion remains adequate to the task of outbalancing the extent of created discrepancy'. However, this mechanism of inclusion/ exclusion is as integral to civil society as it is to the state, since in the late modern era one is often more afraid of organised radicals such as patriot leagues, anti-abortionists, anti-immigrant groups, religious fundamentalists, overzealous animal liberation activists, moral majorities of all kinds, or even simply of dubiously formed voluntary neighbourhood watch groups. While there might be an open and intensive debate as to whether late modernity is characterised by explicit or implicit symbolic violence (Bourdieu, 1997), what is clear is that coercion and the perpetual threat of violence remain as integral to this era as they were in premodern times.

Ideology and late modernity

The fact that the relationship between coercion and production is more complex than Gellner suggests does not imply that the attitude to violence has not dramatically changed through time. On the contrary, Gellner is absolutely right that coercive practices go very much against the grain of modern life. Social mobility and its corresponding egalitarian normative structure underpinned by values of humanism, fairness, merit and individual and/or collective autonomy stand in stark contrast to the hierarchical brutality and cruelty of the traditional world. Whereas excessive violence did not require much justification in the agrarian era, modernity does not usually tolerate open and loud pronouncements of hatred and calls for murder. However, principled demonisation of violence in modernity does not imply its factual decline, as modernity was witness to more bloodshed than any previous epoch. It is rather that this paradoxical situation demands more potent and elaborate mechanisms for justification of coercive behaviour. One could argue that there is a form of cognitive dissonance at the heart of modern nation-states – endorsing harmony while exercising destruction – that had to be unravelled in such a way as to earn mass appeal. And that mighty device was made available with the birth of modern, predominantly secular equivalents of religious belief – that is, political ideologies.

The two central normative pillars of the traditional world – institutionalised and state-sponsored religious doctrine, and the widely shared belief in the divine origins of rulers – have for the most part crumbled with the arrival and maturation of modernity. When they have not completely disappeared, they have blended with or transformed into new, often more elaborate and structured sets of ideas, values and practices that characterise modernity – ideological belief systems. While modernity was responsible for the proliferation of diverse, robust and sophisticated ideological doctrines such as socialism, liberalism, conservatism, environmentalism, feminism or religious fundamentalism, it is nationalist ideology (in all its guises) that became the dominant ideology of the modern epoch. More then anybody else, Gellner (1964, 1983, 1994, 1997) has demonstrated why this is so, and why it had to be so. The stark polarity of Agraria and Industria so nicely depicted in the Big Ditch thesis is perhaps most convincing here. As Gellner rightly argues, the traditional world was politically, economically, and most of all *socially* too hierarchical and stratified to allow for any significant degree of congruence between polity and culture.

The pre-Enlightenment universe, a European world crushed by the ideas and practices of the French Revolution, was a world characterised by a clear and strict division between two social realms – a small nobility (including top clergy) preoccupied with status enhancement, and the multitudes of illiterate peasantry with little or no social and geographical mobility. These were indeed two separate universes – one of 'high' Latin speaking culture, anxious to recover the glory of the Roman Empire under the guise of Christianity, and the other a huge microcosm of 'low' oral cultures of the peasant agricultural producers, whose means of communication were clearly limited by the existence of numerous unstandardised (and often mutually incomprehensible) vernaculars. To bring these two utterly diverse worlds together into one commonly shared cultural realm required a true miracle. So nationalism provided that miraculous glue and was in itself a miracle of modernity. The fact that in today's world very few individuals question the division of human beings into members of particular ethno-national collectivities is a powerful reminder of how globally internalised this (historically recent) transformation is.

While Gellner's diagnosis and his depiction of this astonishing transformation is without doubt highly valuable, his analysis of what happens to ideology in general – and nationalism in particular – in late modernity is more problematic. First, his view that advanced industrial society is legitimised almost solely through perpetual economic growth, underpinned and sustained by the cognitive dominance of science, is again too narrow to accommodate the complexities of human action. While economic well-being is a powerful source of individual motivation, it is surely not the only (and very often not even *the* most important) determinant of collective behaviour. Ideologically driven and politically conscious social movements have sprung up as often among the wealthy middle classes (e.g. anti-globalisation, environmental, animal rights, pro/anti-hunting and pro/anti-abortion groups) as they have among disadvantaged groups. The general public in highly industrialised parts of North America and Europe often tend to be as polarised and politically divided as those in Africa and South America (over many highly non-economic issues, such as the division of church and state, morality, sexuality, or gun control). The fact that they often live in different types of political orders determines whether these deep ideological conflicts remain more quiescent or end up in open bloodshed, but they do not obliterate what is a universal and trans-historical human quality – a propensity towards political discord and sundry ideological commitments. Hence, human beings are not only, and indeed not even predominantly *Homo Economici*. Their motivation can be as much instrumental as value rational, traditional, habitual or emotional (Weber, 1968, Billig, 2002). While Gellner (1983: 114–22, 1997: 47–8) does concede that nationalism remains an important source of state legitimacy in late modernity, his economism does not allow for unbridled nationalist explosions beyond the era of early industrialisation. As he puts it: 'The sharpness of nationalist conflict may be expected to diminish', 'the late industrial society ... can be expected to be one in which nationalism persists, but in a muted, less virulent form' (Gellner, 1983: 121–2). Or 'in advanced industrial society, some processes are set in motion which do, or may, diminish the intensity of ethnic feelings in political life' (Gellner, 1997: 47; also 1996: 122). This problematic view is premised on the assumption that violent nationalism is a property of the periphery undergoing the process of late and uneven industrialisation, and not an integral element of all modern societies. Thus instead of associating nationalism solely with the separatist doctrines and political movements that aim at the establishment of the new state, one has to analyse the nationalisms of metropolitan centres, colonial powers, and post- and quasi-imperial states. As John Hall rightly points out, even secessionist nationalism comes about more often 'from a reaction to the authoritarianism of empires than from the social inequality faced by a culturally distinct group' (Maleščvić and Hall, 2005: 569).

The fact that non-secessionist nationalism often – but crucially, not always – tends to be banal rather than explosive does not, as Billig (1995: 7) rightly points out, suggest its inherent wholesomeness. On the contrary, banality is far from harmless: 'Banal nationalism can hardly be innocent [as] it is reproducing institutions which possess vast armaments [that] can be mobilised without lengthy campaigns of political preparation'. Just as in his understanding of the historical relationship between coercion and production, here also Gellner operates with a teleological and an epistemologically unsound view of human actions. If modernity requires a degree of cultural uniformity which, through trans-generational socialisation and state-sponsored educational systems, moulds individuals into genuine and sincere nationalists, then it is highly unlikely that as long as these processes are set in motion, nationalism will become less relevant or that 'ethnic feelings will diminish'. Why would they? The infrastructural powers of modern nation-states – together with their tight grip on education, information and intelligence services – have only increased, and the nationalist doctrine has now spread worldwide both vertically (to include all social strata) and horizontally (to include the remotest parts of the globe).

Long periods of inter-state peace and the lack of open warfare between the economically and/or politically most advanced states does not in itself indicate the evaporation of nationalist feelings, or the disappearance of a nation-centric vision of the world. On the contrary, such nation-centricity has become such a pervasive cognitive framework (Brubaker, 1996, 2004) that it has penetrated everyday practices in the lives of most people around the globe, even in their most intimate settings. Spectacular events such as 9/11, politically sensitive assassinations, or dramatic incidents of ethno-national humiliation (both individual and collective) are excellent indicators of how easily one can mobilise nationalist sentiment and turn indiscernible banality into arrant virulence. This point is especially important in the context of Gellner's argument (1997: 47) about the potential convergence of nationalisms in late modernity, where 'advanced industrial cultures may come to differ, so to speak phonetically without differing semantically'. However, this can never be a question of different formal appearances hiding similar substances, since ideological conflicts are regularly very much about real life issues, reflecting deep social divisions and profound political differences. Here again we encounter a substantial degree of teleology in Gellner's argument, where advanced economics is seen as replacing politics and culture.

Although the rhetoric, symbolism and ritualism of particular nationalisms might often be very similar, this is not a good indicator of their substantive cores. The birth and maturation of modernity ensured that we live in an ideological age, where lasting ideological conflicts continue to rage both internally (within particular nation-states) and externally (between different nation-states and larger units of trans-communal solidarity). As a result, nationalism becomes an essential requirement of modern politics – a meta-ideology, a realm of an intensive struggle for hegemonic control by all political forces ranging from the extreme right to the extreme left. Today, no serious political movement and ideology – left *or* right – can afford to be delegitimised as 'unpatriotic' or 'treasonous'. Equally, every state or political order as diverse as Islamic Iran, Communist Vietnam, Monarchist Nepal or liberal democratic Greece or United States must legitimise itself first and foremost in nationalistic terms. So not only does nationalism not lose any of its magical appeal in late modernity – actually, it intensifies this appeal – more importantly, it becomes an essential arena and a battleground for different political forces where, as Billig (1995: 27) puts it, the battle for nationhood becomes a battle for political hegemony.

Nationalism between high and low culture

Although highly valuable in the depiction of the Big Ditch cultural transformation, the sharp distinction Gellner makes between pre-industrial, low vernacular cultures and the high culture of modernity has less to offer when approaching late modernity. While I have no dispute with Gellner's argument about the normative dominance and necessity of a single standardised high culture, his view (1983: 117) that 'in the industrial age only high cultures in the end effectively survive' is more problematic. The 'national' high culture does posit itself as a normative ideal of late modernity; but some forms of parallel popular culture not only remain within modernity, but actually become a prevailing pattern of everyday living.[22] Obviously this is not an oral village-based polyvalent folk idiom. Rather, it is a relatively standardised mass culture of an often (but not always) passive majority, which is in some ways parasitic upon its high 'national' equivalent. In other words, what Gellner terms 'high culture of the industrial age' is in fact two layers of standardised cultures – the 'authoritative' layer of an ideal type of national culture which, with modernity, democratisation and principled egalitarianism, becomes publicly recognisable and nominally valued as important, and the 'mundane' layer of everyday life, which is superficially infused with and remains largely dependent on its normative ideal.

The 'authoritative' layer is usually articulated in the creation of widely or even globally recognised 'national' art (the works of prominent painters, composers, writers, architects, etc.); 'national' successes in science, technology or medicine; and exemplary cases of 'national' leadership, heroism, morality or beauty, to name but a few. Verdi's operas, Van Gogh's paintings, Mozart's symphonies and requiems, Tolstoy's novels – today these are globally recognised not only as exceptional works of artistic genius, but also as essential building blocks of the distinct and prestigious national 'high' cultures of Italy, Holland, Austria and Russia respectively. Similarly, the military leadership of Napoleon, the scientific discoveries of Newton or Darwin, the moralistic images of John Paul II, or the superhuman heroism of Nelson Mandela are potent symbols of national identification for many individuals as they are seen to represent exemplary cases of what it means to be French, English, Polish or South African.

The mundane layer is premised on acknowledging these national 'icons,' but largely at the level of what E. Laclau (1996) calls 'empty signifiers' with a powerful ethno-political resonance. Thus, the mundane layer is one where national icons and various symbolic events are invoked through the culture of television soaps, tabloid newspapers, instant news, public ceremonies and rituals. In other words the general public often recognise the national significance of 'high' culture and jealously guard its 'national authenticity', but for the most part they do not live through or experience in any actual way the 'authoritative' layer. Reading Shakespeare or Dostoyevski is not required as long as one is able to invoke them as prestige-enhancing weapons in a global status struggle between 'nations'. The realm of the mundane is one of relatively homogenous mass society that borrows clichés and images from its 'authoritative' counterpart. However, this realm can never become a high culture in Gellner's sense of the word, since its very existence is premised on a significant degree of distance from the national ideal type. In some ways the 'mundane' layer of the standardised high culture is parasitic upon its 'authoritative' counterpart – but as Edensor (2002: 5) rightly points out (and documents this very well in his book), once the nation-state building project is officially complete, 'the mass media and the means to develop and transmit popular culture expands dramatically, and largely escapes the grip of the state, being transmitted through commercial and more informal networks'. Thus he shows how elements of vernacular, pre-modern culture can be re-appropriated by non-establishment groups working outside existing state structures and offering alternative nationalist projects. In a British context, one such alternative project involves celebrations of pagan goddesses, tree worship, ritualistic observation of druidic rites, and visits to pagan sites such as Stonehenge in order to convey 'the spirit of a pre-Christian Britain' in opposition to 'official Christian and over-rationalist constructions of national identity' (5).

However, what is essential here is the fact that, both internally and externally, the 'authoritative' layer is the subject of constant and fierce ideological conflicts between movements which aim to articulate, reorganise and hierarchically order 'national icons and events' through a particular ideological prism. In this respect, as I have argued in Chapter 4, nationalism becomes a central operative ideology of the modern age, supplementing (rather than replacing) dominant normative ideologies of modernity – liberalism, socialism, conservatism or religious fundamentalism. Since nationalism, in all its diverse guises, has become a dominant ideological mainstay of modernity, no serious political movement can afford to be seen as lacking in it. In this context, what matters is the ability to enunciate popularly recognisable images of national importance ('national icons and events') in a way which would suit the aims and ambitions of a particular political movement without alienating the collective perceptions of these national images and hence losing mass support. In other words, the rich repertoire of historical events (such as major victories, heroic defeats, and spectacular events of individual or collective bravery) and personalities (rulers, soldiers, saints, poets, scientists and other charismatics) has to be invoked and reinterpreted in a particular ideological light, so as to fit in with the movement's own meta-narrative of national development.

Hence, despite their official commitment to internationalism and a global proletarian unity, all successful communist movements had to incorporate powerful nationalistic symbols into their ideological narratives. The most obvious examples of this trend would be Stalin's extensive reliance on traditional Russian ethno-national myths, culminating nicely in Eisenstein's films *Alexander Nevsky* and *Ivan the Terrible*; the 'socialism with Chinese characteristics' of Deng Xiaoping; the re-designation of the Cuban Communist party from the 'party of the working class' to the 'party of the Cuban nation'; or the North Korean *Juche* ideology of national self-reliance. This form of strong nationalist appeal underpinning the official ideology is equally present in other supposedly universalist movements, such as Iranian state Islamism (Abrahamian, 1993, Ram, 2000) or American civic and liberal democratic creed (Lieven, 2004). In both of these cases, as in many others throughout the world, nominal trans-national messages of universalism expressed vigorously at the normative, official level are regularly 'translated' on the operative, popular level through alluring nationalist images – whether as Khomeini's constant appeals to the 'immemorial Iranian nation', or the jingoistic Jacksonian nationalism that views the Americans as a 'chosen people' engaged in a messianic mission against and/or on behalf of the inferior 'Others'.

The successful pursuit of a particular ideological project requires intensive reliance on, and hegemonic incorporation of, national symbols.

What is crucial for the mundane layer – that is, for the nationalism of popular culture – is not the actual knowledge about individual heroes or heroic events but rather the fact that they function as a formal object of national prestige, internally and/or externally. Since the pool of exceptional individuals who are globally recognisable is rather limited, most ideological movements have to work with – or even completely invent – distinctively national figures. These individuals, groups or events often operate according to a different status scale, which for the most part does not apply externally. James Connolly and Padraig Pearse, for example, are both publicly recognised – at the 'authoritative' as well as the mundane level – as national martyrs in Ireland, while they would obviously not have such resonance outside of the country. Similarly the image of Oguz Khan holds a special significance for Turcophone societies, while beyond their borders he remains largely unheard of. Jose Marti is revered by most Cubans as the father of their nation, as is Ante Starčević for Croats; but to people outside of Cuba and Croatia, these names generally mean next to nothing. At the same time, external status categorisation requires universal approval, where figures such as Copernicus or Einstein – whose greatness is undisputed – become universal currency of the international status struggle.

The relationship between the 'authoritative' and mundane layers is always complex. Although mundane forms of nationalism borrow from and depend heavily upon the 'authoritative' layer, the intensive informalisation of traditional 'high' culture and the virtual explosion of mass culture in late modernity has meant that 'low' culture is now in a position (as never before) to penetrate the pantheon of 'high' culture. Not only have images of Marilyn Monroe, Ronaldo or U2 today become intertwined with those of Steven Hawking, Picasso or Tchaikovsky as potent, internationally recognised symbols of distinct nation-states and their respective cultures, but equally so have the representatives of traditional high culture found their way into popular culture.

All this is not to posit that the two levels have become indistinguishable, as various analysts such as Edensor (2002) suggest; they clearly have not, as only certain images from 'low' culture achieve durability, continuous attention and wider recognition as potential objects of national 'high culture'. But it does suggest the inherent complexity of this relationship. The ongoing democratisation of cultural tastes and the intensive development and spread of new and widely available technologies of communication have had a deep impact on this relationship. Despite talk of globalisation and an emerging cultural uniformity, however, this process, far from diluting the national sentiment, actually reinforces the nation-centric vision of the world (as Smith (1995), Billig (1995), and others rightly point out), with these very same symbols often used as precious 'currency' in ethno-national status struggles. While David Beckham or Frank Sinatra may be global icons who transcend national borders, worshipped as they are by millions throughout the world, they are unambiguously recognised as the products of a very specific English or American (popular) culture. In this respect they formally perform a similar function to that of Beethoven, Michelangelo or Cervantes, in enhancing the prestige of distinct nation-states. What makes them different – and what still separates 'high' and 'low' cultures – is the actual *content* of these symbolic figures, as it requires conceptual and lived engagement with the works of these individuals. The official national canon of 'high' culture can be broadened to incorporate certain figures and events of popular culture; but in the long run, the last word still rests with powerful state institutions such as ministries of culture, national academies, universities, and the cultural and political elites that have a decisive impact on the articulation of the dominant national narrative.

All of this suggests that standardised national 'high' cultures of modernity are much more complex than Gellner's theory implies. Industria does require logical coherence and science to maintain economic growth – but it can never be sustained by scientific reason alone, as we are not only economic but also ideological and political animals. It is precisely here, in late modernity, that we see how 'truth butters no parsnips and legitimises no social arrangements'. Not only does the late scientific/industrial world remain distinctly nation-centric, if not straightforwardly nationalist; the distinction between 'high' and 'low' culture replicates itself in modernity too. This is obviously not the same hereditarily imposed cultural divide of the medieval world – nevertheless it, too, maintains intensive group polarities, both internally and externally. Gellner (1988: 272) was absolutely right in claiming that 'social cohesion cannot be based on truth,' since genuine knowledge refuses social subservience whereas 'publicly accessible truth fails to separate members of community from non-members'. But as the constant proliferation of modern wars and ideological conflicts demonstrate, this applies as much to Industria as it did to Agraria.

Conclusion

Ernest Gellner offers a powerful diagnosis of the transition to modernity. This truly was an unprecedented and highly improbable episode in the history of humanity, initially affecting small parts of the European continent and then gradually taking hold around the world. In many respects the dawn of modernity was a genuinely miraculous series of events and processes – bringing about the birth of scientific method and logic of reasoning, a sophisticated division of labour, cumulative technological growth, the egalitarian concept of universal justice, meritocracy, social mobility, and the standardisation of national cultures underpinned by the almost exclusively semantic nature of labour. However, despite this compelling diagnosis, Gellner's overall understanding of modernity is overly optimistic. In order to show how extraordinary this transition was, he overestimates the role of production and underestimates the position of coercion and ideology in modernity. While revolutionary changes of historical conditions and social contexts can and do change human beings, they cannot obliterate their trans-historic qualities, such as the universal susceptibility to social conflicts and ideological allegiances. Social conditions can alter our behaviour, but they can never turn us into a different species.

Thus, modernity is not immune to 'fears' and 'falsehoods'. On the contrary, both violence and ideological doctrines flourish in the age of (late) modernity. Instead of their evaporation and replacement by economic production, culture and coercion acquire rather different, modernity-resistant forms. In place of sadistic cruelty against socially or religiously inferior individuals, one finds systematic mass extermination ideologically bolstered by the latest scientific doctrines and most sophisticated technologies available. This is not to suggest that modernity has only one, dark side – obviously not, as it is an age of unparalleled economic and technological progress, openness, civility, and reason. However, many of these developments were built upon, arose simultaneously with, or gave rise *to*, mass scale slaughter and ideological fanaticism. Human history is, perhaps, a story of a dramatic shift from an inexorable, gregarious confinement of *Gemeinschaft* to atomistic solitary incarceration of *Gesellschaft* (Gellner, 1998); but this tells us much more about the structural transformation of the *means* and very little about the *ends*, since the motives and actions of modern human beings are not so dissimilar from their ancestors. The fact that modern man acts as a far more rational and solitary creature than his predecessors does not automatically imply a lack of stern ideological zeal and belligerence. Far from it, as we will see in the remaining chapters of this book.

Part III
Experiences

Part II

Experiences

7

Institutionalising Ethnicity and Nationess

Introduction

One of the main arguments set out in the first two parts of this book is that ethnicity and nationess have much more to do with ideology than identity. I have tried to show why this is important, both at the conceptual and theoretical levels. Not only is it that ethnic groups and nations are not pre-given and static forms of human collectivity, as most social analysts now agree, but also that ethnicity and nationess for the most part do not irresistibly emanate from the individual's ingrained need to belong. There is nothing inevitable in the complex relationship between individuals, groups and their 'cultural shells'. Collective cultural difference is not, and sociologically speaking can never be, a mere synonym for ethnicity or nationess. And this is not simply because of the highly dynamic and fuzzy quality that cultures themselves exhibit, but also because of the contingent and arbitrary character of how and why certain practices or artefacts are chosen from the nearly unlimited repertoire that cultures provide. Thus, when a claim is made to safeguard one's identity this has very little if anything to do with culture but a great deal to do with politics. For ethnicity and nationess are not what they are often presented to be – a set of specific cultural demands – but something rather different: politically motivated forms of social action. In other words the social researcher can never take popular claims for cultural authenticity for granted as, with most appeals to 'cultural roots', one is not on the terrain of identity but of ideology. Whereas the first two parts of this book have analysed the conceptual, operational and theoretical bases of identitarianist discourse, this last section will focus on the empirical consequences of what might be somewhat parodically called 'identity in action'.

Since the uncritical glorification of 'identity' is not only confined to academia but has become a dominant vocabulary of everyday life it is important to explore how such a discourse operates beyond the academic environment. In other words the focal point of this last part of the book is to analyse the political implications of 'identity talk', and in particular how the claims to cultural authenticity are articulated by the dominant social agents as well as by the institutions of the modern state. Drawing critically on some leading sociological theories of social change I explore the role of political elites, intellectuals and structural and ideological forces in the institutionalisation of cultural difference. By looking at such processes as modernisation, democratisation, geopolitical or historical transformations, together with the nature of radical individual and collective status alterations in the context of two relatively recent cases (the disintegration of Yugoslavia and Rwandan genocide), I aim to emphasise the political consequences of 'identity talk' and particularly their direct translation into rigid identitarian-state directed policies. To put it simply, the aim here is to illustrate some possible corollaries of the institutionalisation of 'ethnic and national identities'.

First I explore the links between the collapse of the Yugoslav federal state and the policies that institutionalised strong forms of ethnicity and nationess in the decades before the state's demise (Chapter 7). Second I analyse the role and responsibility of organic, state created identitarian intellectuals in this process of nation-formation (Chapter 8). Finally I examine the role of modern identitarian ideologies, modern technology and status transformations in the policies of ethnic cleansing in Bosnia and Rwanda (Chapter 9).

Return of the repressed?

Our first case study, which is the object of inquiry in this chapter is the sudden unexpected collapse of the Yugoslav federal state. Although the break-up of Yugoslavia has been extensively analysed and is the subject of a voluminous literature, there is still a profound lack of sociologically grounded analyses. With a few notable exceptions such as Sekulić (1997, 2004), Gordy (1999), Vujačić (1996), and Ron (2003) most of the existing accounts are either overly descriptive historical studies which make little attempt of analytical generalisations, or are simply more or less sophisticated political pamphlets intent on the 'blame game', tending to attribute too much coherence and intention to the contingent interplay of events and actors involved. Considering the overall aim of this book my focus here will not be an attempt at complete explanation of this complex and multifaceted episode. Instead I will concentrate only on the peculiar nature of Yugoslav federalism and its role in fostering the state's dramatic collapse. Although this constitutes only a small segment of the larger Yugoslav puzzle I argue that the development of this relatively unique state structure coupled with the distinct operative ideological narratives of state-centred nationalism have had a decisive impact on the sudden and bloody break-up of the federation.

Popular images of the collapse of Yugoslavia were fuelled by dominant journalistic accounts and many academic works (i.e. Glenny, 1992, Kaplan, 1993, Vulliamy, 1994, Ignatieff, 1997), together making the assumption that Yugoslavia disintegrated because it was a multi-ethnic state with a long history of mutual animosities that were kept under control by the iron fist of the communist government. The logic behind this highly popular view is that, as in the rest of the communist word, here too cultural difference was suppressed, and with the collapse of the authoritarian structure the inherent ethnic dissimilarities re-emerged in the form of violent clashes. This view is false on at least four accounts. First, as Brubaker (1998) points out, despite the journalistic obsession with the 'return of the repressed' view of the post-communist world, depicted as intrinsically violent and prone to never ending ethnic conflicts, the overwhelming majority of states in Central and Eastern Europe have not experienced inter-ethnic violence. The mass media's stereotypical portrayals of the region, together with its overemphasis on the spectacular and the brutal, have contributed significantly to a popular imagination of the former 'communist East' as almost innately predisposed to inter-ethnic animosities and violence. What happened in the Caucasus and the former Yugoslavia was more exception than rule as both, two and fifteen new states that emerged from the collapse of Czechoslovakia and the Soviet Union respectively, were created with little or no inter-ethnic bloodshed at all. In historical terms this was unprecedented as states and empires rarely collapse with so little violence.

Second, the view that cultural difference and conflict are somehow necessarily linked is profoundly unsociological. Although as human beings we are political animals prone to discords, competition and conflict, there is nothing inevitable in ethnicity and nationess that necessitates inter-group clashes. As Cohen (1969: 199) puts it, human beings do not kill each other simply because they have different cultural habits; this happens only when they associate such differences with real political or economic inequalities. More recent research (Gagnon, 2004, Gilley 2004) has cast serious doubts on the very concept of 'ethnic conflict', problematising stereotypical representations of the various (largely non-affluent) regions in the world arguing that such representations obscure rather than explain. The fact that two groups of people speak different languages, share different wedding rituals or eating habits does not automatically imply that they will engage in inter-group conflict. If this was the case, given that no society is absolutely culturally homogenous, we would live in a permanent state of war. The view that Yugoslavia disintegrated because it was constituted of culturally diverse ethnic groups and nations is, sociologically speaking, utter nonsense.

Third, the claim that the outburst of inter-ethnic violence in the former Yugoslavia is a continuation of historically deeply embedded animosities is factually wrong. In fact apart from the more recent past, culminating in the atrocities of the Second World War,[23] the groups inhabiting the Yugoslav state had little history of direct mutual animosities. Through most of their history they have been subjects of different imperial powers (primarily Ottomans and Habsburgs) and, historically their collective memory of hostilities and anger were aimed primarily at those respective powers and their representatives and far less at their ethnic neighbours who were often in the same inferior position.[24] Invoking medieval religious divides between Eastern Orthodoxy, Roman Catholicism and Islam, distinct imperial legacies or Balkan wars from the beginning of the twentieth century to explain recent atrocities is a typical example of what Goffman (1968: 9) describes as a stigmatic strategy of retrospective interpretation, that is an 'after the fact' explanation whereby one's past behaviour is reinterpreted on the basis of present typifications and current events. In this respect the former Yugoslavia was no different to many other states and societies as one can easily trace inter-group conflicts in the past of nearly any society. Why has 'ethnic conflict' happened in Yugoslavia but not in Romania which has an even longer history of inter-ethnic animosity and has a substantial and territorialised Hungarian ethnic minority. What about Slovakia and its large Hungarian minority? Or the Baltic states where more than one-third of their entire population consists of ethnic Russians? Drawing historical parallels between the 'powder keg' Balkans at the beginning and the end of the twentieth century might be interesting to the ill-informed subscriber of Orientalist thinking (Said, 1978, Todorova, 1997), but a reified geography can hardly be the source of any meaningful explanation.

Finally and perhaps most importantly for the general argument of this chapter is the view that ethnicity and nationess were somehow suppressed under communism. Although communist states are traditionally perceived as trans or supranational, being ideologically guided by the universalism of Leninist and Marxist doctrine which privileges class over ethnicity, the relationship between class and ethnicity in state socialism was far more ambiguous. As I have argued briefly in Chapter 4 and more extensively elsewhere (Malešević, 2002) there is an important distinction to be made between the normative or official ideological narrative of the particular political order and its operative, which is to say institutionalised, counterpart. While communist states have for the most part preached proletarian internationalism on the normative level, nationalism and especially ethno-nationalism was a cornerstone of their operative ideology and an important source of internal legitimacy. This is particularly visible when representations of dominant social actors are broken down into their normative and operative layers. For example depictions of class enemies – normatively abstract entities such as 'the bourgeoisie' or 'capitalists' – are depicted at the operative level as tangible ethno-national enemies which threaten 'our country'. At the same time the universalist notion of the trans-national working class or working people that features prominently in the normative ideology, is transformed into our 'heroic' and 'chosen people' at the operative level. So instead of an abstract 'egotistic bourgeoisie', one encounters a concrete physical threat represented in the form of British or American imperialist 'spies' and 'traitors'. Stalin's notion of 'kulaks' epitomises this ambiguity where kulaks are both an economic category (exploiters of the poor peasants) but also an ethno-political category (un-patriotic traitors of the homeland bent on 'sucking the blood from the Russian people'). In other words state socialism was not immune to nationalism and ethnocentric discourses.

On the contrary, as Brubaker (1996) has convincingly argued, communist states have devised by far the most sophisticated organisational mechanisms for the institutionalisation of ethnicity and nationess as a category of everyday experience. Thus the Soviet Union was a federal state with 15 states that had constitutionally guaranteed right to independence, 15 distinct legislatures and administrative systems, 15 academies of sciences and arts and other cultural and scientific institutions, 15 communist party leaderships together with separate institutional party machineries, 15 titular nations and all other distinctive signs of culturally underpinned sovereignty. Even more importantly, Soviet citizens were socialised and cognitively chained into a complex system of social classifications where 'ethnic nationality' became not only a statistical category but also a legal position and an 'obligatory ascribed status', assigned at birth on the basis of ethnic descent, recorded in all personal documentation and regularly used to control the access to jobs and higher education (Brubaker, 1996: 31). As a result ethnicity and nationess have become a dominant cognitive perspective of social reality deeply ingrained in the everyday practices of individuals living under such a system.

Much of this argument applies to the Yugoslav case as well. Here too ethnicity and nationess were structurally reified with the help of the communist state: there were eight ethno-nationally distinct legislatures and state bureaucracies, eight academies of sciences and arts, eight party leaderships and so on. However, decoupled (1948) from the rest of the communist world the Yugoslav state structure was ideologically forced to develop even more complex and elaborate state mechanisms of cultural institutionalisation. As will be demonstrated later in this chapter, the peculiar character of this unprecedented institutionalisation of cultural difference had a decisive role to play in the eventual disintegration of the federal state. Hence the argument I develop is exactly the opposite of what is often assumed – Yugoslavia did not collapse because it was an artificial conglomerate of disparate ethnic groups with a long history of mutual antagonism, held in check only by a totalitarian regime. Instead the roots of the collapse are to be found in the very ideas, structures and processes that were created by the state and its political system. Inspired by the modernist ideology of Kardeljist Marxism[25] on the normative level, and sustained by state-sponsored nationalism on the operative level, the Yugoslav state embarked on a process of radical transformation of state organisation which saw an initially highly centralised entity (in 1945) becoming an exceptionally decentralised, and in many respects a confederate, state by the early 1980s. Thus, the roots of state collapse are to be found in its idiosyncratic state organisation which was gradually created as an ad hoc set of arrangements to avoid genuine democratisation. In other words the intensive and, in many respects, unprecedented institutionalisation of cultural difference was a direct (even if not necessarily intended) outcome of specific policies whereby the power elite of communist Yugoslavia used decentralisation as a means of avoiding democratisation and liberalisation. Under pressures from below to further democratise society, the rulers of Yugoslavia shifted the question of popular political participation to the level of inter-republic relations. By giving more power to party elites within the individual republics instead to its citizens, the party preserved its monopoly within the political system. Thus, what took place was not genuine decentralisation, but rather quasi-decentralisation which produced a set of loosely linked but internally highly centralised and, eventually culturally homogenising, units – the individual republics. To avoid democratisation power was not devolved to citizens of individual republics but to the party elites of each constitutive unit. However, before we engage with our empirical material it is necessary to briefly review the explanatory potential of some leading sociological theories of ethnicity and nationess in accounting for the Yugoslav collapse.

The sociology of ethnicity and nationess

The changing nature of relationships between social groups based on ethnicity and nationess is the subject of dispute among social analysts. Some authors such as M. Banton (2000) and M. Hechter (1986, 1995) interpret the shifts in ethnic cohesion and ethnic animosities in terms of the behaviour of rationally motivated actors who manipulate cultural similarities for individual benefits. In this perspective it is argued that human beings are utility maximisers who will regularly aim to exploit their ethnic group membership as a manoeuvre in the process of shaping their individual life chances. Thus, sudden support for the creation of an independent, ethnically based nation-state is explained as a rational outcome for instrumentally driven agents who are forced to make dramatic choices under 'imperfect market' conditions. In the rational choice model of explanation it is this chaotic, Hobbesian environment that helps to influence the transformation of popular beliefs which are formed on the basis of incomplete information. Although this approach is perhaps suitable in explaining the motives and behaviour of some individuals in the final stages of Yugoslav collapse and war, it offers a profoundly ahistorical standpoint which is unable to account for the structural and historical conditions that have created such a chaotic situation in the first place. Rational choice models tend towards *ex post facto* types of explanation and tautological reasoning which is often unfalsifiable (Smelser, 1992, Malešević, 2004). This perspective might shed some light on the processes of individual choice formation in time of severe 'ethnic conflict' but it can tell us very little about the macro-structural changes that led to the collapse of the federal Yugoslav state.

If rational actor models are overly micro-individualist the neo-Marxist theories of ethnicity, in both of its dominant varieties – political economy perspective (Bonacich, 1976, Miles, 1989) or Gramscianism (Hall, 1986, Solomos, 1995) – are distinctly macro-structural attempts at explanation.

The view of ethnic relations and nationess as inherently linked to the contradictory nature of capitalist production, where cultural difference masks class inequality so that it becomes a weapon of socio-economic domination, has at best limited application to the state socialist environment. If class is conceived, as it is in neo-Marxist theories, as something linked to ownership of the mode of production, then a society where the economy had no autonomy and where disparities in personal wealth are small and politically largely insignificant, as was the case in communist Yugoslavia, then there is no room for understanding ethnic animosities and state collapse in terms of hidden class conflict. Even reformulated economistic accounts such as those of 'internal colonialism' that stress territorially confined economic disparities, uneven development, ethnic division of labour and economic exploitation of a culturally distinct periphery by the metropolitan centres (Stone, 1979, Hechter, 1999) find little empirical backing in the Yugoslav context. The first secessionist movements emerged in the most and the least advanced parts of the country – Slovenia and Kosovo, that is the region benefited enormously from the federal system of economic distribution of wealth (Kosovo), and the region that contributed the most to this system (Slovenia). Although stark regional economic inequalities did contribute to the process of state disintegration this had less to do with class structure and much more with the changing popular perceptions of inequalities. It was the political instrumentalisation of these popular perceptions with the openly stated claims that other republics are exploiting 'our' position in the federation that would later serve to justify a variety of intra- and inter-state policies. However, as with the rational choice models this is an after-fact which provides no explanation for state collapse.

Non-instrumentalist theories such as symbolic interactionism (Blumer and Duster, 1980, Lal, 1995), functionalist systems theory (Parsons, 1975, J. Alexander, 1980, 2002) and anti-foundationalism (Goldberg, 1993, Carter, 1997, C. Alexander, 2000) focus their attention less on objective economic or political sources of inter-ethnic animosity and much more on the subjective perceptions and discourses of individual or social actors. While interactionists emphasise transformations in the mutual collective interpretations of social reality and pinpoint how individuals attain and change there inter-ethnic 'definitions of the situation', functionalists are concerned with the stability of commonly shared cultural values and the role that inter-group solidarity plays in ethnic relations. The variety of anti-foundationalist positions on ethnicity and nationess also stress the cultural underpinnings of 'identity formation'. However instead of aiming to provide an explanation their ambition is to decon-struct the hegemonic narratives into which discourses on ethnicity and nationess are shackled. Thus in their account of the sudden break up of the Yugoslav state such perspectives are likely to accentuate the norma-tive power of ideas, values and discourses in shaping the environment for the intensive polarisation of ethnic collectivities. For interactionists the key issue is the dramatic change in the collective definitions of the group situation among individuals who found themselves in a position of switching their group loyalties from Yugoslav to Serbian, Croatian or Slovenian. For functionalists the source of the conflict and state collapse are to be found in the inherent fragility of the common cultural system (the lack of pan-Yugoslav ideology and practice) at the macro state level. For anti-foundationalists the crumbling of rationalist, universalist, and Enlightenment-inspired doctrine of Marxism, together with its utopian grand vista, was a prelude for the articulation of alternative hegemonic narratives such as exclusivist and mutually antagonistic ethnic nation-alisms. Although all these insights contribute to understanding the causes of Yugoslav disintegration their epistemological idealism (func-tionalists and interactionists) or radical relativism (anti-foundationalists) hinder their explanatory potential as they are unable or unwilling to account for the decisive role that tangible political power plays in ethnic relations. If we were to concentrate our attention only on the transfor-mations of popular beliefes and perceptions, or on competing discourses and narratives displayed in the process of Yugoslav breakdown, we would miss the role of political entrepreneurs, cultural elites such as intellectuals and religious leaders, the impact of the state's contradictory organisational structure, and the historically conditioned collective sta-tus alterations. Yugoslavia did not disintegrate only because people's perceptions changed or one meta-narrative replaced another. Rather it is some very material sets of events and processes such as radical constitu-tional change in 1974, the death of its charismatic and omnipotent authority Tito in 1980 or the rise of Milošević in mid-1980s that, among many other events, had such a profound impact on the change of these popular perceptions.

This last point brings us logically to the two remaining and highly compatible sociological theories of ethnicity and nationess which seem most valuable in elucidating the Yugoslav case: elite theory and the neo-Weberian perspective. To put it simply and in stark terms, elite theory studies ethnic relations and nationess as a form of power relation where cultural difference is mobilised for political ends (Cohen, 1981, Brass, 1991). The political theories of ethnicity stress the competition of elites for tangible material resources and their manipulation of cultural, religious, or linguistic symbols for political purposes. As A. Cohen (1969) argues: 'ethnicity is essentially a political phenomenon, as traditional customs are used only as idioms, and as mechanisms for political alignment'. With the help of cultural or religious symbols, large sectors of the population are mobilised on an ethno-national basis and confronted with other groups who are now perceived solely as culturally distinct and thus potentially threatening. Through ethno-national mobilisation a particular elite manages to ideologically articulate cultural difference as a political difference and gives political meaning and significance to culture by reifying and then politicising its content. As Brass (1991: 26) explains the political instrumentalisation of ethnicity is more likely to occur in societies that undergo dramatic and uneven social change. Under such conditions 'ethnic self-consciousness, ethnically-based demands, and ethnic conflict can occur only if there is some conflict between indigenous and external elites and authorities or between indigenous elites'.

The political interpretations of ethnic relations and nationess are particularly convincing when state socialist societies and their offspring are analysed. Since these societies were characterised by the dominance of politics over all other realms of social life, with the economic sphere lacking autonomy, and where the decisions of major political actors (i.e. the communist party, charismatic leaders, political bureaucracy) were crucial for the direction of the development of the society, it is obvious that the analysis of these social actors can yield a better understanding of this phenomenon. However, overemphasising a single group of social actors (political entrepreneurs) is paradoxically both the strength and weakness of this approach. As I have argued elsewhere (Malešević, 2004: 120–5) the evident simplicity of elite theory in many respects embodies Occam's razor principle, where the simplest solution often is the right one. This indicates its substantial value in locating the concrete individuals responsible for initiating or spreading 'ethnic hatred' and violence. It is no accident that the International War Crimes Tribunals in Nuremberg, Hague or Arusha successfully operated very much on these principles of individual responsibility. However, the point made here is not about legal or moral issues but the epistemological implications of these institutions as they are forced to rely on the most trustworthy knowledge claims available. The mass scale violence which often accompanies state collapse is without doubt a multifaceted and complex phenomenon involving numerous individual and social agents, and entailing events which may be unprecedented, messy and (partially) intended, so that tracing individual responsibility behind particular instances of state collapse is a powerful epistemological ally of elite theory. Nevertheless the weakness of this approach is apparent in its underestimation of mass action: whereas elites are portrayed as strong willed, diverse and creative, the population at large is depicted as submissive, completely dependent, homogenous and incapable of meaningful action. The fact that political entrepreneurs and other elite groups are often the dominant social agents whose actions determine the course of historical events has very little to do with individual qualities of those in power and, as Michels (1962) was well aware, more to do with one's structural position. In other words it is the concentration of power in modern bureaucratic organisations that has decisive impact on the ruler's actions. The modern bureaucratic state is a powerful institutional mechanism which can relatively easily turn into an unstoppable behemoth. In addition to this, the behaviour of elites very often goes hand in hand with the tacit consent of the silent majorities. Hence as will be shown in this chapter elite theory can tell us a great deal about the motives, actions and behaviour of individual and collective agents, but to provide a fuller account of the Yugoslav tragedy one has to look in particular at the institutional organisation of the modern state. To get the grips of this, elite theory needs to be supplemented by neo-Weberian accounts.

What is distinctive about neo-Weberianism is its emphasis on the multiplicity of forms of ethnic attachments which can range from class, caste, estate to status groups (Rex 1986). Nevertheless with the intensive development of modern bureaucratic social systems status categorisation often operates as the prevailing form of both in-group solidarity and out-group social exclusion, stretching from inter-personal relationships to the geopolitics of state prestige. Weber (1968) saw ethnic groups as amorphous entities whose formation is almost entirely dependent on social action. He rightly argued that ethnic collectivities are quasi-groups grounded in a particular belief in common descent which becomes socially meaningful only through collective, political action. The key catalyst of this social action is the near universal practice of monopolistic social closure: the restricted character of status membership creates a condition whereby individuals are in a position to close access to symbolic or material benefits to the outsiders. In this context 'any cultural trait, no matter how superficial' can be used for the initiation of monopolistic social closure (Weber, 1968: 388). Building on these ideas contemporary neo-Weberians such as Parkin (1979), Rex (1986, 1996a) and Collins (1986, 1999) emphasise the role of status transformations in the changing relations between human collectivities. Following Weber they operate with a dynamic understanding of ethnicity and nationess, moving away from essentialist views that treat ethnic groups as solid and corporeal 'identity carriers' towards the perception of nationess and ethnicity as a potential social attribute. However despite its potent explanatory weight neo-Weberianism is not without its weak points. Apart from the fragmented character of this theory and its occasional overemphasis on the role of status groups (which is not of immediate relevance here, see Malešević, 2004: 136–41) the crucial problem is the lack of a coherent political explanation of the processes of ethnic group mobilisation. Despite seeing political motives as decisive for social action and attributing great importance to modern bureaucratic systems, neo-Weberian theories of ethnicity and nationess make little connection between the micro sociology of individual action and the macro sociology of geopolitics and state formation. Even though they emphasise the political, in the fragmented nature of the theory much of this emphasis is lost. In addition their understanding of monopolistic social closure is too economistic as it is reduced to being an instrumental mechanism for the collective self-benefit rather than a concept with wider application, including political control, symbolic domination or the politically induced transformations in status hierarchies. Hence to attempt a more comprehensive explanation of the Yugoslav turmoil it will be necessary to enhance neo-Weberianism with elite theory and vice versa, but also to occasionally go beyond these interpretative horizons.[26] To put it bluntly, in this chapter the relationships between ethnicity and nationess on the one hand and state organisation and articulation on the other will be analysed from the perspective of neo-Weberian elite theory. In other words, the emphasis will be placed on the political factors which had a bearing on the changing relationships between distinct collectivities in the federal state. The aim is to look at the dominant social and political actors and their motives, as well as at the structural, organisational mechanisms and institutional constraints in reference to ethnicity and nationess and territorial arrangements of the state.

The structure of Yugoslav federalism

The relationship between ethnicity, nationess and federalism in communist Yugoslavia was complex. While sharing some similarities with other state socialist states such as the USSR and Czechoslovakia, the direction of its development shows more in the way of differences than similarities with these countries.[27] Expelled from the rest of the communist world at a very early stage (1948)[28] in the development of post-Second World War Europe, Yugoslavia had to ideologically adapt and develop a different model of state socialism including its distinct federal arrangements. Claiming to be a more genuine expression of socialist society, the Yugoslav state leadership had to demonstrate abroad and at home that its political system was more in tune with the origins of Marxist doctrine and hence more just, free and equal to all its citizens as well as its constitutive units than its Soviet or (later on) its Chinese counterparts. For that reason, the rulers engaged in the periodical reform of its economic and political system as well as its constitutional structures. While beginning as a very centralised state in 1945, Yugoslavia was gradually transformed into a loosely formulated federation, that by the time of its bloody collapse in 1991, had many actual features of a confederate state. In terms of the relationship between ethnicity, nationess and federalism, one can distinguish between three phases in the development of the Yugoslav state: (a) the period of gradual but constant decentralisation at the macro level which lasted from 1945 to 1974; (b) the period of radical macro decentralisation and simultaneous micro centralisation from 1974 to 1987 and (c) the gradual disintegration of the state from 1987 onwards that ended up in a wars of 1991–99.

From party centralism to macro decentralisation 1945–74

Unlike the Kingdom of Serbs, Croats and Slovenes established in 1918 as an essentially a Greater Serbian project, the new Yugoslav state set up by Tito and the Communist Party recognized the existence and rights of all other major ethnic collectivities, in particular Montenegrins and Macedonians who, because of their predominantly Orthodox religion, were previously seen as Serbs. In 1971 Bosnian Muslims were also given the right to express themselves as a legally distinct ethno-national collectivity.

The aim of the central government was to legitimise itself, on the one hand by providing each constitutive ethnic and national collective with 'its own state', largely along the lines of 'their' historical territories, and on the other hand by unifying different ethnic groups and nations in a single state that would be more sensitive to ethnicity and nationess than its monarchist predecessor. Hence, the country became officially a federation of six republics: Slovenia, Croatia, Bosnia and Herzegovina, Serbia (also having two autonomous provinces – Kosovo and Vojvodina), Montenegro and Macedonia.

Although recognising the specificities of each ethno-national collectivity, the new regime also aimed at emphasising the similarities between these groups. This was not an easy task to achieve, partially because of traditional and historic differences among these groups, among which the most often invoked are the following: most Slovenes and Croats declare to profess Roman Catholicism, were under the control of the Habsburg Empire for several centuries, were more exposed to Western and Central European social and cultural influences, had a more developed industrial infrastructure, and were proportionally more urbanised. In contrast to this are the regions where majority of the individuals declare themselves as Serbs, Montenegrins, Macedonians and Bosniaks/Bosnian Muslims. Historically these regions were subjects of the Ottoman Empire, had a less developed industry, were less modernised and urbanized and have traditionally belonged to Eastern Orthodox Christianity (majority of Serbs, Montenegrins and Macedonians) or Sunni Islam (majority of Bosniaks/Bosnian Muslims). However, what was common to all of these groups was, allegedly, the same Slavic roots (the widely shared myth of common origins) and the oral as well as the literary culture and language related to this common Slavic ancestry. With the exception of Slovene and Macedonian – two languages which are different though not incomprehensible to other South Slavic speakers, the other four ethno-national collectivities communicate through the same language.[29] These cultural and linguistic similarities, together with the shared history of anti-imperial struggle, were further linked by the new state rulers to the Enlightenment and Romanticism inspired pan-Slavic ideals of the nineteenth century and the Illyrian movement,[30] preaching the idea that all the south Slavs originate in the same Illyrian tribe, and thus articulating a powerful common narrative of Yugoslav 'brotherhood and unity'. However the foundation of this cohesive narrative was rooted firmly in a tangible historical event: unlike most other post-Second World War East European states communist Yugoslavia was a self-liberated country. The fact that Nazi and fascist occupation was defeated by an organised pan-Yugoslav communist partisan resistance movement led by Tito solidified the structure of this common narrative. As neo-Weberians such as Collins (1986, 1999) emphasise, military victories raise the prestige of state rulers and enhance the internal legitimacy of the social order.

Nevertheless to successfully govern the new regime with all of these elements, integrative and disintegrative, had to be framed as a coherent account. As a result, in 1945 federalism was offered as a solution that would not only recognise the differences between distinct ethno-national collectivities but would also ensure that the common state remained intact. However, the new constitution also ensured that all central powers were in the domain of the federal government, which in fact meant in the hands of the communist party. Until 1948–49 Yugoslav federalism was largely a copy of the 1936 Soviet model. The Constitution of the Federal People's Republic of Yugoslavia (1946) included in its first article the Leninist idea of the right to self-determination on the part of individual republics, and hence *de jure* the right to secession from the federal state. Every constitutive republic in the federation had its own constitution, which though designed and approved by the parliament of that individual republic, had to be in agreement with the federal constitution. As in the Soviet constitution, the republics had a large degree of autonomy on paper, while in reality power was highly centralised at the federal level.

The political and ideological clash with the Soviet Union meant that Yugoslav leadership needed stronger popular support at home. In order to secure this support, the party was forced to liberalise its policies as well as to accommodate republican party leaderships by decentralising some of its powers. Thus, the new 1953 Constitutional law was more decentralised and ensured that some crucial areas such as economy, media and educational policy, were decided at the level of the republics and not solely at the federal level. The political, economic and constitutional changes were accompanied by intensive industrialisation and political liberalisation, producing the most dynamic development in Yugoslav history with GDP growing at 8.1 per cent annually during the period 1953–60. Thus the economic growth in the early years of communist rule coupled with the later international recognition of Yugoslavia's special position in the Cold War further strengthened the social status of both its leadership as well as its population on world stage. Resisting the might of the Soviet Union worked, in Weberian terms, as an essential ingredient of internal leadership cohesion, as a powerful source of the leadership's legitimacy, and as a popular status boost for the Yugoslav citizens at large.

However, the republics did not develop at an equal pace. The historically more advanced regions of the north (Slovenia, Croatia and Serbian province of Vojvodina) developed faster and more intensively then the rest of the country. To accelerate the development in the poorer regions, the federal government introduced a joint redistributive fund to which the wealthier republics had to contribute more than the others. This fact, together with the simultaneous and gradual decentralisation of the state impacted on the politically induced popular perception in Slovenia and Croatia that they had to carry an enormous burden. At the same time, the communist leaderships of the southern republics played on the popular feeling that they have been exploited by the richer republics of the north. This issue was to become a central point of disagreement in the 1960s.

The new constitution of 1963 did not solve this problem, instead reflecting the ambiguities and existing conflicts that had accumulated in the post-war period. Although the constitution maintained and even extended most of the rights given to individual republics in the constitutional law of 1953, it redefined and neutralised their status as sovereign states. Instead, the republics were now defined as 'state socialist democratic communities' (Caca, 1988: 164). Party leaderships in Slovenia and Croatia viewed this as a step backward, one which, together with the economic stagnation of the late 1960s,[31] contributed further to conflict between republics' leaderships. The rulers of the richer republics were opposed to making contributions to the fund for the underdeveloped republics. In the 1960s first the Slovenian and, later on, the Croatian leadership started opposing the policy of redistribution of economic resources and demanded further decentralisation. The Croatian party leadership particularly opposed the existing currency system and pressed the federal leadership for a new system that would give each republic greater control over its foreign currency assets (Stokes, 1993: 227). For Croatia, this was a crucial issue because of its disproportional income revenue from tourism. As external, macro structural geopolitics stabilised with the Cold War detente between NATO and Warsaw pact states, so the appetites of local, republican leaderships were wetted shifting the geopolitical tension to micro, Yugoslav intra-state level. To mobilise popular support the leaderships of individual republics such as Slovenia and Croatia, where living standards were considerably higher, were now in a position to implicitly play on the higher social status of its population. However since economic or political arguments could be seen as egoistic and inegalitarian, and thus in breach of egalitarian socialist ethics, so the leaderships provided silent support for the intellectual articulation of political and economic demands by casting these as cultural demands: instead of economic or political captivity it was the lack of authentic cultural expression that was voiced – the position of Croatian language, the enunciation of cultural heritage and similar themes.

The federal state responded by accepting a number of constitutional amendments that gave more authority to the republics and provinces. In addition, important changes took place with respect to the main power holder: the League of Communists of Yugoslavia (LCY). Thus, for example, in 1968 the congresses of the republican branches of the LCY were held before the federal congress. As Hodson *et al.* (1994: 1539–40) emphasise, 'this step was important in reversing the tendency of the republican congresses to simply ratify and adopt the policies decide by the federal congress'. However, by the end of the 1960s resistance to centralisation had developed in Croatia into an ethno-national movement led by the leadership of the Croatian branch of the LCY.[32] In the early stages of the 'rebellion', Tito and the federal leadership attempted to accommodate demands made by the protesters. So, for example, in 1971 each republic was given *de facto* veto power on the decisions made on the federal level (Hodson *et al.*, 1994: 1540). However, this and other moves did not satisfy protesters, and Tito changed his position and crushed the movement, removing its leading members from power. Despite this draconian attitude towards the leaders of the Croatian national movement, Tito and the federal party leadership basically accepted most of the demands made by the leadership of 'Croatian Spring' and initiated the radical change of the Constitution in 1974 which essentially devolved all important powers to the republics and provinces. In addition the new constitutional arrangement shifted from civic to much more ethnic definitions of nationhood. For example in the Croatian case what was previously constitutionally referred to as 'a community of people living in Croatia' became, after the constitution of 1974 a 'community of the Croatian nation, Serbian nation in Croatia and other nationalities who live in Croatia' (Uzelac, 2006: 167).

The new and final constitution of socialist Yugoslavia defined the units of federation as 'states based on the sovereignty of the people' (Caca, 1988: 164). For the first time, sovereignty was deduced from the individual republics to federation and not vice versa as it was the case before 1974. In addition to the powers they already had, such as education, media policy and economy, the republics acquired most of the powers that were in the domain of the federal government such as political system, finances and distribution of public funds, social services, policing, civil protection and defence, and jurisprudence. Apart from foreign policy and military organisation, all major decisions were now in the hands of the republics. Effectively, from 1974 Yugoslavia had many more elements that would define it as a confederate state than what was implied by its official name – federation. In most respects this was the end of any meaningful external trans Yugoslav geopolitics, heralding the escalation of a new internally shaped geopolitics of semi-independent republics and their respective leaderships.

From macro decentralisation to micro-centralisation 1974–87

Instead of solving the existing problems, the reform of the federation and the implementation of the new 1974 constitution only accelerated the proliferation of conflicts between the republics and the federation. First, to avoid further rebellions like the Croatian Spring, the party radically decentralised the federal state, but at the same time it strengthened its own role and further micro-centralised its branches all over the country. As Golubović (1988: 256) rightly points out, 'the IX congress of LCY (1969) has reaffirmed directive role of the party apparatus and legalised the route to re-etatisation'. With these changes the Yugoslav state became what some commentators termed 'policentric etatism'.

Second the constitutional change opened up the problem of the party–state relationship. Whereas the state was now radically decentralised, the party was still organised according to the Leninist principle of democratic centralism. As Bilandžić (1985: 411) rightly predicted, since both of these institutions were engaged in decision-making process and were supposed to act as a single unit, changing the principle of organisation and function for one (the state) and not for the other (the party) would lead to the situation where one would break-up the other.

Third, while the new Constitution has completely decentralised the federal state, it preserved the existing centralised modes of decision making within the federal units. In other words, the outcome of the reform of federation was not genuine decentralisation or democratisation, but rather micro-centralisation at the level of the republics. In other words trading democratisation for decentralisation created a new geopolitical reality whereby individual republics acquired nearly independent statehood and hence their leaderships found themselves in an inevitable position of acting along the principles of *raison d'état*. However, since the party itself was still a highly centralised organisation, as long as it was in control it could prevent disintegrative tendencies. The charismatic authority of Tito and other veteran party leaders and war heroes, and the strength of another centralised institution – the military – helped to maintain the federation for another few years.

The problem with the constitution of 1974 was not, as many Serb nationalists would later claim, that it was designed to undermine the Serbian position within the federal state or to 'humiliate' and 'disperse Serbian people'. Instead the implication of the constitution was that it had the opposite affect: it institutionalised the principle of ethnically defined nationess as a central organising element of the political system and hence unwittingly provided an institutional mechanism for the expansion of all future (ethno)nationalisms. While the monopoly on the articulation of this principle was still firmly within the party which decided all important issues regarding the direction of ethno-national policies, that was not initially recognised as a problem. However once the party started loosing its support base and as power started shifting from party to state the outcomes of policies that institutionalised cultural difference were to become blatantly clear. Since the state was completely decentralised and since the party itself was gradually losing its legitimacy among the Yugoslav population, the party leaderships of individual republics were provided with the institutional tracks for the future action: they could switch with relative ease from the universalism of an all-state ideology to the individual particularisms of their own republics. They successfully attempted, and were organisationally in a position, to gain legitimacy by shifting their problems outside of the borders of their respective republics. Hence, economic stagnation or the lack of political liberties were now interpreted by the republic's party leaderships as a result of 'an unequal position of our republic within the federation'. The message was simple: 'It is the neighbouring republic (Croatia, Serbia, Slovenia, and so on) that hinders our development'. Decentralisation of the state soon produced a quasi-multiparty system, with eight communist parties having virtual monopoly over their territories, creating eight distinct and increasingly culturally homogenising statelets. This situation was soon to lead to further and more intensive conflict between the party leaderships of individual republics.

Tito's death in 1980 marked a new phase in the development of the Yugoslav state. This was the period of economic stagnation, huge inflation, the rise of an enormous unemployment rate and political unrest in Serbia's Kosovo. GDP fell from 8.8 per cent in the period 1956–64 to 0.4 per cent in the period 1980–84 (Cohen, 1993). The country also had huge international debts and the gap between the developed north-west and the undeveloped south-east continued to widen. The effects of the new constitutional arrangements were most apparent in the area of economic policy. The republics conducted their own economic policies and the fact that 65 per cent of all borrowings abroad were made by republics and provinces themselves indicates how decentralised the state had become (Dyker, 1990). The death of Tito meant that the last source of (charismatic) authority, and the last element binding the party leaderships and keeping them from serious conflicts, was gone. From now on, the struggle for political control would only intensify.

It is important to emphasise here that, despite large-scale unrest in Croatia in the late 1960s and early 1970s, relations between individual representatives of distinct ethno-national collectivities living in Yugoslavia, unlike those between the party leaderships, were reasonably good. As all available surveys in this period show, the levels of social distance between the main ethno-national groups were very low if non-existent and the rate of intermarriage was relatively high. Thus, in a 1964 survey, 73 per cent of the sample described relationships between Yugoslav ethnic groups as good. Similarly, in a 1966 survey 85.3 per cent of those who declared themselves as Croats and 81.7 per cent of those who identified themselves as Serbs showed slight or negligible ethnic distance towards other ethnic groups living in Yugoslavia (Dyker, 1979). The results of surveys conducted in the 1980s showed a similar pattern (Katunarić, 1986, 1987). In addition, the rate of inter-ethnic marriage for the period 1962–89 was regularly high. The average percentage of exogamous marriages was 12.63, ranging from as low as 6.98 in Kosovo to 25.95 in Vojvodina (Botev, 1994). The real conflicts were at the top, rather than at the bottom, of the social pyramid.

The mid-1980s brought first significant criticism of Tito's policies and the state's highly decentralised structure. In 1986 a group of academics from the Serbian Academy of Arts and Sciences drafted a document 'Memorandum' which set up the basis of Serbian ethno-nationalism. The document attempted to show that post-war Yugoslavia was developed as an anti-Serb project and that 'Yugoslavia, in its present form was no longer an adequate solution to the Serbian question' (Silber and Little, 1995: 30). The document was especially critical of the 1974 constitution, seeing it as intentionally designed to weaken Serbia by giving its two provinces semi-state status. It also insisted that Serbia's political weakness was reflected in its 'economic subjugation' by Slovenia and Croatia. The Memorandum provoked outrage in the other republics but was backed by influential Serbian intellectuals and received a silent support from some members of the Serbian LC Central Committee.

Indirectly promoting the ideas presented in the Memorandum and relying on the growing dissatisfaction with the political system, as well as economic and political crises in Kosovo, Slobodan Milošević managed in 1987 to gain power within the Central Committee of Serbian branch of LC. However paradoxically and unlike his predecessors, Milosevic built his support base not among the party members and through the usual institutional channels, but principally among the masses by organising 'spontaneous' street demonstrations, first in Kosovo and Belgrade and than in Vojvodina, Montenegro and the Serbian populated areas of Croatia and Bosnia. Even though Milošević was in many ways an institutional creation of the socialist, decentralised, bureaucratic and culturally homogenising state, his support base was largely outside these institutions. Nevertheless despite his 'ordinary' and 'anti-bureaucratic' rhetoric his policies were, although extreme, nothing more than a logical conclusion to the direction Yugoslav federalism had taken. The gradual and radical decentralisation of the state provided an institutional shell which was slowly but surely filling with the specific cultural content needed to politicise and acquire mass support. Once political space was fully opened and the proverbial gloves came off, it was easy and tempting to play the ethno-nationalist card. So, Milošević who was first to realise that Tito was dead, was also the first communist leader since the Croatian Spring to break the taboo of speaking to an audience consisting solely of one ethnic group (Serbs) and openly using ethno-national rhetoric. The involvement of the new leadership of Serbian LC in the organisation of large-scale demonstrations on an ethno-national basis meant that, from now on, politics would not be confined to party meetings and declarations. Pandora's box was definitely opened.

The Results of Micro-Centralisation 1987–91

The intensive decentralisation of the federal state and the simultaneous micro-centralisation at the level of the individual republics in a one-party state situation inevitably led to fragmentation of the central party structure. After Tito's death, it was just a matter of time before individual party elites started fighting for political control over the federal centre.

Since Croatian political space was silenced after the purges of 1971, with new cadres elected and promoted on the basis of anti-nationalism, so politics oriented towards ethnic mobilisation could only develop in other two major centres – Belgrade (Serbia) and Ljubljana (Slovenia). Between 1987 and 1989, Serbian LC leadership supporters organised a number of street demonstrations in Kosovo, Vojvodina and Montenegro and managed to replace their party leaderships with those loyal to Milošević. In this way, Serbia controlled four out of eight votes in the federal collective presidency and could block any decision at the federal level. This so-called anti-bureaucratic revolution provoked outrage in the other republics and especially in the most developed and most Westernised Slovenia. Hence, this period was characterised by constant political struggle between a rising Serbian nationalism promoted by Milošević and the Serbian party leadership and a liberal and moderate, but also nationalist-oriented, Slovenian leadership led by M. Kučan. Under the influence of civil society groups and a change of general political climate, Slovenian party leadership was more ready than any other LC leadership for democratisation and radical political change.

The changes that the new Serbian leadership undertook were finalised in March 1989 when a number of crucial constitutional amendments were adopted in the Serbian parliament. In doing so, Serbia took virtual control of Kosovo and Vojvodina, reducing their autonomy to a minimum and thus becoming more powerful than the other republics in the federation. In addition, the Serbian government took over a number of functions that were in the domain of the federal state, such as appointing its own foreign minister. This was a precedent that other republics were to follow. Slovenian, and later on, Croatian reaction was swift. The Slovenian party leadership proposed a set of constitutional changes that were aimed at weakening the federal centre even further, by establishing an 'asymmetrical federation' in which Slovenia would take over from the federal government the right, among other things, to decide how to allocate the republic's wealth. By adopting these amendments Slovenian party leadership strengthened even further the definition of Slovenia's sovereignty in the 1974 constitution.

Slovenian and Croatian rulers were also the first to organise genuine democratic elections in early 1990. The elections brought oppositional ethno-nationalist parties into power with programmes that were clearly secessionist. By the end of that year, elections had been held in each republic. In Bosnia and Herzegovina and Macedonia, ethno-nationalist parties also gained majorities and formed new governments, whereas in Serbia and Montenegro the LC changed its name to the Socialist Party and the Democratic Socialist Party, respectively, and won elections.

The new anti-communist rulers in Slovenia and Croatia were now even less inclined to accept the concept of Serbian leadership for the reorganisation of the federal state. In the face of the Serbian leadership's demand for a more centralised state, they responded with the idea of fully fledged confederation. New Bosnian and Macedonian governments attempted to mediate between the two sides by proposing a compromise repeatedly rejected by the Serbian or the Slovenian side.

In this situation, the institutions of the federal government were gradually losing significance and power. The collective presidency was paralysed and no group had a majority,[33] and the federal parliament was basically illegitimate since no federal elections had taken place. The only relatively functional federal institutions were the office of Prime Minister A. Marković and the army. However, neither of these two could succeed in preserving the federal state. The prime minister was losing the backing of the republics, while the army was internally divided not only along ethno-national lines but also between reformists (clearly a minority) and hardliners.

Since the federal institutions had become dysfunctional, the negotiations on the status of the new organisation of the common state were held directly between the presidents of the republics. When, after many such meetings, with the failure to reach agreement, Slovenian and later Croatian leadership, following successful referenda, decided in 1991 to proclaim their independence.

The break up of the federal state

The results of the first democratic elections of 1990 further polarised the political and constitutional crisis in the federation. The newly elected governments in Slovenia and Croatia not only differed ethno-nationally from those in Serbia and Montenegro but much more importantly also became ideological adversaries. While the north-west was now governed by right-wing nationalists whose primary aim was to secure an independent ethno-national state, to change the economic and political system and to try to join the EU and other Western associations, the south-east was ruled by the same old left-wing nationalists whose principal goal was to preserve the existing economic and political system and to establish its hegemony within the federation, showing little interest in joining Western alliances. Thus what can be seen here is the political, not the cultural underpinning of the conflict. Decades of intensive decentralisation together with the institutionalisation of cultural difference created an environment whereby ethno-nationalist appeals to cultural distinctiveness and status superiority had much more resonance than any economic or political argument.

To invoke these sentiments of status superiority and rigid cultural difference, both sides were firmly determined to use all means available. For this reason, both the Serbian and Croatian ruling elite, which had become the main representatives on both sides, took the control of the mass media and engaged in the delegitimisation of each other by means of an intensive media war. But the targets of delegitimisation were not so much adversary governments as entire ethno-nationally defined populations – Croats and Serbs. For the first time since the Second World War, traditional and historical cultural differences, such as religious denomination (Roman Catholicism versus Serbian Orthodox Church), script (Latin versus Cyrillic), and dialect (predominately Serbian *ekavian* versus Croatian *ijekavian*), were used to politically delineate the two ethno-national collectivities.[34] Hence, at the level of the masses, the political struggle was articulated as a cultural struggle: an ideological clash wrapped up in the discourse of identity. The message disseminated in the media was not that 'we cannot live with them because they do not share our ideas about political and economic organisation of our society' but, rather, that 'we cannot live with them because they are culturally, religiously and historically different or inferior to us'. Why was it that this appeal so quickly mobilised millions of individuals under the banner of ethno-nationalism?

The answer lies in the idiosyncratic organisational nature of the Yugoslav federal structure which unwittingly provided the institutional channels through which the protean force of ethno-nationalism could grow and expand. In order to avoid democratisation and liberalisation the old decentralising state attempted to keep peace by accommodating local/republican elites and diffusing popular pressure from the metropolitan centre to regional authorities. In this process it supplied the bureaucratic and institutional vessels for local party leaderships to build their power base by delegitimising the centre or the leaderships of other republics. To be successful in this fierce but subtle inter-state struggle they were gradually forced to use and further institutionalise cultural difference as a powerful political tool. Once this political door was prised open there was no turning back. The new non-communist leaderships took over where their communist predecessors left off, stretching this cultural chip to the extreme and breaking all taboos by openly invoking rhetoric and actual policies of monopolistic social closure.

The apparent success of new political elites was also grounded in their ability to exploit the past for contemporary purposes. While the old communist regime was opposed to the use of historic, religious and cultural symbols of an ethno-national nature, these were also preserved in the collective memory of many family networks and, the new elite was in a position to unashamedly manipulate these symbols. Communist symbolism was quickly replaced with the supposedly old ethno-national symbolism – flags, coats of arms, religious motives, old national heroes and myths including public reburial of ethno national 'saints and scholars'. Because of their emotional appeal and ambiguity these symbols were relatively easily connected to some imaginary golden ethnic past by invoking directly or indirectly images of common ethnic origin as well as status superiority. In the case of Serbs and Croats, this past is symbolically traced to 'vast' medieval kingdoms of Serbia under Tsar Dušan and Croatia under king Tomislav. As A. Cohen (1979: 103) underlines 'it is this ambiguity in their meanings that forges symbols into such powerful instruments in the hands of leaders and groups in mystifying people for particularistic or universalistic or both purposes'. Symbols become mighty weapons in a power struggle because of their inherent 'irrationality' and their connection to the real or imaginary objects and acts that affect human feelings. By promising the symbolic or real restoration of the 'vast' ethno-national territories the elites were in position to mobilise mass support. Insisting that 'Croatia is for Croats only' implies both symbolic and physical control over the particular stretch of territory and is an embodiment of the claim for monopolistic social closure.

Next, because the communist regime had not allowed subtle discussion on the Second World War massacres and genocide committed by the Ustasha regime against the Serbian population in the Nazi-sponsored Independent State of Croatia, nor the crimes committed by the Serbian Chetnik para-militaries against Bosnian Muslim and Croatian civilians, this space was also open for the new elites. Since these topics were in many respects official taboos but at the same time alive and well in the collective memory, the new elites in power were in position to crudely manipulate these images and provoke fear. With the help of ethno-symbolism, new enemies replaced old ones. Instead of the 'capitalists', 'fascists' and 'Western imperialists', the new sources of fear became the revamped Ustashas/Croats, Chetniks/Serbs and Islamic Fundamentalists/Bosnian Muslims.

In the situation of political uncertainty, economic hardship and state collapse, the intensive attachment to an ethno-national group, and animosity and hatred directed at other 'threatening' ethnic groups, became the only source of security and certainty. The instrumentalisation of these emotions and interests by political elites was particularly evident in the mass media. The dissemination of propagandistic messages had a direct influence on entire populations, provoking old fears – for example, that the new Croatian state is just another version of the Nazi-sponsored and Ustasha-run Independent State of Croatia, or that all Serbs are Chetniks who only want to subjugate, exploit and oppress Croats as happened in the case of monarchist Yugoslavia.

Some of the actual policies of the new governments contributed further to these fears and showed the patterns of monopolistic social closure at work. The new Croatian constitution of 1990 defined the Republic of Croatia solely as a state of ethnic Croats and not as state of all its citizens, or as it had been in the constitution of the Socialist Republic of Croatia, as 'the state of Croats and Serbs living in Croatia'. The new ruling party, the Croatian Democratic Community (HDZ), removed Serbs from important state institutions, introduced the Latin alphabet as the only officially recognised script, and immediately changed political symbols and the names of the streets, thus fuelling nationalism among many Serbs in Croatia. All these actions led to the widely held perception among many individual Serbs in Croatia that, if Croatia becomes independent, they would become second-rate citizens. So, when in 1991 Slovenian and Croatian leadership declared their independence, local Serbian leaders in the territories where the Serbs had an alleged majority did not recognise the new Croatian government and started establishing their own institutions. With the backing of the Yugoslav army, now clearly pro-Serbian, they proclaimed their independent state of 'Serbian Krajina'. Although the creation of this para-state owes a great deal to geopolitical actions on the part of leadership of Serbia this does not explain its local mass support. It is the fear of humiliation and status degradation inbuilt in the newly emerging mechanisms of social closure that can better account for the popular support among many Serbs in Croatia.

In its last gasp the federal government tried to stop the Slovenian leadership from seceding. Since Slovenia had no politically significant minorities, its rulers could quickly and easily negotiate the secession with the Serbian side. This, however, was not the case with the Croatian secession. Having a large Serbian minority whose self-proclaimed leadership had already established its own institutions in the rural areas of state, Croatia could not follow Slovenia without conflict with the Serbian side, a conflict which developed into full-fledged war in the second half of 1991. After six months, the war was partially stopped by UN intervention which confirmed the status quo. The period 1992–94 was one of non-war non-peace in Croatia, and in 1995 the Croatian army conducted two military offensives, crushed the 'Serbian Krajina' para-state and established the authority of the Croatian state in these territories.

A more horrific war followed in Bosnia and Herzegovina. The open conflict between the Serbian and Croatian government could not but affect this multi ethnic republic. As events started to unfold, the Serbian side in the new Bosnian government followed the position of the Serbian government in opposing the joint institutions, whereas the Bosnian Muslim/Bosniak[35] and Croatian ruling parties followed the views and policies promoted by the Slovenian and Croatian governments. In 1992 when the Bosnia government, following a successful referendum, decided to proclaim independence, war spread to the territories of Bosnia and Herzegovina where again the Yugoslav army openly sided with the Serbian paramilitaries. The Bosnian Serb side proclaimed its independent state *Republika Srpska*, and was supported by the Serbian government, both militarily and financially. The war in Bosnia ended with the Dayton Accord, enforced by NATO and signed by all sides in 1995, dividing the country into two largely self-sufficient entities.

Conclusion

Communist Yugoslavia broke up because it produced in itself structural animosities and conflicts that it could not resolve. To maintain its political monopoly within the state, the party attempted to deal with the accumulated economic and political differences and existing social antagonisms by shifting the emphasis from crucial issues of popular participation towards the question of territorial organisation of the federal state. The party–state evaded the central problems of democratisation and liberalisation by articulating them as questions of decentralisation. In other words, decentralisation was used as an *ad hoc* mechanism for decreasing the pressure from 'below'. In this way, the federal party gradually devolved power to the party leaderships of individual republics and in this process helped create institutional tracks for any future cultural homogenisation. This policy resulted in the establishment of a quasi-multi party situation, with eight hegemonic communist parties competing for the control of the centre. Once the communist façade evaporated, the established cultural shells together with its bureaucratic machinery were available for intensive politicisation. To generate popular support new political elites could now easily switch from 'social equality talk' to 'identity talk' and formulate political demands as cultural demands. Under such circumstances all political issues were soon to become exclusively ethno-national issues. This was a prelude to war and collapse of the joint federal state. Yugoslavia did not collapse because it was an artificial conglomerate of many ethno-national groups. It collapsed because it unwittingly created institutional conditions for the stern politicisation of cultural difference. This is not to say that the communist state created cultural difference *ex nihilo* or that culture was not politicised in previous historical periods and under other socio-political orders. What was distinct about the state socialist experiment was its unprecedented bureaucratisation and the inexhaustible proliferation of new institutional structures. Over-institutionalisation of cultural difference in an environment where no other political space is open led directly to a situation whereby culture became the most obvious and most potent device of elite control. Although ethnicity and nationess are dynamic, fuzzy and amorphous, under such conditions of intensive social action and institutional politicisation, as Weber was well aware, they can quickly transform into powerful social mechanisms of in-group solidarity and out-group exclusion. The break up of the Yugoslav federal state is a potent reminder of what can happen when cultures become institutionally entrenched and when the 'politics of identity' turns into a clarion-call for mass extermination.

8
Identitarian Intellectuals and Ethno-nationalism

Introduction

Whereas in Chapter 7 the emphasis was on the responsibility of political elites and state organisation in the institutionalisation of rigid forms of cultural difference, this chapter will focus on the role of cultural elites, and in particular state-created intellectuals, in the process of intensifying ethno-nationalist mobilisation. Although, as I have argued, the fragmentation of the Yugoslav state had a great deal to do with the legacy of a peculiar institutional design and the way this was exploited by political entrepreneurs, this is only part of a complex story concerning the sudden demise of the state. To more fully understand the dramatic social and political shifts that shaped this process it is also essential to dissect the ideological make up of Yugoslavia's intelligentsia. Here again, as in Chapter 7, my aim is not only to attempt to get to grips with the specificity of the Yugoslav situation but also to use this case study to further analytically dissect the implications of identitarianism in practice. Despite the peculiarities that deepened and widened the scale of this tragedy there is also a universalistic message here – a message which can tell us something significant about the position of organicist state intellectuals in initiating, spearheading and galvanising ethno-nationalist mobilisation. Moreover this can also tell us something about the nature of the modern nation-state and its role in fostering identitarian ideologies. Here too, as in the case of political elites and federalism, our attention will focus on both social agents (intellectuals) and social structures (the state), as only through the analysis of their complex interplay can one understand the dynamics of ethno-nationalism.

When observing Yugoslav intellectuals before and after communism one notices a striking paradox – while the rest of the communist world had well-known and prominent dissidents, communist Yugoslavia had very few. Whereas with the disintegration of the communist order, dissidents either disappeared from countries across Eastern Europe by becoming professional politicians or returned to their previous academic or artistic professions, the new post-Yugoslav states witnessed the emergence of authentic dissidents for the first time. This in itself indicates that Yugoslav society was in some ways unique in the communist world, and that its sudden and horrific disintegration had more to do with its own internal social, political and cultural organisation and structure and less with the global political changes resulting from the collapse of the communist order world-wide. However, its uniqueness did not preclude it from sharing common ideological goals with the rest of the communist world. On the contrary, one of the main arguments of this chapter is that precisely because communist Yugoslavia took its ideology more seriously than the rest of the communist world, so it acquired the preconditions for its dramatic and bloody collapse. Although the political underpinnings of the Yugoslav collapse were discussed in Chapter 7 the intellectual and ideological roots of its collapse must still be explored. Hence the focus of this chapter is the analytical profile of the Yugoslav intelligentsia. The aim is to analyse the role and function of intellectuals, both in the communist and post-communist context in order to answer the following two questions: first why did Yugoslavia not have genuine dissidents, and second why did the great majority of Yugoslav Marxist intellectuals suddenly become ethno-nationalist? These two questions are, as we shall see, deeply linked to one another and directly related to the state's organisational structure.

The chapter is divided into three parts. In the first part I review and compare the two leading sociological theories of intellectuals, those of Z. Bauman and A. Gramsci whose concepts are later critically examined to form the basis of my argument. The second part of the chapter draws on Gramsci's typology of organic and traditional intelligentsia and Bauman's distinction between interpreters and legislators in order to identify and assess the profile of the Yugoslav and post-Yugoslav intelligentsia. Here I argue that Yugoslavia lacked the category of the traditional intellectual (whether legislators or interpreters) and that the dominant type of Yugoslav intellectual was an organic, identitarian, legislator. As a result, the post-Yugoslav states are also characterised by the lack of a traditional intelligentsia and thus in the early post-communist period it was the former organic legislators who became organicistic interpreters. The final part of the chapter summarises the findings and looks at their implications concerning the institutionalisation of cultural difference in the modern nation-state.

Intellectuals and society: Gramsci and Bauman

In order to answer the questions posed in the introduction it is necessary to briefly review the two most influential sociological theories of intellectuals, those of Antonio Gramsci and Zygmunt Bauman. For Gramsci, intellectuals are not necessarily people who have academic qualifications or those in possession of particular intellectual skills, but rather all those who are actively and functionally involved in social thinking. Thus, according to Gramsci, everybody is a (potential) thinker, but what makes one an intellectual is his social position: 'All men are intellectuals, one could therefore say: but not all men have in society the function of intellectuals' (Gramsci, 1971: 9). The term 'intellectual' for Gramsci refers only to 'the immediate social function of the professional category of the intellectuals'. Intellectuals are thus defined by their active role in society, and Gramsci differentiates between two main types of intellectuals: traditional and organic.

Traditional intellectuals are professional intellectuals, that is writers, academics, artists, priests, educationalists or bureaucrats. Their function is to create, to critically articulate and to disseminate 'high culture' to a wider audience, which is to say, to society. In this way they stand as mediators between the state and the public. The first influential traditional intellectuals were ecclesiastics who held a monopoly on truth in the feudal period. With the development of the post-feudal society their place was taken by *noblesse de robe*, that is administrators, scholars, scientists and philosophers who, according to Gramsci, because of their 'special qualification' and 'their uninterrupted historical continuity' perceive themselves as 'autonomous and independent of the dominant social group' (Gramsci, 1971: 7). However, Gramsci argues that their independence and autonomy are fictitious and that their thoughts, ideas and actions are determined by their class position. In other words, traditional intellectuals do not belong to a class of their own (they are not, in Alfred Weber's and Mannheim's (1966) words, 'free-floating') and as such cannot rightfully claim political or class neutrality and detachment. Instead they objectively represent the interests of the ruling class. Regardless of how they see themselves, their structural position, which is in itself determined by the capitalist mode of production, places them in a position of dependence.

In sharp contrast, organic intellectuals do not perceive themselves as 'free-floating' and independent. They are individuals which 'every new class creates alongside itself and elaborates in the course of its development'. These organic intellectuals give to their class 'homogeneity and an awareness of its function not only in the economic but also in the social and political fields' (Gramsci, 1971: 5–6). These individuals are, according to Gramsci, organically linked to a specific class. They are born and socialised within a particular social class and as such they express the interests of their class. They do not address the whole public as traditional intellectuals, but rather communicate to their own class. However, organic intellectuals are not sheer ideologues of their class but are an intrinsic development of the class in itself. They are responsible for building and directing class-consciousness, creating it out of the existing ideological material that every class develops within itself. The organic intellectuals are in a position to shape and disseminate their class ideology not only through philosophy, but also in a form more in touch with the everyday life of their class that is, through existing common sense, religious beliefs or folklore. Unlike traditional intellectuals who are equipped with the established forms, procedures and methodological tools for action and thought, organic intellectuals can free themselves and their class by 'developing a critical consciousness of their situation from within their own current forms of thinking and acting' (Bellamy, 1997: 35).

Zygmunt Bauman's theory of intellectuals focuses less on the class position of the intelligentsia and much more on the structural changes of modernity which is reflected in the emergence of the different types of intellectuals. However, Bauman's definition of an intellectual is much more voluntaristic and agency-centred than the one offered by Gramsci. Thus, unlike Gramsci's conception of intellectuals as derived from their structurally given function, Bauman sees an intellectual as a person who transcends the partiality of his occupation and engages with some universal issues and problems that concern the whole of humanity. In particular, an intellectual is preoccupied with the questions of 'truth, judgement and taste of the time' and 'the line dividing "intellectuals" from "non-intellectuals" is drawn and redrawn by decision to join in a particular mode of activity' (Bauman, 1987: 2). Although voluntaristically defined, the predominance of a particular type of intellectual is still determined by structural factors. However, instead of the economic factors such as Marx and Gramsci's modes of production, the central explanatory force for Bauman is cultural change and the transition from Enlightenment modernity to postmodernity. Bauman argues that the changes in the function of intellectuals together with dominant discursive practices more generally, can be explained by two developments: the formation of the modern bureaucratic state as it was gradually equipped with the power to shape society in line with firmly defined model of order, and the emergence of a reasonably independent intellectual discourse which was to provide the rational tools for the completion of this model. According to Bauman, while these two have operated in relative synchrony in the era of modernity, the break-up in their aims and functions has given rise to the present-day condition of postmodernity. These two periods are also characterised by the predominance of different types of intellectuals. While the principal intellectual of modernity is a legislator, postmodernity is characterised by the emergence of a new species of intellectuals – the interpreter. Their functions are deeply related to the structural conditions of their respective times. Thus, the experience of modernity is, according to Bauman, that of 'an essentially orderly totality', the ambition of which is to predict in order to control events. Successful control implies possession of an objective, factual, testable, and standardised knowledge. The role of the intellectual here is to make 'authoritative statements, which arbitrate in controversies of opinions and which select those opinions which, having been selected, become correct and binding. The authority to arbitrate is in this case legitimised by superior (objective) knowledge to which intellectuals have a better access than the non-intellectual part of society' (Bauman, 1987: 4).

The modern intellectual is thus perceived as being equipped with a cognitive apparatus which differentiates truth from non-truth, proper ethical values from immoral ones, or accurate aesthetic choices from kitsch. As such the intellectuals of modernity are legislators because they are in a position to claim a monopoly over knowledge and to legislate ('scientifically identified and proven') universal values. In this way, according to Bauman, the modern intellectual legitimises existing power relations.

In contrast to this postmodernity is characterised by the collapse of what Lyotard (1984) calls the 'grand meta-narratives'. The postmodern condition is marked by plurality of models of order and a relativity of procedures, practices, strategies and thus knowledge. There is no single, universal truth as promised by the Enlightenment project, and so knowledge claims are legitimated and validated only in reference to particular traditions. The function of the intellectual here is not to legislate for order but rather to interpret and narrate events and actions to the public within a particular tradition. Intellectuals are interpreters and translators of different orders who deploy their expert knowledge to mediate between different traditions. Hence what we experience today is a transition from modernity to post-modernity and consequently a shift from intellectuals-as-legislators towards intellectuals-as-interpreters.

Although Gramsci's and Bauman's theories of intellectuals are often perceived as very different, particularly because of their respective and opposing Marxist and postmodernist positions, there is in fact a similarity to their taxonomy of intellectuals. First, Gramsci's concept of the traditional intellectual corresponds partially to Bauman's notion of the legislator. Traditional intelligentsia such as academics, priests, teachers, philosophers and other professional intellectuals were indeed very often legislators. Their aim and function was not only to intercede between the state and the public but also to order and mould the masses in line with the prevailing blueprint. Because of their 'special qualification' they were necessarily educators, and in the Age of Reason being an educator also means being a manager. In Bauman's words: 'education stood for a project to make the formation of the human being the full and sole responsibility of society as a whole, and especially its lawgivers. The idea of education stood for the right and the duty of the state to form (best conveyed in the German concept of *Bildung*) its citizens and guide their conduct. It stood for the concept, and the practice, of a managed society' (Bauman, 1987: 69). In addition, Bauman's legislators just as with Gramsci's traditional intellectuals, were perceived as individuals responsible for the legitimisation of the existing order, status quo and its corresponding power structures.

Second, it seems that one can look for parallels between organic intellectuals and interpreters as well. The most striking similarity here is the identitarian concept of shared tradition/community. For Gramsci what distinguishes organic from traditional intellectuals is their social origins. They are born within a particular socio-economic and cultural tradition which empowers them to truly represent the interests of their social group. According to Gramsci one can even rate how integrated a particular intellectual is within his social group: 'It should be possible (...) to measure the "organic quality" of the various intellectual strata and their degree of connection with a fundamental social group ... ' (Gramsci, 1971: 12). Analogous to this is Bauman's perception of the interpreters. Unlike the legislator who addresses all humanity, an interpreter is focused on his own community, or in the language of contemporary communitarians, his own identity. There is no universal standard, universal truth or universal context-free knowledge. 'It is in community, rather than in the universal progress of mankind, that the intellectuals of the West tend to seek the secure foundation of their professional role' (Bauman, 1987: 145).

However, even though there is a striking element of similarity between the two sets of concepts to which I will return later in the chapter, there are also analytically relevant differences that allow us to preserve and integrate these two dichotomies. The most important difference here is the point that not all traditional intellectuals were legislators and not all organic intellectuals were interpreters and vice versa. In historical and geographical terms one can think of various mystics, cabalists or alchemists (i.e. Artephius, Paracelsus, Agrippa, Sufi philosophers, Hindu mystics) who were certainly traditional intellectuals but with no legislative agendas. Their social function actually makes them 'traditional interpreters'. Furthermore the historical record is full of examples of intellectuals that were legislators in their aims and action but were 'organically' created by their social groups and were acting on behalf of their intrinsic communities. Probably the most familiar names here are Hegel, Herder, Mazzini, Rousseau, or even Comte. Thus, it is necessary to analytically integrate these two typologies and to speak of traditional legislators and traditional interpreters as well as organic legislators and organic interpreters. This new typology allows us to critically evaluate and discuss Gramsci's and Bauman's preference for interpreters over legislators and organic over traditional intellectuals and to simultaneously identify and explain the social profile of intelligentsia in Yugoslavia and its successor states.

Organic legislators

When the communists took power in 1945 they inherited underdeveloped, agricultural society with an extremely modest academic infrastructure. Yugoslavia had very few university-educated people and most of its population consisted of illiterate or semiliterate peasants. For example, in 1948 67 per cent of the population were involved in agriculture while in the early 1950s 42 per cent of population over ten years of age still had no elementary education (SP, 1986: 12–25). The majority of its intellectuals, most of whom were educated abroad, were living in one of the major cities where the state's three universities were located – Belgrade, Zagreb and Ljubljana. The war and the communist triumph caused most of the non-communist intelligentsia to migrate to the West. The remaining non-communist intellectuals were seen as the potential or actual 'bourgeois enemy' of the new state and were not given a voice in society. On the other hand, the tiny group of communist and leftist intellectuals (the traditional intelligentsia) were disciplined and fully integrated in the apparatuses of the new state, very much in line with Gramsci's notion of the ideological conquest of the traditional intelligentsia (Gramsci, 1971: 10). As a result, in the 1940s the new Yugoslav state had de facto no intellectual class as such. In Gramsci's terminology the traditional intelligentsia was either conquered or wiped out. This was evident throughout the society in a number of ways, from a chronic shortage of teachers in all levels of education, to the virtual non-existence of academy trained artists or the absence of any independent critical thinking about the nature, prospects and development of the new society.

However, in less than thirty years the new state managed to industri-alise, urbanise and modernise its economy as well as establish a new aca-demic and cultural infrastructure. By the late 1970s there were 19 universities with outpost faculties and departments in 74 cities. Over one million people graduated in the period between 1945 and 1984 (JSP, 1986: 115). The changes in the social structure were most spectacular. For example, while the total number of those involved in agriculture dropped from 67 per cent to 20 per cent (JSP, 1986: 12), the number of secondary school and university graduates increased in this period from 7 per cent to 23 per cent and from 0.6 per cent to 5 per cent respectively. While only nine people received a PhD degree in 1945, this figure was close to one thousand for the year 1984 alone (JSP, 1986: 113–16). As all these figures show, in a relatively short period of time the new state created not only a substantial academic and cultural infrastructure, but also a new generation of intellectuals.

In the 1960s, 1970s and 1980s Yugoslav society was characterised by a fairly rich academic, literary and political life. Cultural and informa-tional production was impressive. While in 1945 Yugoslavia had only 10 radio stations, by 1984 there were 202; whereas in 1948 there were 232 academic and cultural journals, by 1984 this figure had increased to 1474; while in 1948 there were only 306 newspapers in circulation this number had increased by 1984 to 3063 (JSP, 1986: 118–20). Although controlled by the party–state apparatus, the newspapers, journals, radio and TV stations could not but facilitate lively discussions and conflicting viewpoints among the newly emerging intelligentsia. Since the state praised itself for being the most liberal in the communist world, it did allow a certain level of free exchange of ideas. Three broadly defined groups of intellectuals emerged in this period: the state intelligentsia, left-wing Marxist critics of the regime and ethno-nationalists. The state intelligentsia was most numerous. These individuals worked on the Communist Party boards, in Marxist Centers, workers universities and other state-sponsored academic and research institutions. Some of them were leading ideologues of the Party doctrine and hence prominent political figures such as E. Kardelj, V. Bakarić or S. Šuvar. Their principal role was to articulate and promote the official party line and to legitimise the actual policies by making reference to Marx's or Lenin's works. Because of the inevitable power struggle within the party structure the role of these people in explaining the 'holy doctrine' of socialist self-management was extremely important, with their debates often fierce but quite subtle.

The most influential among the left-wing groups were the philosophers and sociologists around the *Praxis* journal. The Praxis School (M. Marković, Lj. Tadić, G. Petrović, and others) revitalised the thought and ideas of early Marx's writing with its emphasis on unity of theory and practice and the theory of alienation. This circle of intellectuals had strong international links with leading neo-Marxist circles abroad (such as the Frankfurt School theorists, The New Left Review and other leftist groups and individuals) and saw themselves as fierce critics of the existing bureaucratic socialism in Yugoslavia. Although the group itself was internally diverse its members all shared a commitment to worker control, Marxist humanism and anti-nationalism.[36]

While the Praxis group comprised left-wing critics of the government, one could also notice the emergence of right-wing criticisms of the state's structure and its policies. The new right-wing intellectuals were less organised and effective, in part because of the state's fierce opposition to their ideas and also because of the nature of their action. Most of these intellectuals were promoting ethno-nationalist agendas. However, because of the country's subtle ethnic mosaic and recent war history of mutual antagonisms and ethnically motivated killings, the 'ethno-national question' was largely a taboo in communist Yugoslavia. This was especially the case if promoted outside the party–state channels. The official position was that with the introduction of federalism this question was more or less solved. As a result, leaflets, journals and books published by these right-wing intellectuals were quickly confiscated and banned. They were often under house arrest or imprisoned while at the same time, because of their conflicting and mutually exclusive ideologies (i.e. competing Croatian, Serbian and other nationalisms), they could not or were unwilling to organise at the federal level. Hence, these intellectuals were best known on the basis of their underground publications and court trials such as, for example, the publications of A. Izetbegović,'s *Islamic Declaration* (1970), G. Djogo's *Woolen Times* (1981), F. Tudjman's revisionist publications and interviews to foreign media on the 'Croatian national question', or the series of books by V. Šešelj's on Tito's illegitimate rule and subsequent trials following the publications of these books. This group was perceived by the authorities as the most threatening because of their potential counter-hegemonic role in challenging the widely accepted idea that the 'national question' had been resolved in the Yugoslav federation. Unlike the previous two groups these intellectuals had no sympathy with universalist and internationalist socialist ideals or federalism.

Although in many ways fairly different, these three groups of intellectuals had much in common. Most of them had been created by the state itself. They were usually first- or second- generation migrants from rural areas who went to state schools and universities and were educated and socialised in the milieu of the communist state. Most of them at some point were members of the League of Communists of Yugoslavia (LCY). With the exception of some Praxis philosophers they had very little intellectual contact with the outside world: while the capitalist West was an old ideological adversary, from 1948 the communist East has also become a political enemy; thus international communication and exchange of people and ideas was prevented.

Unlike the rest of the communist world the Yugoslav state embarked on developing a non-Soviet type of socialism. Because of its early expulsion from Cominform and hence the 'legitimate' communist world, the Yugoslav state was forced to take its Marxism more seriously then any other communist country. In order to legitimise its resistance to Soviets it was forced to ground its official and operative ideologies exclusively in the teachings of Marx, Engels and Lenin. The only known form of 'existing socialism' of a Stalinist type had to be abandoned and a new alternative created almost out of nothing. In this way the Yugoslav state had to introduce various new concepts such as 'workers control', 'self-management', 'the delegate system' and similar ideas. These concepts, derived from the works of the classics of Marxism, served to justify state policy at home (to unite Yugoslav communists and left sympathisers around the party leadership) and abroad (to delegitimise Soviet and later Chinese interpretations of revolutionary socialism). This isolation within the communist world and commitment to Marxist purity, combined with a newly urbanised and industrialised society, created preconditions for the development of the Yugoslav state's own class intelligentsia.

In that sense, regardless of their mutually opposing ideologies, all three groups were similar in the way that they were, to use Gramsci's terminology, organically created within their class. Following Lenin directly and Gramsci indirectly, the new state rulers managed to create their own organic intellectuals within a period of thirty years. While the state intelligentsia was the 'pure' product of its policies, the left and the right wing critics were the 'waste' of the same process of creation. These intellectuals could not be traditional in Gramsci's terms because they were not part of the 'uninterrupted historical continuity' and did not perceive themselves to be 'autonomous and independent of the dominant social group' (Gramsci, 1971: 7). Indeed they were the creation of the Yugoslav ruling class and had no intention of addressing humanity in its entirety. Instead they represented, spoke for, and in the name of, the 'Yugoslav (or even narrower Croatian/Serbian) working class'. In line with Gramsci's ideas, state intellectuals also disseminated their ideology through more practical means – school textbooks, newspapers, public gatherings, compulsory meetings at the workplace and so on. Even Praxis intellectuals had little patience with the 'bourgeois ideologies'. All these intellectuals were indeed organically created by their own class.

Most of these intellectuals were also legislators. They perceived their teachings and ideas as unquestionably scientific and true. For the state-backed intelligentsia, Marxism-Leninism was seen as a pure science which had discovered the ultimate laws of history, so that all that was needed was to implement these laws in the context of the Yugoslav state, that is through the policies of socialist self-management. A typical example here would be the following statement from the Manifesto of LCY drafted by leading state intellectuals: 'this program attempts to theoretically formulate, with the help of Marxist analysis, general laws of socialist development and specific forms of revolutionary process in Yugoslavia' (PSKJ, 1977: 44).

Not far from this position were the Praxis intellectuals. Although far more subtle, their guiding principles were fairly similar: to follow the blue print of Marx's early works (i.e. the *Economic and Philosophical Manuscripts* of 1844). Their criticism of state policy was simply a more radical and more purist interpretation of Marx's ideas. Occasionally, as N. Sesardić, shows citing leading Praxis philosopher G. Petrović, their ideas were in line with the official party doctrine: 'in terms of the intensity of the criticism of bureaucracy in general and our bureaucracy in particular, there is no significant difference between what one can read in our philosophical and sociological journals and what has been said for years in the speeches of many LCY leaders' (Sesardić, 1991: 228). The ethno-nationalists also shared this legislative world-view. However, their blueprint was the establishment of an independent nation-state along ethnic principles with ethnic nations also perceived in a rigidly deterministic and law-like naturalistic way. Hence one can read in Tudjman how nations [...] grow up in a natural manner, in the objective and complex historical process, as a result of the development of all those material and spiritual forces which in a given area shape the national being of

individual nations ...' (Tudjman, 1981: 288). For many of them communism and ethno-nationalism were not incompatible, and the true
ethno-national state would be ethnically pure and socially egalitarian.

All three groups thus saw themselves as being in possession of an
essential and supreme knowledge, and as such owning the right to direct
and mould the actions of the masses. They were legislators in the true
sense. In other words, regardless of their ideological differences, the
great majority of Yugoslav intellectuals were both organic in origin and
legislative in aims and practices – they were indeed 'organic legislators'.

At the same time Yugoslavia had very few liberal intellectuals interested in promoting the ideas of pluralism, the rule of law, multi-party
elections, free market, individual freedoms, human rights and similar
values. In other words, Yugoslavia did not have a class of traditional
intelligentsia. This fact will help us explain the sudden and often shocking
transition from Marxism to ethnic-nationalism that occurred from
mid-1980s. While the shift to nationalism on the part of the state intelligentsia was a surprise, the conversion of leading Praxis philosophers to
the Serbian nationalist cause was a shock to many.

Organicistic interpreters

It has often been emphasised that intellectuals played a decisive role in
the prelude to the wars of Yugoslav secession. Intellectuals were responsible for the drafting of the famous *Memorandum of the Serbian Academy
of Sciences and Arts* that set the direction for Serbian ethno-nationalism.
Intellectuals were equally responsible, both silently and actively, for supporting ethnic cleansing in Bosnia and Croatia and later in Kosovo.
Intellectuals were also the chief media propagandists disseminating the
images and language of hatred and fear for the national cause. However,
the loyalty of intellectuals to ethno-national projects is not new. As
A. Smith (1998) argues and convincingly documents 'given their discursive skills, status interests and occupational needs, professionals have
been particularly strong adherents of the nationalist cause'. Throughout
modern history intellectuals have always been leaders of nationalist
movements and were very often blind to the suffering of non-nationals.
What was relatively novel in this case was the sudden and dramatic
ideological shift among the Yugoslav intelligentsia. While, as already
explained, a majority of them were communist state intellectuals,
Marxist critics of the regime, and only occasionally ethno-nationalists,
by the late 1980s and early 1990s the great majority of all intellectuals
had become committed nationalists. Individuals who were diehard

Leninists, Marxists and Kardeljists literally overnight become fierce supporters of the ethno-nationalist ideology. Among them the most surprising was the conversion of some leading Praxis philosophers to the ethno-nationalist cause. Mihailo Marković for example became the vice-president and chief ideologue of S. Milošević's Socialist Party, firmly supporting the militaristic adventures of the Serbian regime in Bosnia and Croatia and arguing that 'it is necessary to reintegrate the territories of the former Yugoslavia wherever Serbs constitute a majority of the population' and that 'the new state border in Croatia must follow the line of delineation between the Serb and Croat peoples' (Marković, 1994: 3). S. Stojanović became an advisor to the nationalist writer, and first president of rump Yugoslavia – D. Ćosić, supporting the policy of the 'exchange of population'; meanwhile Lj. Tadić who in the 1960s wrote that 'Serbian and Croatian nationalisms have remained militant, despotic ideologies that lack political and cultural creativity in all their forms' (Secor, 1999: 5) became a personal friend and main supporter of the indicted war criminal Radovan Karadžić, arguing now that 'ahead of us [Serbs] lies first a spiritual and then a territorial integration', adding that cosmopolitan intellectuals who object to this aim are 'pretentious semi-intelligent people who go so far as to denounce as Serb Nazism the legitimate advocacy of the threatened national interests' (Milosavljević, 2000).[37] How did this conversion happen so quickly?

One can look at the individual cases and explain this change psychologically – that is, pragmatic conversion in order to gain or preserve established socio-economic or political privileges and social status, resentment at blocked promotion under the previous regime, or psychological stress and disorientation produced by the total collapse of communist ideology worldwide. However, since this is not a sporadic event but a mass phenomenon it needs a sociological explanation. This type of explanation can be found in looking at social determinants of this phenomenon: the social origins of Yugoslav intellectuals as well as the structural forces of their social environment. In theoretical terms this means returning to Gramsci and Bauman.

First, as already stated, Yugoslav intellectuals were organic legislators. This means that they were organically created by their social group which in this particular case was the group in power. Unlike other East European intellectuals the Yugoslav intelligentsia was in principle not in conflict with the holders of power. With very few exceptions its intellectuals were employed in the state-sponsored institutions (universities, research institutes, government service agencies, etc.), had decent salaries, their research projects were approved and funded by the party–state, they had access to the mass media, could easily travel abroad, were regularly and with a few complications promoted and have enjoyed social and cultural prestige within the state. More than that, Yugoslav intellectuals have taken an active part in the apparatuses and the policies of the state. They shaped and articulated its laws, they led discussions on the direction of its development, on party boards and in the media, they published literary works, produced paintings and sang operas praising the existing order. In other words, Yugoslav intellectuals were truly the ideological power holders. In Gramsci's words they were created organically by their own class and as such have acted on behalf of their own class.

What happened in the late 1980s and early 1990s is that: (a) their common state disintegrated; (b) their universalist ideology of Marxism-Leninism, as well as its Yugoslav derivative of socialist self-management was discredited in theory and in practice; and (c) their class lost political power and social prestige together with the cultural and social hegemony.

So, how could organic legislators react under these circumstances? Since their common state fragmented into a number of ethnocentric unstable 'statelets' with uncertain borders, so the previous state-centredness had to be abandoned in favour of ethno-national solidarity. Equally so, the legislative universalism of self-management ideology lost its appeal outside of the previous state structure and had to be replaced by a more particularistic ideology, the most readily available being ethno-nationalism. And finally, the loss of political power and cultural hegemony signalled the necessity of ideological conversion. Hence, the sudden and dramatic collapse of the federal state was paralleled with the sudden, dramatic and simultaneous disintegration of the Yugoslav intellectual class as a unified body.

Second, the organic nature of the Yugoslav intelligentsia meant that its conversion was very much determined by its members' social origins. An organic intellectual could not easily become a traditional individual-ist intellectual, one who stands alone in support of particular ideas and practices, regardless of how unpopular these were. According to Gramsci, an organic intellectual is an expression of the group being in itself. This intellectual is both the group's creation and its image, and as such his primary loyalty is to the group itself. While the content of the groups' demands, ideas and principles may change, this does not affect the organic intellectuals' determination concerning the form of these demands, ideas and principles. So, in the eyes of the organic intelli-gentsia there is no real contradiction between yesterday's support for a 'Yugoslav working class' and today's support for the 'Croatian national being'. This indicates that there is a thin line to be drawn between an 'organic intellectual' and an 'organicistic intellectual'.

In the context of dramatic social change the organic intelligentsia becomes an organicistic intelligentsia relatively easily. The nature of organicism is that it contains biological concepts and visions of the social world. In this respect, human beings are perceived as cells of an organism who only exist to maintain and serve the whole, that is, a community, state or nation. An organicist sees organisms as wholes that obey irreducible system-like laws. Society is a living unit with a metabolism and evolutionary strategies of adaptation and survival. Individuals are subordinated to the collective because each part can function only in relation to the whole. There is no individual free will and personality traits are attributed exclusively to collectivities. For an organicist, the individual exists only as part of a biological system so that his actions, meaning and existence are determined by the power of the collective organism. In this sense one organism or collective unit ('a class') can be replaced with another ('ethnic group'/'nation') but not with a non-collective entity ('a free thinking individual').

This shift from organic to organicistic interpretation of reality in Yugoslav and post-Yugoslav intelligentsia was accelerated by the existing traditionalism and the dominance of collective values in Yugoslav society, to which intellectuals were not immune. Intellectuals' apparent 'sudden' glorification of community versus society or rural versus urban, of tradition versus modernity has its social roots in the traditional patriarchal family life and its corresponding values such as authoritarianism and sexism, which even in the 1980s were the dominant mode of thinking in Yugoslavian society. As numerous surveys show (Katunarić, 1986, Šiber, 1988, Pantić, 1990) the levels of authoritarian consciousness and sexism were found to be very high in all parts of the country.

Third, post-Yugoslav intellectuals have become organicists but in the process have also abandoned their legislative ambitions. The total collapse of Marxist universalism, its totalising aims and teleological principles have undermined its scientific authority. The privileged access to the unquestionable truths of Marxism-Leninism that underpinned the claim to legitimacy and status had become worthless. In the new world of post-communism the knowledge claims of intellectuals could no longer appeal to universal principles, and in order to recapture some form of authority they were forced to become interpreters. As interpreters they can only claim to represent the particular truth of their own community, because they can validate these claims only within their community. For example, while the Serbian historian can write a scholarly two volume book on the idea of the Serbs as the 'most ancient people in the world' (Luković-Pjanović, 1990), her findings and arguments will have no academic audience outside of her community. In other words, while the arguments of this book will provoke laughter outside her 'tradition', within that 'tradition' the author will be regarded as a distinguished and authentic scholar who will regularly attract a large (including academic) audience. So, the function of the post-Yugoslav intelligentsia is not to legislate, but to interpret and translate for and within their community. As Bauman would say: 'Inside the community, the philosophers have the right, and a duty, to spell out the rules which decide who are the rational discussants and who are not; their role is to assess the justification and objectivity of views, and to supply the criteria for criticism which will be binding because of those criteria' (Bauman, 1987: 145).

However, post-Yugoslav intelligentsia are not any kind of interpreters, they are organicistic interpreters. The link between organic intellectuals and interpreters that was discussed earlier receives its full expression when organic intellectuals become organicistic intellectuals. The identitarian commitment to a single 'tradition' and a single community becomes binding and exclusionist. Organicistic interpreters perceive their community as an infallible entity in possession of a single and recognisable will. For an organicist interpreter, an ethnic nation represents a united, integral and indivisible cultural and political entity. The ethnic community is perceived in an obscure reduction of eighteenth-century Romanticism goals as a living collectivity to which universal rules and ethics do not apply. One can for example read in Tudjman (1981: 289) how 'nations are the irreplaceable cells of the human community or of the whole of mankind's being' or that 'nations as a whole behave more or less uniformly in a psychological sense, according to their historically acquired impulses for self-preservation' (Tudjman, 1990: 437, Uzelac, 2006: 197). Following indirectly Goethe, Herder and Hegel organicist interpreters stand on the assumption that the truth cannot be found outside of the 'collective spirit', outside of the *volksgeist* but only within 'ourselves', 'ourselves' being an ethnic collective. From this perspective there is no morality beyond the borders of community. In other words, for an organicist Serbian intellectual the Serbs could not commit war crimes because their war goals were noble and divine – to unite all Serbs into a single state. Or again, for a Croatian organicist interpreter the slogan 'all for Croatia and Croatia for nothing', which places ethnic cleansing in the service of the nation, thus transforming it into the fullest expression of patriotism.

Implications

Although Gramsci's and Bauman's concepts and typologies have proved useful in this discussion of Yugoslav intellectuals, they have also been shown to have significant analytical and moral deficiencies. There is a vivid danger in favouring interpreters and organic intellectuals over legislators and traditional intellectuals. As evident from the Yugoslav case, organic intellectuals can easily turn into organicistic intellectuals, which in combination with relativist interpretivism provides the deadliest of cocktails. Gramsci's Marxist recommendations were very much tested in the circumstances of Yugoslav state socialism, providing irrefutable evidence of how the ideological monopoly and cultural hegemony of a single socio-political stratum can lead towards a much greater degree of restriction and control than Gramsci could have ever imagined. The concept of organic intellectuals is in itself exclusionist and as such incompatible with a tolerant, democratic and liberal polity envisaged by both Gramsci and Bauman. The liberating role that Bauman attributes to interpreters in opposition to legislators becomes also invisible and morally unsustainable if accepting the ethical parameters of one's own 'tradition' and one's own 'identity'. While there is an obvious danger in legislators monopolising power and protecting the status quo in the name of universal truth, the danger behind the relativism of interpreters is certainly much greater. While one can debate with traditional intellectuals and rally against legislators, there is no discussion with organic and organicistic interpreters. If one does not belong to their 'community', does not share their 'tradition' and 'identity', was not organically created by it, then one's thoughts and actions are perceived as irrelevant or if relevant then threatening and hence target for elimination. Both Gramsci and Bauman are often blind to the implicit and explicit authoritarianism of organic/identitarian interpreters.

The case of the Yugoslav intelligentsia demonstrates that one should not underestimate the role which traditional intellectuals play in society. They might have legislative aims and ambitions; they could be tied to their class origins and thus mislead us by claiming independence and detachment; they might even be directly bribed, corrupted, may be turncoats, selfish, careerists, traitors, morally degraded, dishonest and so on, but they do perform a crucial role in every society – the role of social criticism. Their motives do not have to be necessarily altruistic (and very often are not) but their argumentative skills, practical and theoretical knowledge, interests at self-promotion and self-protection, status seeking motivation and so on place them in the position of being permanent social critics. As long as society has well-articulated traditional intelligentsia it will be in a position to hear a plurality of voices. Any healthy social order requires a variety of intellectuals and a plurality of intellectual discourses. One needs to listen to traditional, organic, legislative, interpretative, passive, active, bureaucratic, anarchic, creative, boring or mad intellectuals in order to develop one's own thoughts about his/her own society. The biggest danger for every society is to have a monopoly by a single type of intellectual. The hegemony of organic legislators or organicistic interpreters armed with the idea of preserving society as a whole, whether in the form of 'national identity' or 'proletarian unity', any entity that promises to definitively and finally transcend all social conflicts, guarantees a road to hell. Hence, the answer to both questions raised in the introduction to this chapter is the same: because Yugoslavia was much more successful in developing its own organic intellectuals than the rest of the communist world, it never had proper dissidents and it simultaneously laid down the foundation for the metamorphosis of Marxist intellectuals into ethno-nationalist warriors.

The unusual character of Yugoslav state socialism and the country's distinct post-Second World War development might suggest that unexpected rapid transformation of its cultural elites from committed socialists to organicistic nationalists is something rather odd, with little relevance to the rest of the world. However despite all its peculiarities this was no *sonderweg*. The Yugoslav case is simply a more extreme version of something that has become a dominant practice of modern life for the past two hundred years – ideologisation and state-sponsored institutionalisation of inflexible forms of cultural difference. What happened to Yugoslav intellectuals is a vivid illustration of just how far the institutionalisation of rigid communitarian and identitarian ideas can go. As the ontological foundations of most communitarian principles are similar, a quick switch from one form to another as historical conditions change can be expected. When this happens under conditions of post-authoritarian state structures, coupled with the ideological monopoly of a particular doctrine, one is on the terrain of intra-group violence and even possible mass extermination. This is not to say that most contemporary social orders are set to emulate the Yugoslav example. They probably will not. What is claimed here for extreme forms of identitarianism is similar to what Giddens (1985) has already argued for totalitarianism: this remains an ever-present possibility for all modern societies. The intrinsic design of the modern nation-state is built on principles that ultimately predispose cultural homogeneity. As identitarian ideologies, either as all-state (nationalism), sub-state (ethno-nationalism, cultural essentialism) or supra-state (religious fundamentalism) intensify one need not look for answers for their expansion outside of the state structures for it is the makeup of the modern, Enlightenment created, nation-state that is at the heart of identitarian ideologies and subsequent state policies. Let us now explore the darkest face of these ideologies – genocide.

9
Ethnic Cleansing, Nation-building and Modernity

Introduction

Ethnic cleansing and genocidal mass killings are conventionally viewed as a prerogative of the authoritarian, traditional and backward world. However, recent historical and macro-sociological research has convincingly demonstrated that systematic mass scale bloodshed was rarely (if ever) an explicit aim of pre-modern rulers. In other words, as R. W. Smith (1999) puts it, one was killed because of where he was, not *who* he is. It was the arrival of modernity – and its most enduring creation, the Enlightenment inspired nation-state – which generated an environment for the systematic mass extermination of human beings. Not only did ethnic cleansing appear on the historical stage with the birth of a modern nation-state, but mass scale violence is also often unwittingly triggered by the processes of democratisation, liberalisation and modernisation.

This chapter aims to explore the complex and contradictory relationships between modernity and systematic mass killings in the context of nation-state formation in Rwanda and Bosnia. In conceptual terms, the chapter develops an argument through the synthesis of two leading macro sociological theories of genocide, those of Zygmunt Bauman and Michael Mann. I will argue that despite their nominal disagreement, there is in fact a great deal of explanatory compatibility, the fusion of which can help us better understand what happened in Bosnia and Rwanda in the mid-1990s. In particular this concerns four specific arguments put forward in dealing with the nature of Rwandan and Bosnian experience: (a) the modernity of ideological blueprints for nation-state building; (b) the modernity of the means used for their implementation; (c) the processes and ideology of democratisation; and (d) the radical transformation of geopolitics that fosters conflict between mutually incompatible state building projects. While these arguments deal with the structural sources of the Bosnian and Rwandan experiences, they do not tell us as much about the individual and collective motives of the actors involved. Therefore, the analysis of individual and social status transformations is undertaken to identify the changing mechanisms of ethnic group mobilisation in both Rwanda and Bosnia.

Mass killings, state-building and modernity

Unlike its traditional counterparts – empires, city-states or city-leagues – the modern post-Enlightenment state is largely inconceivable without a substantial degree of commonly shared values. While this sense of collective unity and purpose is sometimes articulated through republican ideals or the existence of a vibrant civic culture, it is for the most part a nationalist experience – in all its diverse guises – that shaped and cemented the image of the modern state as we know it. It is no historical accident that the idea of the clearly delineated and territorially bound sovereign state, together with the first attempts at its proper implementation, were born at the same time as the fully fledged ideology of nationalism. Even the once popular term 'nation-state' (which has recently gone out of vogue) is really a very appropriate description of this intimate but often cloaked relationship between the two. Of course, the somewhat awkward construction of 'nation-state' never reflected the reality of the polity's invariably culturally diverse make-up, but it did clearly and poignantly suggest its desired direction of development. In other words, the process of modern state-building is almost unimaginable without the parallel existence of relatively coherent ethno-national projects. As historical experience tells us, nationalism – civic or ethnic, left or right leaning, banal or hot – is the essential glue of state legitimacy in the modern age.

This complex relationship between the state-to-be and nation-to-emerge is premised on an assumption that the new state requires and can only properly function through single standardised cultural idiom (Gellner, 1983, 1997). However, the pure and uninterrupted implementation of such an ideal is severely constrained by both internal and external factors. Internally this includes the complexities of domestic politics such as the difficulties in building and maintaining wide political alliances around a grand national project, general public distaste for the use of excessive violence in implementing this project, its huge economic costs, or institutionally embedded moral principles. Externally, any dramatic attempt at mass social mobilisation is always restricted by local, regional and global geopolitics. As a result, what Gellner (1997: 50) calls 'the marriage of culture and state', and the creation of relative ethnic homogeneity in most modern polities was gradual, incomplete and much less violent than the ethno-nationalist principle of 'one nation-one state' implies. It is this historical contingency, and the substantial time-lag between more dramatic explosions of ethno-national massacres, that largely camouflaged the intrinsic virulence of this 'one nation-one state' principle. To put it simply, the periodic genocidal outbursts of the nineteenth and twentieth century are not an aberrant exception to modernity's rule of nation-state building, – *they are the very rule!* Modern day genocides – from the virtual annihilation of Herreros or Native Americans by the nationalising German and US states respectively, to the extermination of nearly two-thirds of all Armenians in 1915 by the freshly emerging Turkish Republic, the millions killed in the Nazi Holocaust to create the new Aryan *lebensraum*, the Khmer Rouge's butchery in the name of the proletarian nation, to the more recent killing fields of Darfur – are all poignant reminders of what happens when constraints on the implementation of the nation-state principle are lifted. Thus cultural homogeneity – an essential prerequisite of any modern, functional, stable and eventually tolerant polity – is very much premised on the historical obliteration of cultural difference. When this is achieved gradually and slowly, or through largely forgotten historical episodes of mass scale bloodshed, then we accept it as something normal and natural. But when this same principle is applied suddenly in front of our eyes without any restraints we are utterly shocked and disgusted by its savagery.

Thus the root cause of ethnic cleansing and genocide is not (and never was) the intrinsic barbarity of some 'peoples', their authoritarian traditions or politics, their economic or technological backwardness. It is the very process of modernity and the pinnacle of its creation – the idea of the modern nation-state that has set the foundation for all future genocides. Working broadly within the Weberian heritage, two leading contemporary macro sociologists, Zygmunt Bauman (1989, 1991) and Michael Mann (1999, 2001, 2005), provide convincing arguments as to why mass ethnic cleansing is so deeply intertwined with modernity.

Bauman focuses predominantly on the Nazi Holocaust, but he provides a universalist argument. What distinguishes the Holocaust from traditional forms of mass killing is its intrinsic rationality. It is the spirit of Enlightenment, with its engineering aspirations, blueprints and grand vistas that unwittingly created conditions for 'the final solution'. Unlike the sporadic, largely irrational or ritualistic, medieval butchery of 'religious others', random pogroms or gruesome cases of individual brutality, the systematic extermination of a particular ethnic collectivity requires modernity. It requires both a rationally conceived grand project and the most rational means of its implementation – a highly developed division of labour, a well-organised bureaucracy, clearly defined goals and an impeccable technology. The roots of the Holocaust, as Bauman (1989: xiii) puts it, are to be found in the 'emancipation of the political state, with its monopoly of means of violence and its audacious engineering ambitions, from social control – following the step by step dismantling of all non-political power resources and institutions of social self-management'. The principal goal of genocide is not the elimination of a despised enemy; rather, this is a necessary by-product of social engineering, a modernist obsession with implementing a design of the perfect social order. To achieve this utopian state of social perfection one is geared towards the most economical means for its complete and uninterrupted realisation: 'The use of violence is most efficient and cost-effective when the means are subjected to solely instrumental-rational criteria, and thus dissociated from moral evaluation of the ends' (Bauman, 1989: 98). The modern enlightened state acts as a giant gardener, by removing all the grubby and obstructing 'weeds' that spoil the possibility of realising perfect design. What lies at the heart of mass extermination is not such a simple emotion as hatred; genocide, in Bauman's (1989: 17) view, is instead 'a product of routine bureaucratic procedures: means – ends calculus, budget balancing, universal rule application'. Modern ethnic cleansing is systematic, impersonal and 'businesslike' – a process rooted in a technocratically driven culture and governed by the principles of instrumental rationality, where violence becomes nothing more than mere technique.

Michael Mann agrees that systematic mass killings have intensified with modernity, but his focus is less on the means (instrumental rationality) and more on the ends of this process. What is essential here is the role of the state and the process of democratisation. As he puts it: 'Murderous cleansing is most likely to result where powerful groups within two ethnic groups aim at legitimate and achievable rival states "in the name of the people" over the same territory, and the weaker is aided from outside' (Mann, 2005: 33). Thus genocide often comes as a corollary of two competing state-building projects. However, this idea in itself is derived from the modernist ideologies of popular government. The staunchly modern and democratic idea of 'people's rule' has often blurred its meanings where *demos* is regularly read as *ethnos* and where a project of democratisation tends to be implemented as one of ethnic homogenisation. The intrinsic link between the two creates a historical condition where mass scale ethnic cleansing is in fact the 'dark side of democracy'. Liberal democracy, the welfare state, economic sustainability and a tolerant political culture 'were all built on top of terrible atrocities committed against the indigenous "others" – for this was *Herrenvolk* democracy' (Mann, 1999: 25). Hence genocide is not a prerogative of authoritarianism; it is more likely to happen under the conditions of imperfect democratisation and liberalisation. The 1915 genocide of Armenians was not executed by an authoritarian but a multiethnic Ottoman Empire; it was conceived and put into practice by liberalising, secular and Western oriented Young Turks. One of the first twentieth-century genocides was not carried out in the name of Allah or imperial Ottoman glory, but rather in the name of people conceptualised in modern ethno-national terms. However, the transformation of these rivalries from simple ethnic riots to full-blown genocides is always preconditioned by their transposition to the level of the nation-state. It is a democratising nation-state, often deeply divided from within and radicalised by geopolitical pressures such as war, that lies at the heart of modern mass systematic killing.

While Bauman and Mann both argue that large-scale ethnic cleansing is a product of modernity, they strongly disagree over the question concerning the conditions under which it is likely to happen. For Bauman the essential requirements are the existence of a blueprint of an ideal society and the advanced technological means for its realisation. For Mann the focus is on the ideology and process of democratisation as well as the geopolitics which creates conditions for mutually incompatible state-making projects. Let us explore how well these two theoretical accounts work in the context of two recent and nominally different genocidal experiences – Rwanda and Bosnia.

Bosnia and Rwanda between modernity and extermination

A superficial look at the Bosnia and Rwanda from the late 1980s to early 1990s would indicate that they had almost nothing in common. One was located in the heart of Africa, a part of the underdeveloped Third world, predominantly agrarian, over 90 per cent rural (Waller, 1996), overwhelmingly practicing Christian and Roman Catholic – a highly centralised state with a long and turbulent history of colonial experience, and with an unprecedented degree of population density. The other was positioned at the periphery of the European continent, a part of the communist Second world, mostly industrialised with more than 60 per cent of its population living in urban areas (SG, 1986), highly secular while maintaining three very distinct but mostly non-practicing ethno-religious traditions, and part of a functioning but very decentralised federal state with a relatively low degree of population density. The only thing that seemed to unite them was the fact that both were externally deemed to be the embodiment of peace and stability. While Rwanda was often invoked as an example of an orderly, well administered and organised state (Newbury, 1992), Bosnia and Herzegovina was regularly praised and admired for its interethnic harmony and the long tradition of tolerance (Mahmutćehajić, 2000).

As a result, the sudden and dramatic eruption of violence that started in the early 1990s in both states surprised many observers. But the horrific and unprecedented scale of the ensuing slaughter – with extensive practice of ethnic cleansing followed by genocidal episodes in Bosnia between 1992 and 1995, and a fully fledged genocide in Rwanda in 1994 – was an utter and complete astonishment to all. While both cases were seen as shocking, they were largely perceived and stereotypically interpreted as two separate and distinct phenomena – one an indicator of the poisonous legacy of communist authoritarianism and other a post-colonial anarchy of 'primitive tribal hatreds'.

Nevertheless, digging deeper into the structural origins of these dramatic events reveals a great deal of similarity between them. Not only is it that the sources of these extraordinary events are complex and multiple, but also that they are rooted in a common ideological legacy which is broader and much older than that of either communism or postcolonialism. This is the legacy of enlightened modernity. What took place between April and June 1994 in Rwanda and in July 1995 in Srebrenica and Žepa in eastern Bosnia had very little to do with communist authoritarianism or tribal cultures, and a great deal to do with the ideologies and practices of modernity. This legacy requires a detailed analysis in the context of arguments developed by Bauman and Mann.

Ideological blueprints

All attempts at the systematic annihilation of entire groups of people are rooted in a particular belief system. However, unlike their traditional, mostly religious counterparts, modern ideological belief systems are totalising projects of social engineering. Instead of converting, enslaving or periodically destroying the religious 'others' modernity requires the execution of a particular blueprint where the elimination of 'the other' is not the aim itself, but rather the means to achieving the ultimate aim – an ideal state of collective perfection. In both of our cases there is a powerful ideological drive behind the policy of ethnic cleansing.

In Rwanda this can be partially traced back to the colonial codification and institutionalisation of ethnic group differences as hard and tangible categories of collective membership. In 1933 the Belgian colonisers introduced obligatory identity cards with a fixed concept of group membership which were recorded as such in the official census of 1933/34, and have since been used to ideologically distinguish, firmly separate and then grant a privileged position to individuals ('Tutsis') on the basis of their group membership. The resonance of a deeply modern impulse to order, manage and systematise difference in order to control it is clearly visible here. This ideological codification had a profound implication on moulding ethnic relations in post-colonial Rwanda, where cultural difference was intensively politicised in nearly every aspect of social life – making 'Tutsis' virtual masters of the state and justifying their rule through the so-called Hamitic thesis. The core idea behind the 'Hamitic thesis' was the view that the innate superiority of Tutsis (i.e. their alleged delicate and tender physiognomy, noble and aristocratic posture or sophisticated intelligence) was an indicator of their recent migration, as they are 'not really indigenous Africans' but descendents from the cursed son of Noah (Hintjens, 1999: 252).

The intensity of Tutsi ideological and political hegemony gradually created an explosive counter-hegemonic discourse – the ideology of Hutu Power ('Hutu Powa'). The crystallisation of this doctrine was articulated in the poignantly modernist and quasi scientific sounding 'Notes on the Social Aspect of the Racial Native Problem in Rwanda', better known as the 'Bahutu Manifesto of 1957'. Although the manifesto was quite moderate on most issues, it reiterated the essentialist, identitarian, divisions between the two groups and advocated preservation of 'racial' purity. The establishment of institutional Hutu hegemony through the ideological legacy of the Manifesto, enacted through the 'revolution' of 1959–61, further polarised Rwandan society. The Hamitic thesis was now reversed – Hutu Power depicted Tutsis as foreign invaders from Ethiopia, ungrateful feudal parasites who exploited and humiliated the authentic 'sons of the soil', the only true Rwandans: the Hutus. It is this ideological narrative in its most radicalised version that, in the early 1990s, became a dominant doctrine and was later used to justify genocide. As Mamdani (2001: 190) points out 'For Hutu Power, the Hutu were not just the majority, *they were the nation*'. With the publication of the so-called Hutu Ten Commandments in 1990 – which forbade mixed marriages, sexual relations and nearly all forms of social relations between the two groups, and branded as traitors all those who deviated from these rules – the ideological terrain was set for mass extermination.

What is essential here is that both Hamitic and Hutu Power ideology were modern blueprints for the transcendence of difference, removal of ambiguity and the creation of an ethically pure and thus perfect collectivity. This was clearly illustrated with the very gardening metaphors used by *interahamwe* (youth paramilitaries responsible for most of the killings), where mass killing was regularly referred to as 'pulling out the roots of the bad weeds', 'bush clearing' or 'tree felling'. Implementing genocide was nothing more than doing an *akazi gakomeye* (a big job).

In Bosnia, the ideological roots can be traced back partially to the structure of the millet system of the Ottoman Empire as well as the culture-centric administrative divisions of the Habsburg Empire – both of which helped to establish the future institutional tracks for the ethnoreligious identification that emerged with the gradual collapse of the empires and the onset of modernity. The two central ideological movements of modernity, Enlightenment and Romanticism, politicised these institutionalised frames of group membership which found their full expression in the Balkan nationalisms. Hence the nineteenth-century Serbian and Croatian nationalisms were not primarily aiming at the creation of sovereign and autonomous post-imperial free republics, but were rather charting the maximalist borders of their ethnically homogenous Greater Serbias and Croatias. Directly influenced by their metropolitan upbringings in Paris, Vienna or Berlin, they articulated early grand nationalist projects such as *Načertanije* (I. Garašanin), or the unification of Croats of three faiths (A. Starčević). While communist victory softened the ideological message of these ethno-nationalist grand vistas, it never attempted to obliterate them. On the contrary, it worked hard towards its full institutionalisation as a dominant form of cognitive practice (Brubaker, 1996). Instead of fighting ethno-nationalism as its official ideology proclaimed, the communist state rather reified and cemented these narratives and integrated them within a larger metanarrative of a communist blueprint. As argued in Chapter 4 and more extensively elsewhere (Malešević, 2002), while normative ideology did speak the language of a transnational universalism (unity of the world proletariat), operative ideologies remained profoundly particularist and nation-centric (Yugoslavs/Serbs/Croats as a heroic chosen people). This fact helps us understand how the language of a fully blown ethnonationalism could so easily enter elite discourses in the second half of the 1980s and early 1990s, and even more so why it found mass resonance among the wider public. The publishing of the Memorandum of the Serbian Academy of Sciences and Arts in 1986 – drafted by disenchanted former communist zealots – was less a direct battle-cry for a

Greater Serbia (as it is often presented) and more of an unintentional statement on how successful the communist state was in essentialising ethno-cultural differences as political ones. Like the Bahutu Manifesto of 1957, this was a rather moderate document written in the spirit and discourse of quasi-science and Romanticism, an attempt to articulate a visionary blueprint for social change. It advocated the view that 'Serbs have to become a historical subject and that this can be achieved only through the renewal of the national consciousness about their historical and spiritual being' (Jović, 2003: 362). However, regardless of its limited content, the Manifesto was a catalyst for the proliferation of (initially) Serbian (and later) Croatian and Bosniak nationalisms. By the early 1990s, Bosnian society was ideologically deeply divided around three mutually incompatible grand blueprints – the unification of all ethnic Serbs in a single state, the creation of an independent Croatian state incorporating large parts of Bosnia, and a multi-ethnic sovereign state with a Bosniak majority. The fact that Serbian ethno-nationalism was the first to radicalise – and at times became genocidal – had a lot to do with the availability of the much stronger institutional and military state apparatus at its disposal, and correspondingly the need to justify the ruthless implementation of a particular ethno-nationalist blueprint. To be successful it had to depict Bosniaks and Bosnian Croats as blood-thirsty Ustashas and Ottoman era janissaries, hell bent on recreating a fascist era 'Independent State of Croatia' (NDH) or an Islamic state. Thus in the Bosnian case, just as in Rwanda's, one encounters competing ideological blueprints set on realising modernity's goal of a homogenous totality. Here too there is a restless urge to remove cultural variation, destroy uncertainty and order social reality along ethnically 'unmixed' social worlds.

Means of modernity

To successfully implement a particular ideological design, as Bauman stresses, one has to rely on the institutions and technology of modernity. While Bosnia and Rwanda are often seen as technologically and industrially underdeveloped societies, this view is entirely premised on an absolutism that identifies modernity with its most technologically advanced representatives. The fact that a certain society is institutionally and organisationally modern does not necessarily imply that it has to resemble contemporary Japan or United States. What is more important is the preponderance of profoundly modernist principles of instrumental rationality, division of labour, rationalist bureaucracy, and that it applies the most advanced technological tools that it has at its disposal. The fact that Rwandan genocide was perpetuated principally through the use of machetes[38] instead of gas chambers is not an indicator of its pre-modern character. On the contrary, the machete is a highly proficient weapon in a tightly inhabited terrain with enormous population density such as Rwanda. Furthermore this was a modern, mass factory-produced, mass imported (from China in 1993) and mass distributed weapon with multiple uses (for field work and for killing) which was deliberately chosen by state administrators for its low cost and its concealing and controlling (on the part of central authority) capabilities.

Thus, the systematic mass scale killings in Rwanda were achieved relying on the means of modernity. As many analysts (Prunier, 1997, Taylor, 1999, Hintjens, 2001) have observed, 1980s Rwanda was an exceptionally orderly, well administered and tidy society, with very good road and communication networks, highly functioning hospitals and schools in all the main towns, a stable economy, low inflation, negligible foreign debt, and very low levels of corruption. The levels of literacy were quite high in an African context: 'about 70% of men and 50% of women over 15 could read and write' (Wood, 2001: 62). The mass media (radio and newspaper) networks were developed and widespread throughout the country. It should come as no surprise that Rwanda was often referred to as the 'Switzerland of Africa'. More than that, this was an exceptionally centralised state with 'chillingly purposeful bureaucratic control' (Oplinger, 1990: 260), a highly disciplined bureaucracy and a political culture of 'systematic and unconditional obedience to authority' (Prunier, 1997: 141). As a result, the genocide was implemented in a highly centralised way with astonishing speed and ruthless efficiency (Reyntjens, 1996: 245). Most commentators agree that the 'the administrative machinery of the local state was key to organising the series of massacres that constituted the genocide' (Mamdani, 2001: 144). As Prunier (1997: 244–7) points out, sadistic killers were rare – most killers were 'ordinary peasants' who 'were controlled and directed in their task by the civil servants in the central government, *prefets*, *bourgmestres* and local councilors'. Even excesses such as rape and macabre brutality were carried out in a highly rationalised and administered 'Swiss' way ('according to plan and under the supervision of authority' Prunier, 1997: 349). Consequently 800,000 people were killed within less than three months, where 'daily killing rate was at least five times that of the Nazi death camps' (Prunier, 1997: 261). This was a genocide that depended heavily on the organising principles of modernity – the hierarchical and developed division of labour with the strict delegation of tasks, efficient bureaucracy and instrumental rationality in implementing the ultimate goal of ethnic purity.

The Bosnian experience was similar. At the end of the 1980s, Bosnia was in many respects a modern state with quite developed infrastructural powers. The post-Second World War period saw Bosnia developing intensively from an impoverished semi-feudal province of the Ottoman and Habsburg Empires, with high levels of illiteracy and almost non-existent means of transport and education, into a moderately developed economy with an extensive railway system, decent central roads and some highways, impressive communication networks, widespread mass media presence (TV, radio, newspapers), high literacy rates, expanding education system with five established universities and a rapidly growing (mostly heavy) industry. The average annual growth of industrial development from 1948 to 1984 was around 9 per cent; by the late 1980s over 50 per cent of the economy was industry based, with less than 15 per cent of population employed in the agricultural sector; literacy rates jumped from 55 per cent in 1948 to over 90 per cent at the end of 1980s (SG, 1986). While there was only one radio station in 1947, by 1984 there were 45; whereas there were only 21 newspapers in circulation in 1948 there were 359 by 1984; while there were only 900 university students in 1947 there were over 40,000 by 1984 (SG, 1986). Although the Yugoslav federation was an extremely decentralised entity, its individual constituent parts were tightly integrated, with Bosnia being one of the most centralised units. This was also an exceptionally bureaucratised state with a highly developed apparatus of state control and constant proliferation of the institutions of socialist self-management from work places, local municipalities, educational and informational institutions to the top of state structures. Communist Bosnia was the epitome of the Enlightenment dream of scientific and progressive state building with its infinite variety of 'scientific socialist' institutions such as the 'basic organisation of associated labour', 'self-management interest community' or 'contractual organisation of associated labour' (Malešević, 2002: 126).

It came as no surprise then, that these very institutions were used in the implementation of ethnic cleansing. The existing administrative apparatus was essential in the formation of so-called Bosnian Serb autonomous regions (SAO), municipal coalitions, which were created in the early 1990s out of fragments of the local state structure including numerous bureaucratic segments such as a municipal executive committee, the mayor's office, legislative assembly, local police office, and the municipal territorial defence organisation (Ron, 2003: 50–1). The most important bureaucratic vehicle of ethnic cleansing were crisis committees (*krizni štabovi*) which organised the so-called humane exchange of population from 'Serb to non-Serb areas' including the direct transport of people, repossession of their property, and exchange of houses and apartments. Considering the war conditions and the general breakdown of state structures, this was achieved in an unusually systematic and diligent way by carefully documenting every single transaction. The well-researched case (Oberschall, 2000; Ron, 2003) of the ethnic cleansing of Prijedor shows how the activists of the Serbian Democratic Party (SDS) initially formed parallel municipal state structures with the crisis committee at its helm forming an alternative power structure which – in a single night on 29 April 1992, with the help of JNA (the Yugoslav Army) quickly seized control of the entire city, including its central police station, the radio transmitter, and municipal headquarters. Upon establishing its full control the new local government proceeded towards gradual displacement of its non-Serb population by firing them from their jobs, ordering them to wear distinct armbands, forbidding mixed marriages, arresting them and eventually sending them to detention camps (Ron, 2003: 54–6). As documented by Ćekić *et al.* (1999: 162) the mass killings of Srebrenica were similarly perpetuated in a highly systematic and co-ordinated way – separating men and boys from women, organising transport for the deportation of the civilians, and taking control of all civilian institutions. Following a relatively precise schedule of events it took '72 hours to invade, arrest, displace and potentially kill the entire [more than 30,000] Bosniak population of Srebrenica'. This was done in a very orderly fashion by relying on the means of modernity – the advanced division of labour, bureaucratic delegation of tasks, and systematic co-ordination between the military and the local and central government. Thus in both Rwanda and Bosnia ethnic cleaning and genocide required and were made possible by the technological means of modernity.

Democratisation and liberalisation

If democracy is conceptualised simply and broadly as majority rule, then this very principle opens a possibility for what De Tocqueville long ago called a 'tyranny of the majority'. The inclusive notion of rule by the people is often premised on the exclusivist definition of who constitutes the people. More often than not modernity answers this question in ethno-national terms: no *liberté* and *egalité* without *fraternité*.

Hence as Mann (2005: 4) puts it, liberal democracies were built on top of ethnic cleansing via mass murder or through the institutionalised coercion and consequently the 'regimes newly embarked upon democratisation are more likely to commit murderous ethnic cleansing than are the stable authoritarian regimes'. The ideology and practice of democratisation are essential for ethnic cleansing.

The recent events in Rwanda and Bosnia are prime examples of how the democratising states can lead to mass bloodshed. Until this period both Bosnia and Rwanda were single party authoritarian states – one communist, the other an example of what is referred to as 'developmental dictatorship' (Prunier, 1997: 77). Since the military coup in 1973, Rwanda was ruled by J. Habyarimana's MRND (Revolutionary Movement for National Development) and membership was obligatory for every single Rwandan citizen. The state was tightly regulated with an administrative control that rivalled the communist world (Prunier, 1997: 77). The regime penetrated every aspect of social life and periodically organised mass displays of loyalty through so-called animation gatherings (Mamdani, 2001: 142). This was an ideocracy that relied on the two central institutions – the party and the army, both of which were created as authentic, Hutu, organisations of the postcolonial, revolutionary period. There was very little inter-ethnic violence in this authoritarian state.

The Rwandan Patriotic Front (RPF) invasion of Rwanda in October 1990 – coupled with a disastrously declining economy – weakened Habyarimana's position, forcing the MRND and the army to accept the democratisation and liberalisation of political life. Consequently the constitution was changed to allow for multiparty elections, galvanising the development of a vibrant civil society. The early 1990s saw an unprecedented proliferation of political parties, civil society organisations, independent mass media, pressure groups, regional associations and so on. The ruling party became internally polarised and fractured over the direction of social change. Officially it had to embrace the transformation, changing its name to MRNDD, adding 'Democracy' to 'Development' (Mamdani, 2001: 154). In this process, having now to compete for the Hutu vote with far more radicalised Hutu power parties, it too became radicalised. In the context of political uncertainty with the RPF threatening its borders and a deeply polarised society any attempt at multiethnic reconciliation was delegitimised as treasonous. The failure of the coalition government – formed in 1992 to prevent RPF offensives – and their acceptance of (deeply humiliating for the army and radical Hutus), Arusha Accords completely fractured the Hutu political elite. The democratic principle of majority rule was now constantly invoked by rising Hutu power groups to justify the all-Hutu domination, describing Hutus as 'democrats', the 'majority people', the 'great majority', and identifying all Tutsis with the threatening RPF. With the help of powerful propaganda outlets such as the RTLM radio and the *Kangura* newspaper this message became both believable and reassuring to most Hutus. Thus as Mann (2005: 442) puts it, 'danger was presented not by a stable, cohesive, or totalitarian state but by a weakening and ... partially democratising state beset by factionalism and radicalisation'.

The Bosnian case follows a similar pattern. Bosnia and Herzegovina was the least democratic, most illiberal of all the constitutive republics in the Yugoslav federation. Its communist leadership was generally regarded as the most rigid, clamping down on any independent associations and banning political excesses or semi-dissident voices often tolerated in neighbouring Slovenia, Serbia or Croatia. As in Rwanda, here again the two central pillars of institutional power were the party and the army and, just like in Rwanda, both were the cornerstones of the state's revolutionary legacy. This too was an ideocratic state, set on implementing the principles of the dominant ideology of socialist self-management (Malešević, 2002). Despite its pronounced ethno-cultural differences, this was a state with minimal if any inter-ethnic violence.

The worldwide collapse of communism, the dramatic economic decline and the radical transformation of political space in the more developed Yugoslav republics had a deep impact on Bosnian polity, forcing its political rulers towards democratisation and liberalisation. Here too the constitutional changes were swift, allowing multiparty elections. Civil society groups, including autonomous associations, political parties, pressure groups, independent mass media (with new television and radio broadcasters and hundreds of new journals and newspapers), quickly multiplied throughout the country. The ruling communist party (League of Communists) attempted to prevent an internal split between traditionalists and reformers by changing its name into LC – Socialist Democratic Party. The radicalisation of intra-state politics within the Yugoslav federation between its pro-reformist north west (Slovenia and Croatia) and its conservative south-east (Serbia and Montenegro) together with the gradual escalation of violence, further polarised political life in Bosnia (Cohen, 1993, see Chapter 7). As a result the first democratic elections brought into power a coalition of three, and in many respects mutually exclusive, ethno-nationalist parties – SDS, SDA and HDZ. All three were seen as representing the democratic will of 'their people'. With wars in Slovenia and Croatia, the incompatibility of political projects of the three ruling parties – the unification of all Serbs into a single state, the sovereign and independent Bosnia and the unification of Croatian populated parts of Bosnia with Croatia – crystallised to the extreme. All three parties were legitimising their claims by invoking the principles of majoritarian democracy. When parliamentary negotiations on reforming the state structure failed, the strongest of the three (SDS), aided by a now completely Serb-dominated army, embarked on territorial expansion of its rule through war and ethnic cleansing. In this process it relied heavily on propagandistic messages, specifically on the imminent resurrection of the fascist NDH or the Islamisation of the whole of Bosnia, constantly invoking its democratic mandate. Just as in the Rwandan case, in the context of grave political uncertainty these ideas became trustworthy to the majority of Bosnian Serbs. Hence in this case, too, it was a democratising and liberalising state rather than an authoritarian one that provided the environment for the radicalisation of political space and eventually for mass killing.

Geopolitics of competing state projects

Apart from the internal political pressures brought about by the complexities of democratisation, the direction and intensity of inter-ethnic group hostility is also determined by external influences, that is by geopolitics. However as Mann (2005: 6–7) emphasises, it is a predominantly unstable geopolitical environment with factionalised and radicalised structure that leads to war-induced ethnic cleansing. This is more likely to happen when two rival state projects claim sovereignty over the same territory and the weaker group is aided from the outside or the stronger group 'believes it has such overwhelming military power and ideological legitimacy that it can force through its own cleansed state at little physical or moral risk to itself'.

The turbulence of political events and the excessive use of violence in neighbouring Uganda and Burundi had a deep impact on the transformation of ethnic relations in Rwanda. As Mamdani (2001) emphasises, the RPF was formed out of the Rwandan (predominantly Tutsi) refugees who settled in Uganda and who were ideologically and militarily moulded by Museveni's National Resistance Movement. The domestic politics of Uganda shaped the structure and actions of the RPF, and their 1990 invasion had more to do with Ugandan internal politics than with the RPF's goals of Rwandan liberation. The recent history of Burundi had an even more direct impact on the change of collective perceptions in Rwanda. The presence of the most radical, pre-1959 'reactionary' Tutsis in Northern Burundi, who openly advocated the restoration of Tutsi dominance coupled with the outbursts of mass killings of Burundian Hutus in 1972, 1988 and especially 1993 (Hintjens, 1999: 278), including the killing of the first ever democratically elected Hutu president of Burundi (Ndadaye) in a still Tutsi hegemonic state with an overwhelming Hutu majority, directly inflamed the ethnic nationalism of Rwandan Hutus. All these events reinforced and gave popular credence to the Hutu Power view of a so-called Bahima (pan-Tutsi) or Hamitic conspiracy to re-create a feudal-like Tutsi land out of the existing states in the region (Hintjens, 2001). Hence, what one encounters here is a profoundly unstable geopolitical condition in the entire region which directly influenced an already radicalised and factionalised Hutu political elite. The dramatic explosion of mass scale violence leading eventually to genocide had a great deal to do with competing and mutually exclusive projects of state building – a nominal multiethnic parity disguising Tutsi hegemony advocated by RPF, versus the state of 'indigenous' ethnic Hutu majority promoted by a radicalised Hutu establishment. The direct and obvious threat of both Uganda and Burundi supported RPF at the borders of Rwanda created a situation where all Rwandan Tutsis were suddenly perceived as the 'enemy within', allowing the genocide perpetrators to see themselves as the 'true victims'.

The sudden and dramatic break-up of the Yugoslav federation also generated a profoundly unstable geopolitical condition. The political events and the gradual reliance on the rhetoric of violence – and eventually the use of violence itself in Serbia and Croatia – had deep repercussions in Bosnia. With the wars in Slovenia and Croatia, political elites as well as the general population became more radicalised, giving even stronger support to the three incompatible projects of state building. The formation of Serbian paramilitaries in Serbia proper and their well-documented misdeeds in the Croatian war as well as JNA's almost full conversion to the Serbian nationalist cause accelerated an offensive mobilisation on the part of the Bosnian Serb public, as well as the defensive, and later also offensive, mobilisation of Croat and Bosniak populations. The parallel existence of what Brubaker (1996) calls the nationalising homeland states of Serbia and Croatia with their own ethno-national state building projects destabilised Bosnia dramatically. Not only did these hypothetical projects make direct (Greater Serbia or Greater Croatia) or indirect (rump Yugoslavia) claims on its territory, they also engaged in an extensive propagandistic war creating a situation of collective fear among Bosnian Serbs, and later Croats as well. This situation gave way to various conspiracies about 'well prepared scenarios' on the part of Germany or the United States to carve up the Yugoslav state in order to divide Serbs into five states so as to subjugate them, or to establish a so-called green (Islamic) transversal from Istanbul over Albania, Kosovo, Sanjak (in Serbia) and Bosnia, securing a strong Muslim presence in Europe. Thus, just as in the Rwandan case, the regional geopolitical context was dramatically unstable – causing volatility, factionalisation and radicalisation in Bosnia itself. Here too, competing state projects were given ideological and military backing which led to popular belief that 'our' ethnically different neighbours were really exponents of the threatening state building-project, plotting to obliterate us. In this context, although a relative minority, Bosnian Serbs were militarily the stronger side whose political elite acted on the belief that it could rely on an overpowering military might and ideological right (claiming that Muslims are not a real ethno-national group but converted Serbs) to create an ethnically pure state. The stubborn resistance of the other two collective agents was also based on a strong geopolitical motive – their belief, vindicated as it happened, that they would receive support from outside (i.e. Croatia and international community/NATO).

The state, social status and large-scale violence

Despite their conceptual differences and apparent incommensurability (especially voiced by Mann, 2005: 242), these two interpretative frameworks prove to be highly compatible and useful in the attempt to shed light on the causes of dramatic and murderous ethnic cleansing in Bosnia and Rwanda. In other words, there is a significant degree of compatibility between Bauman's and Mann's theories. This should come as no surprise as they both work, though implicitly, within the Weberian tradition of research. Their explanatory difference comes largely from their different degrees of emphasis – while Bauman draws on a culturalist, postmodernist, interpretation of Weber's analytical heritage by focusing on the role of (modern) values and ideas and their products (such as the technology and science), Mann provides a more politically materialist explanation building on the influence of internal and external forces of politics. The fact that these highly compatible approaches are disconnected and often polarised is a symptom of a larger epistemological problem of fragmentation within neo-Weberian theory of ethnicity which cannot be dealt with here (see Malešević, 2004). What is essential for this study is that, as our empirical research on Rwanda and Bosnia demonstrates, the explanatory synthesis of the two models is possible, useful and analytically desirable. It is only when one combines the two that we get a better picture of what took place in Bosnia and Rwanda in the early 1990s. Although this synthesis is necessary, it in itself is not enough. It tells us a great deal about the structural causes of the phenomena – such as the historical roots of the particular belief systems, about the means of implementation, the internal and geopolitical contexts – but it does not tell us as much about the individual and collective motives of social actors. In other words, despite Mann's attempt to identify the profile of the perpetuators of ethnic cleansing whom he classifies as leaders, militants and the 'core constituencies' of ethno-nationalism, or Bauman's study of the psychological reasons for individual and mass obedience, their core arguments are still overly structuralist. Whereas in Bauman agency is a secondary, almost invisible force moulded by the structures of modernity, Mann's agents, although highly present, are too static and too one-dimensional, shaped as they are by the sudden historical and geopolitical transformations. What is missing here is a dynamics of the micro social world: group interactions, the transformation of collective perceptions, social categorisation, and the analysis of social action in general. In the Weberian tradition this relates particularly to the concepts of social status and monopolistic social closure. Both of these concepts are essential to fully understand the social mechanisms behind the sudden and unprecedented mass scale killings in Rwanda and Bosnia.

First, as Weber saw it, ethnic groups are for the most part status groups. They are quasi-groups, amorphous entities whose formation is almost entirely dependent on social action. They are grounded in a particular belief in common descent which becomes socially meaningful only through collective, political action. Social status is dependent on what Weber calls the 'social estimation of honour' which provides individuals with a 'sense of dignity', with a feeling of 'beauty and excellence', and with a sense of privilege. Ethnic group status is intrinsically hierarchical as expressed in what Weber calls 'ethnic honour', a sense of in-group superiority vis-à-vis out-groups. As individuals play the status game, so do the quasi-communities where the social prestige of one's ethnic collectivity is premised on denying such a position to other collectivities. In this way ethnic markers are also available as devices of monopolistic social closure. By this term Weber (1968: 43–4) meant that social relationships are restricted to in-group members by closing off, limiting or pre-conditioning access to material or symbolic benefits to members of out-groups. The monopolistic social closure of relationships is often used to improve the status position of a particular group.

Thus, starting from the assumption that human beings are status anxious creatures, one can attempt to understand the dynamics of inter-group action in Rwanda and Bosnia and especially the degree of ethnic mobilisation that took place in a very short period of time. Taking into account the long history of sharp social status demarcations as well as their dramatic transformations in both Bosnia and Rwanda, the state was heavily involved in status regulation. In Rwanda the near absolute status dominance of Tutsis in the pre-colonial and colonial period was for the most part reversed by the Hutu revolution of 1959. However, to fully understand the importance of social status it is necessary to go back again to the 1930s when Belgian colonisers rigidly fixed and legally underpinned what were until than very flexible sense of group membership. This policy had a dramatic impact on individual and social status as it blocked any future individual status enhancement between the vaguely defined 'inferior' Hutus into status 'superior' Tutsis. As Mamdani (2001: 101) points out: 'After the 1933 census, Hutu and Tutsi were enforced as legal identities. This had a crucial social effect: neither *kwihutra* (the social rise of an individual Hutu to the status of a Tutsi) nor *gucupira* (the social fall from Tutsi to Hutu status) was any longer possible.' The Belgian colonisers had frozen individual status mobility, thus forcing individuals to compete and conflict as members of particular *ethnic* groups. From this moment to improve one's individual standing one had to work on improving the social standing of the group – and as Banton (1983) noticed a long time ago, 'when people compete as individuals group boundaries are weakened but when they compete as groups boundaries are strengthened'. This was a prelude to any future conflict as, on one hand, it intensified collective status competition and on the other provided an institutionalised skeleton around which group mobilisation could take place.

The revolution of 1959 was a first radical attempt to reverse the status hierarchy. The ethnically divisive underpinning of status membership was further reinforced by the new Hutu rulers with the leader of the revolution and the first post-colonial president of Rwanda, G. Kayibanda, advocating 'segregation' and 'confederal organisation' for 'two nations in a single state' (Mamdani, 2001: 127). The new regime established a mechanism of absolute monopolistic social closure, where political participation was confined exclusively to Hutus and all Tutsis were excluded from political life. With the nationalisation of the educational system in 1966 and the rising Hutu middle class, the social closure was extended to other sectors – education, banking, para-state companies and even private businesses. The intensity and speed of this status reversal led to violence which was quashed by the bloodless coup of 1973, when Habyarimana created a more moderate and stable system of status control. The second republic introduced a system of fixed ethnic quotas where Hutus were guaranteed 85 per cent of places in the educational system, civil service, army, regional administration and other state institutions, while Tutsis were allocated between 10 and 15 and a small minority Twa 1 per cent (Hintjens, 1999: 256, Mamdani, 2001: 139). Although this state-induced status equilibrium helped prevent intergroup violence for nearly two decades it also institutionalised status on the basis of group-centricity, thus reinforcing identitarian and very divisive cognitive perceptions and practices of social reality. Despite this period being a vivid improvement on the Kayibanda years, notably for Tutsis, it too was built on group-centric mechanisms of monopolistic social closure where one's ethnic origin completely determined one's individual status position.

The economic collapse of the late 1980s and early 1990s combined with the RPF invasion dramatically undermined this fictive equilibrium, with the Hutu majority experiencing double status degradation. The military defeat of the Hutu majority army meant the instant decline of Hutu social prestige, while the economic downturn further damaged their sense of superiority. Simultaneously, the Tutsi led RPF's military strength together with the emergence of an economically powerful Tutsi independent business class, which was created gradually as Tutsis had limited access to civil service employment and had to rely on the (now booming) private sector, utterly destabilised status hierarchies.[39] Hence the dramatic escalation of intra-group conflict – and especially its unprecedented scale, ending in genocide – had a great deal to do with sudden transformations of social status as well as with collective perceptions of status threat. To understand the intensity of mass killings, one has to engage with the rapid status degradation of the majority Hutu and their potential, as well as the actual status enhancement of Tutsis. Since the status equilibrium was upheld and underpinned by the state, its accelerated alteration by both internal democratisation and external geopolitical change intensified collective fears of potential collective submission, which in turn was further augmented by mass media manipulation, together creating a situation of constant status anxiety among Hutus. Hence the perception of the status threat was not just imagined – in some sense it was very real and, when inflamed by extremist propaganda, led to a situation where mass killers saw themselves as true victims (Gourevitch, 2000).

Bosnia shares this history of state regulated status control. Both the Ottoman and Habsburg Empires have been heavily involved in the institutionalisation and politicisation of ethno-culturally framed status groups. The Ottoman millet system institutionally divided social groups

into semi-autonomous ethno-religious communities, whose entire communication with the state authorities was mediated by its top clergy. On
the other hand it stratified these groupings according to their ethno-
religious compatibility or proximity to the imperial court and the state's
official religion. Thus Bosnian Muslims maintained a higher social
standing then their Orthodox/Serb and Catholic/Croat counterparts.
Despite late attempts at the ethno-political unification of Bosnian collectivities, and Benjamin Kalay's ambition to create a single ethno-
national group in Bosnia, the Habsburg Empire was constructed and
functioned as a realm of culturally specific administrative units, thus in
many respects reinforcing the legacy of the Ottoman Empire. Moreover,
it fostered a sense of ethno-religious status hierarchies by privileging
Roman Catholic Croats at the expense of two other ethnic collectivities.
Monarchist Yugoslavia, itself created as an ethnic (greater Serbian) project, further strengthened this sense of state regulated status hierarchy by
enhancing the social prestige of the Serbian collectivity over the others.

There is a lot of similarity here with the Rwandan colonial and post-
colonial experience, as in both cases one can witness a striking state
supported transformation of social status hierarchies. In a similar vein to
Habyarimana's state, Tito's Yugoslavia also created a system of proportional ethnic representation, thus cementing ethno-cultural categorisa-
tions as political identities. The Yugoslav federal state had a highly
complex system of ethnic representation that involved the rotation of
party apparatchiks at both the federal and state (Bosnian) levels in
governmental institutions, civil service, party central committees, and
places of work, as well as at the level of municipal and local government.
Bosnia was remarkable in this respect, as it implemented the most rigid
system of status control by making compulsory ethnic rotation on all
these levels so as to have equal representation of Serbs, Croats and
Muslims/Bosniaks in nearly all state and non-state institutions. As a
result this republic was the least ethnically stratified in the Yugoslav
federation. The large-scale research done by Katunarić (1991) and others
demonstrates that, unlike Croatia, which had a higher percentage of
Serbs among military and police,[40] Bosnia had a very egalitarian
structure of ethnic composition in all major sectors of society, with
proportional representation among the top echelons of the social structure evident in areas such as top government offices, high ranking positions of state companies, professionals, and leading military and police
posts. The situation was similar at the lower levels of the social pyramid.[41] Consequently the social distance between the three major
groups, as measured regularly by many researchers from the 1960s to

1990s (i.e. Katunarić, 1986, Šiber, 1988, Pantić, 1990), was negligible or very mild.

Here too, as in Rwanda, two developments – one external and one internal – dramatically altered inter-ethnic relations. First, the extraordinary downfall of the Yugoslav economy in the 1980s, which especially affected Bosnia's predominantly heavy industry leading to staggering levels of unemployment and the rise of ethnic nationalisms in Serbia and later in Croatia. Both of these processes had a deep impact on status transformation in Bosnia. The internal and geopolitical uncertainty which came together with post-communist democratisation and liberalisation crushed the existing status equilibrium of the authoritarian period by weakening the external guarantor of this equilibrium – the impartial state. This externally and internally imposed uncertainty created an environment of collective status anxiety, and a very real and material threat of monopolistic social closure on the part of the other ethnic group. In the Bosniak and Croat case, that meant the establishment of Serbian dominance in Milošević's Yugoslavia while for Bosnian Serbs the objective threat was an independent Bosnian state with Bosniak and Croat majority. Here again, just as in Rwanda, the rhetoric of new ethno-nationalist political elites and their reliance on tightly controlled mass media further inflamed status uncertainties. In this case, too, the main perpetuators of mass killings saw themselves as the real victims. In both Rwanda and Bosnia the extensive use of violence and mass extermination of the 'others' was justified as a pre-emptive action on the part of a group that 'felt threatened'.

So what is remarkable about both of these cases is that mass violence did not result from economic exploitation of one ethnic group over another, or from strict monopolistic ethnic closure on the part of one group, or from lack of a political voice. Rather systematic mass killings erupted after a relatively long period of ethnic group harmony and status equilibrium imposed by the state structures. It was the collapse of these state structures that generated 'status vacuum' – which, together with the ideology and technology of modernity, democratisation and an intensively changing geopolitical environment, moved collective actors towards mass extermination.

Conclusion

The paradox of nation-state building is that the full and adamant implementation of this Enlightenment-inspired and profoundly modernist principle is very much premised on the eradication of cultural difference.

Whether cultural uniformity is an openly stated goal or simply a by-product of a peculiar form that modernisation took in eighteenth- and nineteenth-century Europe, and then spread around the globe, has less relevance now. What is more important is that contemporary episodes of systematic mass violence, such as those of Rwanda and Bosnia, owe as much if not more to this very principle as they do to the particular historical circumstances of their geographical location. Thus, modern-day genocidal outbursts are not so much the result of individual or collective hatreds or any other kind of social pathology – they are unwitting outcomes of something that is structurally embedded in modernist principles (uncompromising ideological blueprints) and modern technological apparatuses, together with the most sophisticated bureaucratic mechanisms of the modern state. The mass extermination of 'cultural others' also often depends on sudden and incomplete democratisation and on the geopolitical environment when prone to dramatic political change. Internally, the mechanisms of massive collective mobilisation require radical escalations and general transformations in the social status and prestige of ethnically conceptualised collective and individual actors. The horrors of Rwanda and Bosnia are not something that happens in a faraway, authoritarian and backward world of unfinished past, it is something that has a great deal to do with the elementary principles and values on which the foundation of our post-Enlightenment world is built – this is the Janus face of modernity.

Concluding Remarks

Although the recognition of cultural difference is usually seen as a source of self-liberation and collective emancipation there is a darker side to identity politics which has received far less attention. Instead of a 'celebration of difference', many identity projects, couched as they are in discourses that reify and essentialise, and often institutionalised by powerful structures of the modern state, tend either to reinforce group centric views of social reality or reproduce blinkered and discriminatory forms of domination. The rhetoric of identity often becomes a potent device for the ideological justification of political inequality, and in the most extreme cases, for mass murder. However, regardless of how unintentional such an undesirable outcome is, identity is very far from being an innocent, technical term. Instead its nearly universal and all embracing popularity, apparent normality, and general acceptance are the very ingredients that constitute its ideological power.

The principal aim of this book has been to put identity claims under rigorous scrutiny: to explore the conceptual, theoretical and methodological value of this concept, to locate its geographical origins and its historical functions and, most of all, to come to terms with its sociological and political consequences. While an attempt was made to indicate the pronounced conceptual and operational weaknesses of this idiom, the principal focus of my analysis was the ideological potency of its rhetoric. Whether its use is confined to particular social movements, individual political entrepreneurs, religious and cultural organisations, political parties, pressure groups, terrorist networks, global enterprises or bureaucratic apparatuses of the modern nation-state, 'identity talk' is a paramount discourse of our age. It is apparent that everybody, from refugees in the villages of Darfur, Islamists of Hamas, Californian border patrol militias, European Commissioners, Swamis and Hindu priests, Chinese communist apparatchiks to the British Chancellor of the Exchequer legitimise their actions and policies with reference to the preservation and protection of a particular identity.

And this is precisely why identitarianism is so appealing both to those at the disseminating as well as those at the receiving end of its message. To articulate a distinctly political claim as a cultural/identity claim is to empty it of its particularistic, divisive and normative content, to make something which is fundamentally conflictual seem much more consensual and natural. This ideological process, as I have tried to show, is not the result of a simple manipulation on the part of a ruling elite or the 'false consciousness' on the part of those who follow, nor is it necessarily linked to particular economic processes or specific political orders. Rather its ideological potency is universal as it is grounded in the workings and structures of our modern, post-Enlightenment age whose institutional design and value bifurcation constantly foster the politicisation of cultural difference.

For the last two hundred years or so the territorially demarcated, bureaucratically administered and sovereign nation-state has been the prevailing norm of political organisation, while the politicisation of culture has proven to be the essential source of its internal and external legitimacy. Although in normative terms the political and cultural elites of the state may incline to a variety of universalist political doctrines of social organisation, the institutional shell of the nation-state forces them towards infusing these doctrines with a hefty dose of culturally coloured particularism. It is this, often subtle translation of the universalist normative doctrine into its particularist operative, nationalist, form that is at the heart of successful state legitimisation. In other words, regardless of the nominal or substantive difference between various political orders and state elites, no serious political authority can afford to ignore identity. Any claim to legitimacy which is not in some way grounded in the dominant operative ideology of modernity – nationalism – is likely to fail. Whether civic, ethnic or banal, nationalist narratives continue to be the most forceful operative ideology of our age.

Seminal theorists of nationalism such as Gellner and Smith have taught us well how and why nationalism has acquired such a privileged ideological position in the post-traditional world. Yet by decoupling ideology from coercive forms of power they both espouse an overly optimistic view of late modernity where nationalism and strong ethnic bonds are seen either as something that will gradually diminish in influence (Gellner, 1997: 47) or else provide the only guarantor of a free society in the modern era (Smith, 1995: 147). The experience of late modernity indicates otherwise.

Not only is it that nationalism has not disappeared or managed to safeguard individual or collective liberties, but as a backlash to globalising tendencies and changing geopolitical environments, it has actually expanded and mutated into a variety of forms, and many of these are anything but benign. The identitarian rhetoric of ethnicity and nationess has now been extensively incorporated not only by state or state seeking actors but also by local, regional and global movements with religious, economic, gender or nativist agendas, from Queer nation, Dalits of India, Padania, Inuit or Métis nationhood to Hizb ut-Tahrir's and al-Qaeda's vision of a global Islamic caliphate for the entire 'Muslim nation'. More importantly, concrete attempts at the institutionalisation of these principles have poignantly confirmed just how thin the line between the politicisation of culture and violence actually is.

This is not to say that ethnicity and nationess are inherently conflictual or that cultural difference automatically implies hostility. Certainly not. What I argue is that what often starts out as harmless recognition or 'celebration of difference' under grinds of the administrative 'iron cage' and specific historical and geopolitical conditions can easily slide into collective brutality. Any organised political attempt to mould ethnicity and nationess, that is, to structurally tamper with the intrinsic ambiguity of cultural difference, may in the long term prove to be a recipe for disaster. As ambiguity is a sine qua non of cultural difference, so any venture aimed at rigid legislation and inflexible institutionalisation, either through its excessive affirmation or complete denial, is ultimately counterproductive. When such actions are underpinned by post-authoritarian state structures, ideological monopolies, organicistic intellectuals and mass mobilisation, as the Rwandan and Yugoslav cases demonstrate so well, then we are likely to find ourselves at the gates of hell. What is crucial to recognise here is that mass extermination is not a perverse side effect of an otherwise innocuous and profoundly admirable process called identity politics; instead, in many respects, it is its very core.

Notes

1. The fact that only a few years ago (in 2001) when I initially ran this internet search there were 4 million entries and that in four years this has multiplied by more than 23 times is in itself an excellent indicator of the continuous explosion of popular interest in 'identity'.
2. The mathematical example would look something like this: because 2 is the same as 2 the difference between 2 and 2 is 0. This implies that this 2 is simultaneously defined by its difference from non 2 and its similarity to itself (2). According to Goddard (1998) this entails that difference (from zero difference to nonzero differences) defines the whole structure of identity.
3. Although Weinreich has developed his own research tools designed to study identity ('Identity Structure Analysis'- ISA) I have not used this empirical tool here but have only operationalised his definition and model of ethnic identity. This has been done with the purpose to secure methodological compatibility with Isajiw's concept of ethnic identity.
4. These factors have been generated with the help of principal component analysis while the relationship between the two factors has been established with the help of canonical analysis.
5. These three factors have been yielded with the help of principal component analysis. For more about the methodology and the sample structure used in this research see Malešević (1993, 1994) and Malešević and Malešević (2001).
6. Typical example includes the following: 'Greece furnishes a good example of an ethnic national identity' while 'the United States is the standard example of a plural national identity' (Smith, 2001b:32–34).
7. While classics of post structuralism such as Foucault, Baudrillard, Lyotard, Deleuze and Guattari are uncompromising in their rejection of ideology arguing that 'there is no ideology and there never has been' (Deleuze and Guattari 1988:4), post-Marxists such as Laclau and Mouffe (1985) make some attempt to incorporate the concept of ideology into their discourse theory.
8. As Torfing (2005:158) points out Foucault operates with a quasi-transcendental conception of discourse as his early archaeological form of discourse analysis argues that 'the discursive rules of formation are conditioned by nondiscursive relations. However, the criteria for distinguishing the discursive realm from the nondiscursive and the nature of the "conditioning relation" remain unclear'.
9. On the basis of meticulous empirical research D. McAuley (2005) convincingly argues that al-Qaeda's discourse is predominantly focused on the three following topics: Arabian peninsular nationalism, the glorification of the tribal way of life and Saudi Arabia's place in the world economy.
10. See Abercrombie *et al.* (1978:160, 1980:150–80) for their explicit claim that media and educational system are not important: 'the apparatuses of transmission of belief are not very efficient in reaching the subordinate classes'; '... any ideological incorporation is a *secondary* effect on development of the

educational system'; ' the evidence of media influence is so thin and subject to so many caveats that our conclusion must be that the media are not significant ...'.

11. Other researchers such as Zubaida (1993) and Abrahamian (1993) have also found Khomeini's discourse as relying much more on nationalist than Islamic images.

12. Rudyard Kipling's original epigram is: 'What do they know of cricket who cricket only know?' (Billig, 2005:4).

13. For a more detailed analysis of the relationship between classical sociological theory and ethnic relations and nationalism see Malešević (2004) and Guibernau (1995).

14. Although H. Kohn (1944) and J. Plamenatz (1973) were clear predecessors in differentiating between these two types of nationalist experience, unlike Smith they lack a coherent sociological account of the two trajectories around which the these two types developed.

15. For a more detail criticism of this determinist logic of reasoning see Haugaard (2002).

16. There is a more explicit nominal shift from deterministic and static concepts in Smith's latest major work *Chosen Peoples* where for the first time he speaks of nations in terms of 'series of processes' (24) rather than relatively fixed categories. However even in this work his empirical analyses remain chained to a teleological and finalist logic of argumentation with pronouncements such as '*once a national identity has been created* [sacred foundations and cultural resources] may be regarded as its guarantors and guides' (258, my italics).

17. For a more extensive criticism of this research strategy see chapters 1 and 2.

18. This tight link between the social/national and the sacred is most explicit in Smith's later works where one can read how 'more durable foundation for the persistence of national identities' can be provided '*only by the sense of the sacred* and the binding commitments of religion.' Smith, *Chosen Peoples*,4–5 (my italics).

19. More precisely the syntagm used is 'European miracle', because the tectonic social change that took place occurred only in Europe. But as Gellner (1989:1) clarifies: 'The phrase should not be read – the *European* miracle. It must be read – the European *miracle*. We know not what we do, and we do not know what hit us. We cannot take credit for it.'

20. C. Hann (2001) identifies more affinities between Gellner and Geertz, such as their commonly shared holistic notion of 'a culture'.

21. Despite the popularity of cinematic representation of traditional warfare as bloody, brutal and mass scale, as Mann (1986:141) argues – and documents well in his book – the victories and defeats in agrarian societies were very often decided with little fighting: 'Battles were usually unnecessary: Skirmishes showed the rough balance of force, the defenders' counsels were divided, someone opened the gates'.

22. Gellner is not unique in his neglect of popular culture. As Edensor (2002) shows, none of the leading theories of nationalism devotes much attention to analysis of popular culture.

23. Even in this case the large-scale bloodshed was directly influenced by the events of the Second World War and actions of leading powers, Nazi Germany and fascist Italy, who occupied much of the monarchist Yugoslavia

and it is highly likely that without this geopolitical background this bloodshed might not have happened at all.

24. For example despite the nominal privileges that Bosnian Muslims had under
Ottoman rule over their Christian neighbours, Serbs and Croats, in reality
this extended only to a very small minority of aristocrats (*agas* and *beys*)
while everybody else, Muslims and non-Muslim alike, was considered to be
raya (underclass).

25. Edvard Kardelj was the chief ideological architect of communist Yugoslavia.
On the role of Kardelj's model of state development see Rogel (1985), Jović
(2003) and Uzelac (2006).

26. For a more extensive discussion of all of these theories see S. Malešević (2004)

27. For example Yugoslavia did not have the concept of 'titular nation' or the
system of internal passports which were crucial in the institutionalisation of
ethno-national federal units in the Soviet Union. See more about the Soviet
case in Brubaker, 1996.

28. In 1948 after the Tito–Stalin split the Yugoslav Communist Party was
expelled from the Cominform and Eastern European communist states broke
off relationships with the Yugoslav state.

29. With the break-up of the common state in 1991 the common language,
Serbo-Croat, has also officially disintegrated into Serbian, Croatian and
Bosnian, with Montenegrin on the way, although the differences between
these supposedly three or four languages are no greater than those between
American and British English. It is also important to note that there are differences in dialects among Serbo-Croat speakers but they cross cut ethnic
borders. The only linguistically significant difference is that most Serbian
and Montenegrin speakers predominantly use Cyrillic script whereas Bosniak
and Croat speakers almost exclusively use Latin alphabet.

30. See more about the ideology of the Illyrian movement in Uzelac (2006).

31. In the period 1966–70, the growth of the GDP has fallen from 8.1 per cent to
5.8 per cent. See: *SP* (1986:10)

32. The Croatian ethno-national movement (also known as 'Maspok' or
'Croatian Spring') was launched in 1967 with a declaration about the
position and name of the Croatian language and very soon spread to include
various groups: separatist economists who wanted to see an independent
Croatian state, liberals who demanded change of the political system, students and cultural workers who stood for cultural purism and the separation
of the Croatian language and culture from its amalgamation with the Serbian
language and culture.

33. Since Serbian leadership had control over four votes (Serbia, Vojvodina, Kosovo
and Montenegro) the voting would usually end up in a deadlock — 4:4).

34. For more about the delegitimisation strategies used during the war in former
Yugoslavia see S. Malešević and G. Uzelac (1997) and S. Malešević (1998).

35. From 1990 onwards the term Bosniak (not Bosnian which refers to all
citizens of Bosnia-Herzegovina) was used more often by Bosnian Muslims to
describe their nationality.

36. The Praxis School was certainly the most important theoretical development
in communist Yugoslavia. From its beginning it included a fairly diverse
group of academics, mostly from the Universities of Belgrade and Zagreb. The

Belgrade group (M. Marković, S. Stojanović, Lj. Tadić, Z. Golubović, D. Mićunović, M. Životić, N. Popov and T. Indjić) was in some ways more radical and as a result suffered harsher treatment by the authorities when in 1974 all eight members were expelled from the University and the journal *Praxis* was banned. The Zagreb group, the original creators of the school, including M. Kangrga, G. Petrović, R. Supek, D. Grlić, B. Bošnjak, I. Kuvačić and P. Vranicki, was from the beginning much more anti-nationalist but some of their representatives were also less critical of the authorities. For a personal account of the school's origins see Kangrga (2001).

37. One should also note that not all Belgrade based Praxis philosophers have become nationalists. Some like M. Životić and N. Popov were leading opponents of Milošević's regime and ethno-nationalist policies in Serbia.

38. D. Stone (2004:47) disputes that most people were killed by machetes: 'In fact most of the murdered were slain by being shot, machetes being used to 'finish off' already dying victims, or toward the end of genocide, when the numbers to be killed were smaller'. Current government sources deny this indicating that 38 per cent were killed with machetes and only 15 per cent by firearms (Straus, 2004), but it is hard to say whether these figures can be trusted since the government has interest in emphasising the gruesomeness of the crime.

39. This was a conscious policy of the rulers. As Prunier (1997:151) points out: 'it was better for the President to have a prosperous Tutsi business class that having independently powerful Hutu businessmen who would have autonomous political ambitions of their own and eventually pursue them'.

40. This trend of higher ethnic Serbian representation in the military was also a feature of the entire Yugoslav federation although, as Cohen (1995:182) shows, this was gradually changing as the number of Croats and other groups was increasing while the number of Serbs was decreasing.

41. There was a slight under-representation of Bosniaks among the professionals and overrepresentation among manual labourers and farmers (Katunarić, 1991: 377).

References

Abercrombie, N. (1990) 'Popular Culture and Ideological Effects', in N. Abercrombie, S. Hill and B. S. Turner (eds) *Dominant Ideologies*. London: Unwin Hyman.

Abercrombie, N. and Turner, B. S. (1978) 'The Dominant Ideology Thesis', *British Journal of Sociology*, 29 (2):149–70.

Abercrombie, N., Hill, S. and Turner, B. S. (1980) *The Dominant Ideology Thesis*, London: Allen & Unwin.

Abercrombie, N., Hill, S. and Turner, B. S. (1983) 'Determinacy and Indeterminacy in the Theory of Ideology', *New Left Review*, 142: 55–66.

Abercrombie, N., Hill, S. and Turner, B. S. (1986) *Sovereign Individuals of Capitalism*. London: Allen & Unwin.

Abercrombie, N., Hill, S. and Turner, B. S. (eds) (1990) *Dominant Ideologies*. London: Unwin Hyman.

Abrahamian, E. (1993) *Khomeinism*. Berkeley, CA: University of California Press.

Alexander, C. (2000) *The Asian Gang*. Oxford: Berg.

Alexander, J. (1980) 'Core Solidarity, Ethnic Outgroup, and Social Differentiation: A Multidimensional Model of Inclusion in Modern Societies', in J. Dofney and A. Akiwowo (eds) *National and Ethnic Movements*. London: Sage.

Alexander, J. (1987) 'The Centrality of the Classics', in: A. Giddens and J. H. Turner (eds) *Social Theory Today*. Cambridge: Polity.

Alexander, J. (2002) 'On the Social Construction of Moral Universals: The "Holocaust" from Mass Murder to Trauma Drama', *European Journal of Social Theory*, 5 (1): 5–86.

Althusser, L. (1994) 'Ideology and Ideological State Apparatuses (Notes towards an Investigation)' in S. Žižek (ed.) *Mapping Ideology*. London: Verso.

Anderson, B. (1983) *Imagined Communities*. London: Verso.

Apple and Weis, L. (eds) (1983) *Ideology and Practice in Schooling*. Philadelphia, PA: Temple University Press.

Armstrong, J. (1982) *Nations before Nationalism*. Chapel Hill, NC: University of North Carolina Press.

Banton, M. (1983) *Racial and Ethnic Competition*. Cambridge: Cambridge University Press.

Banton, M. (2000) 'Ethnic Conflict', *Sociology*, 34 (3): 481–98.

Barrett, M. (1991) *The Politics of Truth: From Marx to Foucault*. Cambridge: Polity.

Barth, F. (ed.) (1969) *Ethnic Groups and Boundaries: The Social Organization of Culture Difference*. London: George Allen & Unwin.

Barthes, R. (1993) *Mythologies*, London: Vintage.

Baudrillard, J. (1988) *Simulacra and Simulations*. Cambridge: Polity.

Bauman, Z. (1987) *Legislators and Interpreters*. Cambridge: Polity.

Bauman, Z. (1989) *Modernity and the Holocaust*. Cambridge: Polity.

Bauman, Z. (1991) *Modernity and Ambivalence*. Cambridge: Polity.

Bauman, Z. (1996) From Pilgrim to Tourist – or a Short History of Identity, in: S. Hall and P. du Gay (eds) *Questions of Cultural Identity*. London: Sage.

Bauman, Z. (1997) *Postmodernity and its Discontents*, Cambridge: Polity.

Bauman, Z. (2004) *Identity*. Cambridge: Polity.

Baumeister, R. (1986) *Identity: Cultural Change and the Struggle for Self*. Oxford: Oxford University Press.

Beck, U. (1991) *Risk Society*. Cambridge: Polity.

Beeler, J. (1971) *Warfare in Feudal Europe 730–1200*. Ithaca, NY: Cornell University Press.

Beetham, D. (1991) *The Legitimation of Power*. London: Macmillan.

Bellamy, R. (1997) 'The Intellectual as Social Critic: Antonio Gramsci and Michael Walzer', in J. Jennings and A. Kemp-Welch (eds) *Intellectuals in Politics*. London: Routledge.

Bendle, M. F. (2002) 'The Crisis of "identity" in High Modernity'. *British Journal of Sociology*, 53 (1): 1–18.

Berger, P. and Luckman, T. (1966) *The Social Construction of Reality*. New York: Anchor Books.

Bevir, M. (1999) 'Foucault and Critique: Deploying Agency against Autonomy' *Political Theory* 27(1): 65–84.

Bhabha, Z. (1994) *The Location of Culture*. London: Routledge.

Bilandžić, D. (1985) *Historija SFRJ: Glavni procesi 1918–1985*. Zagreb: Školska Knjiga.

Billig, M. (1995) *Banal Nationalism*. London: Sage.

Billig, M. (2002) 'Ideology, Language and Discursive Psychology', in S. Malešević and I. Mackenzie (eds) *Ideology after Poststructuralism*. London: Pluto.

Billig, M. (2005) *Laughter and Ridicule: Towards a Social Critique of Humour*. London: Sage.

Billig, M. *et al.* (1988) *Ideological Dilemmas: A Social Psychology of Everyday Thinking*. London: Sage.

Blair, T. (1999a) 'The Pride of Britain Awards' 20 May, *http://www.number-10.gov.uk/news.asp*.

Blair, T. (1999b) 'Broadcast to the Nation on Kosovo' 26 March, *http://www.number-10.gov.uk/news.asp*.

Blair, T. (1999c) 'Britain in Europe' 14 October, *http://www.number-10.gov.uk/news.asp*.

Blair, T. (2000) 'Celebrating the Angels' Heroism' 2 March, *http://www.number-10.gov.uk/news.asp*.

Blumer, H. (1969) *Symbolic Interactionism: Perspective and Method*. Englewood Cliffs, NJ: Prentice Hall.

Blumer, H. and Duster, T. (1980) 'Theories of Race and Social Action', in *Sociological Theories: Race and Colonialism*. Paris: Unesco.

Bonacich, E. (1976) 'Advanced Capitalism and Black/White Relations in the United States: A Split Labor Market Interpretation', *American Sociological Review*, 41:34–51.

Botev, N. (1994) 'Where East Meets West: Ethnic Intermarriage in the Former Yugoslavia 1962 to 1989', *American Sociological Review*, 59: 461–80.

Boudon, R. (1982) *The Unintended Consequences of Social Action*. London: Macmillan.

Boudon, R. (1989) *The Analysis of Ideology*. Cambridge: Polity.

Bourdieu, P. (1990) *The Logic of Practice*. Cambridge: Polity.

Bourdieu, P. (1997) *State Nobility*. Cambridge: Polity.

Brass, P. (1991) *Ethnicity and Nationalism*. New Delhi: Sage.

Breuilly, J. (1993) *Nationalism and the State*. Manchester: Manchester University Press.

Browning, C. (1992) *Ordinary Men*. London: Penguin.

Brubaker, R. (1996) *Nationalism Reframed*. Cambridge: Cambridge University Press.

Brubaker, R. (1998) 'Myths and Misconceptions in the Study of Nationalism', in J. Hall (ed.) *The State of the Nation: Ernest Gellner and the Theory of Nationalism*. Cambridge: Cambridge University Press.

Brubaker, R. (2004) *Ethnicity without Groups*. Cambridge, MA: Harvard University Press.

Brubaker, R. and Cooper, F. (2000) 'Beyond "Identity", *Theory and Society*' 29 (1):1–37.

Bulmer, M. (2001) 'Ethnicity', in A. S. Leoussi and A. D. Smith (eds) *Encyclopedia of Nationalism*. London: Transaction.

Caca, Dj. (1988) 'Ustavni koncept Socijalistickih Republika i Socijalistickih Autonomnih Pokrajina', in *Ustavni razvoj Socialisticke Jugoslavije*. Belgrade: Eksportpres.

Cameron, K. (ed.) (1999) *National Identity*. Exeter: Intellect.

Carter, B. (1997) 'Rejecting Truthful Identities: Foucault, "Race" and Politics', in M. Loyd and A. Thacker (eds) *The Impact of Michel Foucault on the Social Sciences and Humanities*. London: Macmillan.

Carrithers, M. (1992) *Why Humans have Cultures*. Oxford: Oxford University Press.

Cekic, S. *et al.* (1999) *Srebrenica 1995: Dokumenti i svjedocenja I*. Sarajevo: Institut za istrazivanje zlocina protiv covjecnosti i medjunarodnog prava.

CIRI (1979) *The Constitution of the Islamic Republic of Iran*, http://www.salamiran.org/IranInfo/State/Constitution/.

Cohen, A. (1969) *Custom and Politics in Urban Africa*. Berkeley, CA: University of California Press.

Cohen, A. (1979) 'Political Symbolism', *Annual Review of Anthropology*, 8: 87–113.

Cohen, A. (1981) *The Politics of Elite Culture*. Berkeley, CA: University of California Press.

Cohen, A. P. (1985) *The Symbolic Construction of Community*. London: Routledge.

Cohen, L. (1993) *Broken Bonds: The Disintegration of Yugoslavia*. Boulder, CO: Westview.

Collins, R. (1986) *Weberian Sociological Theory*. Cambridge: Cambridge University Press.

Collins, R. (1992) *The Sociological Insight*. Oxford: Oxford University Press.

Collins, R. (1999) *Macrohistory: Essays in Sociology of the Long Run*. Stanford, CA: Stanford University Press.

Connor, W. (1994) *Ethnonationalism*. Princeton, NJ: Princeton University Press.

Connor, W. (2004) 'The Timelessness of Nations'. *Nations and Nationalism* 10(1/2): 35–48.

Connor, W. (2005) 'The Dawning of Nations', in A. Ichijo and G. Uzelac (eds) *When is the Nation?* London: Routledge.

Copi, I. (1979) *Symbolic Logic*. New York: Macmillan.

Cori, R. and Lascar, D. (2000) *Mathematical Logic*. Oxford: Oxford University Press.

Crawford, K. (2000) 'History Textbooks and the Construction of National Memory: A Comparative Analysis of Teaching the Second World War' *Curriculum* 21(1): 26–39.

Crawford, K. (2001) 'Constructing National Memory: The 1940/41 Blitz in British History Textbooks', in *Internationale Schulbuchforchung*. Hannover: Verlag Hahnsche Buchhandlung.

CSFRY (1974) *The Constitution of the Socialist Federal Republic of Yugoslavia.* Belgrade: DDU.

Čulinović, F. (1959) *Stvaranje nove Jugoslavenske drzave.* Zagreb: Grafički Zavod Hrvatske.

Dandeker, C. (1990) *Surveillance, Power and Modernity.* Cambridge: Polity.

Daniel, E. V. (1984) *Fluid Signs: Being a Person the Tamil Way.* Berkeley, CA: University of California Press.

Delanty, G. (1996) 'Beyond the Nation-State: National Identity and Citizenship in a Multicultural Society – A Response to Rex' *Sociological Research Online.* 1(4). http://www.socresonline.org.uk/1/3/1.html#2.3.

Deleuze, G. and Guattari, F. (1988) *A Thousand Plateaus.* London: Athlone.

Dickens, P. (2000) *Social Darwinism.* London: Oxford University Press.

Douglas, M. (1970) *Natural Symbols.* London: Barrie and Rockliff.

Douglas, M. (1992) *Purity and Danger.* London: Routledge.

Doyle, A. (2002) 'Ethnocentrism and History Textbooks: Representation of the Irish Famine 1845–49 in History Textbooks in English Secondary Schools', *Intercultural Education* 13(3): 315–30.

Durkheim, E. (1976[1915]) *The Elementary Forms of Religious Life.* London: George Allen & Unwin.

Durkheim, E. (1933) *The Division of Labour in Society.* New York: Macmillan.

Durkheim, E. (1986) *Durkheim on Politics and the State.* Edited by A. Giddens. Cambridge: Polity.

Dyker, D. (1979) 'Yugoslavia: Unity out of Diversity?', in A. Brown and J. Gray (eds) *Political Culture and Political Change in Communist States.* London: Macmillan.

Dyker, D. (1990) *Yugoslavia: Socialism, Development and Debt.* London: Routledge.

Edensor, T. (2002) *National Identity, Popular Culture and Everyday Life.* Oxford: Berg.

Eisenstadt, S. N. (2000) 'The Reconstruction of Religious Arenas in the Framework of "Multiple Modernities" '. *Millennium* 29(3): 591–611.

Eisenstadt, S. N. (2002) 'The Construction of Collective Identities and the Continual Reconstruction of Primordiality', in S. Malešević and M. Haugaard (eds) *Making Sense of Collectivity.* London: Pluto.

Elias, N. (1983) *The Court Society.* Oxford: Blackwell.

Elton, G. (1992) *The English.* Oxford: Blackwell.

Elster, J. (1985) *Making Sense of Marx. Cambridge: Cambridge University Press.*

Eriksen, T. H. (2004) 'Place, Kinship and the Case for Non-Ethnic Nations', *Nations and Nationalism* 10(1/2): 49–62.

Eurobarometer (2000) *How Europeans see Themselves.* Brussels: European Commission.

Evans-Pritchard, E. (1965) *Theories of Primitive Religion.* Oxford: Clarendon Press.

Ewing, K. P. (1990) 'The Illusion of Wholeness: Culture, Self, and the Experience of Inconsistency', *Ethnos* 18(3): 251–78.

Fenton (2003) *Ethnicity.* Cambridge: Polity.

Foucault, M. (1977) *Discipline and Punish: the Birth of the Prison.* London: Allen Lane.

Foucault, M. (1980) 'Truth and Power', in C. Gordon. (ed.) *Michael Foucault, Power/Knowledge.* Brighton: Harvester Press.

Fox, N. (1998) 'Foucault, Foucauldians and Sociology', *British Journal of Sociology*, 49(3): 415–33.

Freeden, M. (1996) *Ideologies and Political Theory: A Conceptual Approach*. Oxford: Clarendon Press.

Freeden, M. (2003) *Ideology*. Oxford: Oxford University Press.

Gagnon, V. P. (2004) *The Myth of Ethnic War*. Ithaca, NY: Cornell University Press.

Geertz, C. (1964) 'Ideology as a Cultural System', in D. Apter (ed.) *Ideology and Discontent*. New York: Free Press.

Geertz, C. (1973) *The Interpretation of Cultures*. New York: Basic Books.

Gellner, E. (1964) *Thought and Change*. London: Weidenfeld and Nicolson.

Gellner, E. (1983) *Nations and Nationalism*. Oxford: Blackwell.

Gellner, E. (1988) *Plough, Sword and the Book: The Structure of Human History*. London: Collins Harvill.

Gellner, E. (1989) 'Introduction', in: J. Baechler, J. A. Hall and M. Mann (eds) *Europe and the Rise of Capitalism*. Oxford: Basil Blackwell.

Gellner, E. (1994) *Encounters with Nationalism*. Oxford: Blackwell.

Gellner, E. (1996) *Conditions of Liberty: Civil Society and its Rivals*. Harmondsworth: Penguin.

Gellner, E. (1997) *Nationalism*. London: Phoenix.

Gellner, E. (1998) *Language and Solitude: Wittgenstein, Malinowski and the Habsburg Dilemma*. Cambridge: Cambridge University Press.

Giddens, A. (1978) *Durkheim*. London: Fontana Press.

Giddens, A. (1985) *Nation-Sate and Violence*, Cambridge: Polity.

Giddens, A. (1987) 'Structuralism, Post-Structuralism and the Production of Culture', in A. Giddens and J. Turner (eds) *Social Theory Today*. Cambridge: Polity.

Giddens, A. (1991) *Modernity and Self-Identity*. Cambridge: Polity.

Giddens, A. (1992) *The Transformation of Intimacy*. Cambridge: Polity.

Gilley, B. (2004) 'Against the Concept of Ethnic Conflict', *Third World Quarterly* 25(6): 1155–66.

Gleason, P. (1983) 'Identifying Identity: A Semantic History', *The Journal of American History* 69(4): 910–31.

Glenny, M. (1992) *The Fall of Yugoslavia*. London: Penguin.

Goddard, I. W. (1998) *The ID Matrix and the Conservation of Identity* http://dev.null.org/psychoceramics/archives/1998.02/msg00002.

Goffman, E. (1968) *Stigma: Notes on the Management of Spoiled Identity*. Harmondsworth: Pelican.

Goffman, E. (1969) *The Presentation of Self in Everyday Life*. London: Allen Lane.

Goffman, E. (1975) *Frame Analysis*. Harmondsworth: Peregrine.

Goldberg, D. (1993) *Racist Culture: Philosophy and the Politics of Meaning*. Oxford: Blackwell.

Goldhagen, D. (1996) *Hitler's Willing Executioners: Ordinary Germans and the Holocaust*. New York: Knopf.

Golubović, Z. (1988) *Kriza identiteta savremenog jugoslovenskog društva*. Belgrade: Filip Višnjić.

Gordy, E. (1999) *The Culture of Power in Serbia*. University Park: Penn State University Press.

Gouldner, A. (1970) *The Coming Crisis of Western Sociology*. New York: Basic Books.

Gourevitch, P. (2000) *We Wish to Inform You That Tomorrow We Will Be Killed with Our Families: Stories from Rwanda*. London: Picador.

Gray, P. and Little, R. (1997) *Germany 1918–1945*. Cambridge: Cambridge University Press.

Gramsci, A. (1971) *Selections from the Prison Notebooks*. London: Lawrence and Wishart.

Greenfeld, L. (1992) *Nationalism: Five Roads to Modernity*. Cambridge, MA: Harvard University Press.

Guibernau, M. (1996) *Nationalisms*. Cambridge: Polity.

Guibernau, M. (2001) 'National Identity and Modernity', in A. Dieckhoff and N. Gutierrez (eds) *Modern Roots: Studies of National Identites*. Hampshire: Ashgate Press.

Guibernau, M. (2004) 'Anthony D. Smith on Nations and National Identity: A Critical Assessment', *Nations and Nationalism* 10(1/2): 125–42.

GUMG (Glasgow University Media Group) (1985) *War and Peace News*. Milton Keynes: Open University Press.

Gutierrez, N. (2001) 'The Study of National Identity', in A. Dieckhoff and N. Gutierrez (eds) *Modern Roots: Studies of National Identites*. Hampshire: Ashgate Press.

Habermas, J. (1987) *The Philosophical Discourse of Modernity*. Cambridge: MIT Press.

Hall, J. A. (2002) 'A Disagreement about Difference', in S. Malešević and M. Haugaard (eds) *Making Sense of Collectivity*. London: Pluto.

Hall, J. A. (1988) *Powers and Liberties: The Causes and Consequences of the Rise of the West*. Harmondsworth: Penguin.

Hall, J. A. (1989) 'States and Societies: The Miracle in Comparative Perspective', in J. Baechler, J. A. Hall and M. Mann (eds) *Europe and the Rise of Capitalism*. Oxford: Basil Blackwell.

Hall, S. (1986) 'Gramsci's Relevance for the Study of Race and Ethnicity', *Journal of Communication Inquiry* 10(2): 5–27.

Hamnett, I. (2001) 'Durkheim and the Study of Religion', in: W. S. F. Pickering (ed.) *Emile Durkheim: Critical Assessments of Leading Sociologists*. London: Routledge.

Handler, R. (1994) 'Is "identity" a useful cross-cultural concept?', in: J. R. Gillis (ed.) *Commemorations: The Politics of National Identity*. Princeton, NJ: Princeton University Press.

Handler, R. and Segal, D. (1990) Jane Austen and the Fiction of Culture: An Essay on the Narration of Social Realities. Tuscon, AZ: University of Arizona Press.

Hann, C. (2001) 'Gellner's Structural-Functional-Culturalism', *Czech Sociological Review* 9 (2): 173–82.

Harris, H. (1995) 'An Experimentalist Looks at Identity', in H. Harris (ed.) *Identity*. Oxford: Clarendon Press.

Hastings, A. (1997) *The Construction of Nationhood*. Cambridge: Cambridge University Press.

Haugaard, M. (2002) 'Nationalism and Modernity', in S. Malešević and M. Haugaard (eds) *Making Sense of Collectivity*. London: Pluto.

Hechter, M. (1999) *Internal Colonialism: Celtic Fringe in British National Development*. London: Transaction.

Hechter, M. (1986) 'Rational Choice Theory and the Study of Race and Ethnic Relations', in J. Rex and D. Mason (eds) *Theories of Race and Ethnic Relations*. Cambridge: Cambridge University Press.

Hechter, M. (1995) 'Explaining Nationalist Violence', *Nations and Nationalism* 1(1): 53–68.

Herman, E. and Chomsky, N. (1994) *Manufacturing Consent: The Political Economy of the Mass Media*. London: Vintage.

Hill, S. (1990) 'Britain: The Dominant Ideology Thesis after a Decade', in N. Abercrombie, S. Hill and B. S. Turner (eds) *Dominant Ideologies*. London: Unwin Hyman.

Hintjens, H. (1999) 'Explaining the 1994 Genocide in Rwanda' *Journal of Modern African Studies* 37 (2): 241–86.

Hintjens, H. (2001) 'When Identity Becomes a Knife: Reflecting on the Genocide in Rwanda', *Ethnicities* 1(1): 25–55.

Hirst, P. (2001) *War and Power in the 21ˢᵗ Century*. Cambridge: Polity.

Hobsbawm, E. (1992) *Nations and Nationalism since 1780*. Cambridge: CUP.

Hodson, R., Sekulić, D. and Massey, G. (1994) 'National Tolerance in the Former Yugoslavia', *American Journal of Sociology* 99(6): 1539.

Holsti, K. (1991) *Peace and War: Armed Conflicts and International Order 1648–1989*. Cambridge: Cambridge University Press.

Hopkin, J. (2001) 'The World according to Geography Textbooks: Interpretations of the English National Curriculum', *International Research in Geographical and Environmental Education* 10(1): 46–67.

Howard, M. (1976) *War in European History*. Oxford: Oxford University Press.

Hroch, M. and Maleckova, J. (2001) 'Nation: A Survey of the Term in European Languages', in A. S. Leoussi and A. D. Smith (eds) *Encyclopedia of Nationalism*. London: Transaction.

Huntington, S. (1968) *Political Order in Changing Societies*. Yale: Yale University Press.

Ignatieff, M. (1997) *The Warrior's Honor: Ethnic War and the Modern Conscience*. New York: Henry Holt and co.

Isaacs, H. (1976) 'Basic Group Identity: The Idols of the Tribe', in N. Glazer and D. Moynihan (eds) *Ethnicity: Theory and Experience*. Cambridge, MA: Harvard University Press.

Isajiw, W. (1974) 'Definitions of Ethnicity', *Ethnicity* 2(1):111–24.

Isajiw, W. (1990) 'Ethnic Identity Retention', in R. Breton, W. Isajiw, W. Kalbach and J. Reitz (eds) *Ethnic Identity and Equality: Varieties of Experience in a Canadian City*. Toronto: University of Toronto Press.

Jenkins, R. (1996) *Social Identity*. London: Routledge.

Jenkins, R. (1997) *Rethinking Ethnicity*. London: Sage.

Jenkins, R. (2002) 'Different Societies? Different Cultures? What are Human Collectivities?', in S. Malešević and M. Haugaard (eds) *Making Sense of Collectivity*, London: Pluto.

Jenkins, R. (2004) *Social Identity*, revised second edition. London: Routledge.

Jones, E. (1981) *The European Miracle*. Cambridge: Cambridge University Press.

Jović, D. (2003) *Jugoslavija – država koja je odumrla*. Zagreb: Prometej.

JRRT (2004) *The State of British Democracy*. York: The Joseph Rowntree Reform Trust.

Kallis, A. 1999 'Coping with the Uncomfortable Past: A Comparative Analysis of the Teaching of World War II and the Role of Historical Education in the

Construction of a "European' identity" ', in A. Ross (ed.) *Young Citizens in Europe*. London: CICE.

Kangrga, M. (2001) *Šverćeri vlastitog života*. Belgrade: Republika.

Kaplan, R. (1993) *Balkan Ghosts: A Journey through History*. New York: St. Martin's Press.

Kasapović, M. (1996) 'Izbori – kontekst i rezultati' *Erasmus*, 18(1): 5–12, October issue.

Katunarić, V. (1986) 'Sistem moći, socijalna struktura i nacionalno pitanje' *Revija za Sociologiju* 28(2): 75–90.

Katunarić, V. (1987) 'Autoritarnost – Etnocentrizam – Seksizam i društvene grupe' *Revija za Sociologiju* 29(1): 603–10.

Katunarić, V. (1991) 'Uoči novih etno-političkih raskola – Hrvatska i Bosna i Hercegovina', *Sociologija*, 33(3): 373–85.

Kedourie, E. (1960) *Nationalism*. London: Hutchinson.

Keegan, J. (1999) *The First World War*. London: Pimlico.

Khomeini, I. (1985) *Islam and Revolution*. London: KPI.

Kohn, H. (1944) *The Idea of Nationalism*. New York: Macmillan.

Kumar, K. (2003) *The Making of English National Identity*. Cambridge: Cambridge University Press.

Laclau, E. (1996) *Emancipation (s)*. London: Verso.

Laclau, E. and Mouffe, C. (1985) *Hegemony and Socialist Strategy*. London: Verso.

Lal, B. B. (1995) 'Symbolic Interaction Theories', *American Behavioral Scientist* 38(3): 421–41.

Lane, C. (1984) 'Legitimacy and Power in the Soviet Union Through Socialist Ritual', *British Journal of Political Science* 14 (1): 207–17.

Lancaster, S. and Lancaster, T. (1995) *Britain and the World*. London: CPL.

Leach E. (1961) *Pul Eliya: A Village in Ceylon*. Cambridge: Cambridge University Press.

Larrain, J. (1994) 'The Postmodern Critique of Ideology', *The Sociological Review* 42(2):289–314.

Levi-Strauss, C. (1975) *The Raw and the Cooked*. New York: Harper and Row.

Lewins, F. (1989) 'Recasting the Concept of Ideology: A Content Approach', *British Journal of Sociology* 40(4): 678–93.

Liebknd, K. (1989) 'Conceptual Approaches to Ethnic Identity', in K. Liebkind (ed.) *New Identities in Europe*. Aldershot: Gower.

Lieven, A. (2004) *America Right or Wrong: An Anatomy of American Nationalism*. Oxford: Oxford University Press.

Lijphart, A. (1968) *The Politics of Accommodation: Pluralism and Democracy in the Netherlands*. Berkeley, CA: University of California Press.

Linz, J. and Stepan, A. (1992) 'Political Identities and Electoral Consequences: Spain, the Soviet Union and Yugoslavia', *Daedalus* 121(2):123–39.

Linz, J. and Stepan, A. (1996) *Problems of Democratic Transition and Consolidation: Southern Europe, South America and Post-communist Europe*. Baltimore, MD: John Hopkins University Press.

Llobera, J. (1994) 'Durkheim and the National Question', in W. S. F. Pickering and H. Martins (eds) *Debating Durkheim*. London: Routledge.

Lukes, S. (1973) *Emile Durkheim*. Harmondsworth: Penguin.

Luković-Pjanović, O. (1990). *Srbi, narod najstariji*. Belgrade: Glas Srba.

Lyotard, F. (1984) *The Postmodern Condition: A Report on Knowledge*. Manchester: Manchester University Press.

Mackenzie, J. (1989) *Imperialism and Popular Culture*. Manchester: Manchester University Press.

Mahmutćehajić, R. (2000) *Bosnia the Good: Tolerance and Tradition*. Budapest: CEU Press.

Malešević, S. (1993) 'Percepcija "etnickog porijekla" i "zivotnih ciljeva" kao determinanti etnickog identitieta', *Revija za sociologiju* 24(1–2): 87–99.

Malešević, S. (1994) 'Percepcija etnickog identiteta: Aplikacija jednog modela' *Migracijske teme* 10(1): 31–55.

Malešević, S. (1998). 'Ustashas and Chetniks: Delegitimization of an Ethnic Enemy in Serbian and Croatian War time Cartoons', in C. Lowney (ed.) *Identities: Theoretical Considerations and Case Studies*. Vienna: IWM.

Malešević, S. (2002) *Ideology, Legitimacy and the New State: Yugoslavia, Serbia and Croatia*. London: Frank Cass.

Malešević, S. (2004) *The Sociology of Ethnicity*. London: Sage.

Malešević, S. and. Hall, J. A. (2005) 'Citizenship, Ethnicity and Nation-states', in C. Calhoun, C. Rojek and B. Turner (eds) *The Sage Handbook of Sociology*. London: Sage.

Malešević, S. and Malešević, V. (2001) 'Ethnic Identity Preceptions: An Analysis of Two Surveys', *Europa Ethnica* 58(1–2):1–16.

Malešević, S. and G. Uzelac (1997) 'Ethnic Distance, Power and War: The Case of Croatian Students', *Nations and Nationalism* 3(2): 291–98.

Malinowski, B. (1926) *Myth in Primitive Psychology*. Westport, CT: Negro Universities Press.

Mann, M. (1986) *The Sources of Social Power I: A History of Power from the Beginning to A.D. 1760*. Cambridge: Cambridge University Press.

Mann, M. (1988) *States, War and Capitalism: Studies in Political Sociology*. Oxford: Blackwell.

Mann, M. (1993) *The Sources of Social Power II: The Rise of Classes and Nation-States, 1760–1914*. Cambridge: Cambridge University Press.

Mann, M. (1995) 'A Political Theory of Nationalism and its Excesses', in Periwal, S. (ed.) *Notions of Nationalism*. Budapest: CEU Press.

Mann, M. (1999) 'The Dark Side of Democracy: The Modern Tradition of Ethnic and Political Cleansing', *New Left Review* 235 (May-June): 18–45.

Mann, M. (2001) Explaining Murderous Ethnic Cleansing: The Macro-Level, in M. Guibernau and J. Hutchinson (eds) *Understanding Nationalism*. Cambridge: Polity.

Mann, M. (2003) *Incoherent Empire*. London: Verso.

Mann, M. (2005) *The Dark Side of Democracy: Explaining Ethnic Cleansing*. Cambridge: Cambridge University Press.

Mannheim, K. ([1936]1966) *Ideology and Utopia*, London: Routledge & Kegan Paul.

Mamdani, M. (2001) *When Victims Become Killers: Colonialism, Nativism and the Genocide in Rwanda*. Princeton, NJ: Princeton University Press.

Marcuse, H. (1964) *One-Dimensional Man: Studies in the Ideology of Advanced Industrial Society*. Boston: Beacon Press.

Markovic M. (1994) 'Inteligencija je uz narod', *Politika* 10(April): 3–4.

Markus, G. (1991) 'Concepts of Ideology in Marx', in Kroker, A. and M. (eds) *Ideology and Power in the Age of Lenin in Ruins*. New York: St. Martin's Press.

Marshal, T. H. (1992[1948]) *Citizenship and Social Class*, London: Pluto.

Marx, K. and Engels, F. (1982) *The German Ideology*. London: Lawrence & Wishart.

McAuley, D. (2005) 'The Ideology of Osama Bin Laden: Nation, Tribe and World Economy', *Journal of Political Ideologies* 10(3): 269–87.

McNeill, W. (1984) *The Pursuit of Power*. Chicago, IL: University of Chicago Press.

Mead, G. H. (1934) *Mind, Self and Society from the Standpoint of a Social Behaviorist*. Chicago, IL: University of Chicago Press.

Michels, R. (1962) *Political Parties*. New York: Free Press.

Miles, R. (1989) *Racism*. London: Routledge.

Miller, W. (1991) *Media and Voters*. Oxford: Oxford University Press.

Milosavljevic, O. (2000) 'From the Memorandum to "Collective" Responsibility', in: *Serbian Elite*. Belgrade: Helsinki Odbor za ljudska prava u Srbiji.

Mouzelis, N. (1999) 'Modernity: A Non-European Conceptualisation', *British Journal of Sociology* 50(1): 141–59.

*** *(1997) Naša Borba*, 17 February, p.1.

Newbury, C. (1992) 'Rwanda: Recent Debates Over Governance and Rural Development', in M. Bratton and G. Hyden (eds) *Governance and Politics in Africa*. Boulder, CO: Lynne Rienner.

Nisbet, R. (1976) 'Introduction', in E. Durkheim ([1915]1976) *The Elementary Forms of Religious Life*. London: George Allen & Unwin.

Oberschall, A. (2000) 'The Manipulation of Ethnicity: From Ethnic Cooperation to Violence and War in Yugoslavia', *Ethnic and Racial Studies* 23(6): 982–1001.

Oplinger, J. (1990) *The Politics of Demonology*. London: Associated University Press.

Ozkirimli, U. (2000) *Theories of Nationalism*. London: Macmillan.

Ozkirimli, U. (2003) 'The Nation as an Artichoke? A Critique of Ethnosymbolist Interpretations of Nationalism', *Nations and Nationalism* 9(3): 339–55.

Pantić, D. (1990) *Promene vrednosnih orijentacija mladih u Srbiji*. Belgrade: IDN.

Parfit, D. (1995) 'The Unimportance of Identity', in H. Harris (ed.) *Identity*. Oxford: Clarendon.

Pareto, V. (1966) *Sociological Writings*. Oxford: Basil Blackwell.

Parham, T. and Helms, J. (1981) 'The Influence of Black Students' Racial Identity Attitudes on Preferences for Counselor's Race', *Journal of Counseling Psychology*. (28): 250–57.

Parkin, F. (1979) *Marxism and Class Theory: A Bourgeois Critique*. London: Tavistock.

Parsons, T. (1991) 'A Tentative Outline of American Values', in R. Robertson. and B. S. Turner (eds) *Talcot Parsons–Theorist of Modernity*. London: Sage.

Parsons, T. (1937) *The Structure of Social Action*. New York: Free Press.

Parsons, T. (1951) *The Social System*. New York: Free Press.

Parsons, T. (1975) 'Some Theoretical Considerations on the Nature and Trends of Change of Ethnicity', in N.Glazer and D. P. Moynihan (eds) *Ethnicity: Theory and Experience*. Cambridge: Harvard University Press.

Paul, M. and Fischer, J. (1980) Correlates of self concept among Black Early Adolescents, *Journal of Youth and Adolescence* (9): 163–73.

Pešić, V. (1995) 'Društveni i državni aspekt multikulturalnosti u Bosni i Hercegovini', in B. Jakšić (ed.) *Interkulturalnost*. Belgrade: IFDT.

Phinney, J. (1992) 'The Multigroup Ethnic Identity Measure: A New Scale for Use with Diverse Groups', *Journal of Adolescent Research* (7): 156–76.

244   *References*

Phinney, J. and Alipuria, L. (1996) 'At the Interface of Cultures: Multiethnic/ multiracial High School and College Students', *Journal of Social Psychology* (136): 139–58.

Pickering. W. S. F. (2001) 'The Eternality of the Sacred: Durkheim's Error?', in W. S. F. Pickering (ed.) *Emile Durkheim: Critical Assessments of Leading Sociologists*. London: Routledge.

Plamenatz, J. (1976) 'Two Types of Nationalism', in E. Kamenka (ed.) *Nationalism: The Nature and Evolution of an Idea*. London: Edward Arnold.

Poggi, G. (2000) *Durkheim*. Oxford: Oxford University Press.

Popper, K. (1957) *The Poverty of Historicism*. London: Routledge & Kegan Paul.

(1977) *Program Saveza Komunista Jugoslavije*. Belgrade: Komunist.

Prunier, G. (1997) *The Rwanda Crisis 1959–1994: History of a Genocide*. London: Hurst.

Ram, H. (2000) 'The Immemorial Iranian Nation? School Textbooks and Historical Memory in Post-Revolutionary Iran', *Nations and Nationalism* 6(1): 67–90.

Rex, J. (1980) 'The Theory of Race Relations: A Weberian Approach', in *Sociological Theories: Race and Colonialism*. Paris: Unesco.

Rex, J. (1986) *Race and Ethnicity*. London: Open University Press.

Rex, J. (1996a) *Ethnic Minorities and the Modern Nation State*. London: Macmillan.

Rex, J. (1996b) 'National Identity in the Democratic Multicultural State' *Sociological Research Online* 1 (3) http://www.socresonline.org.uk/1/2/1.html.

Reyntjens, F. (1996) 'Rwanda: Genocide and beyond', *Journal of Refugee Studies* 9(3): 240–51.

Robson, W. (1993) *Britain 1750–1990*. Oxford: Oxford University Press.

Rogel, C. (1985) 'Edvard Kardelj's Nationality Theory and Yugoslav Socialism', *Canadian Review of Studies in Nationalism* 12(2):343–57.

Roland, A. (1988) *In Search of Self in India and Japan*. Princeton, NJ: Princeton University Press.

Ron, J. (2003) *Frontiers and Ghettos: State Violence in Serbia and Israel*. Berkeley, CA: University of California Press.

Rose, N. (1999) *Governing the Soul*. London: Free Association Books.

Said, E. (1978) *Orientalism*. New York: Random House.

Sartori, G. (1969) 'Politics, Ideology and Belief Systems', *American Political Science Review* 63(1): 398–411.

Schmitt, C. (1976) *The Concept of the Political*. New Brunswick, NJ: Rutgers University Press.

Secor, L. (1999) 'Testaments Betrayed: Yugoslav Intellectuals and the Road to War', *Lingua Franca* 9(6): 1–15.

Sekulić, D. (1997) 'The Creation and Dissolution of the Multinational State: The Case of Yugoslavia', *Nations and Nationalism* 3(2):165–79.

Sekulić, D. (2004) *Sukobi i tolerancija*. Zagreb: Jesenski i Turk.

Seliger, M. (1976) *Ideology and Politics*. London: Allen & Unwin.

Selimbegović, V. (2000) 'Alija i Armija, dva oka u glavi', *Dani* 176 (October): 4–7.

Sesardić, N. (1991) *Iz analiticke perspektive*. Zagreb: SDH.

Shils, E. (1968) 'The Concept and Function of Ideology', *International Encyclopaedia of the Social Sciences* 7: 66–76.

Shlapentokh, V. (1982) 'The Study of Values as a Social Phenomenon: The Soviet Case', *Social Forces* 61 (4): 403–17.

Siber, I. (1988) *Psihologijski aspekti medjunacionalnih odnosa*. Zagreb: Kulturni Radnik.

Silber, L. and Little, A. (1995) *The Death of Yugoslavia*. London: Penguin & BBC.

Simmel, G. (1955) *Conflict and the Web of Group Affiliations*. New York: The Free Press.

Smelser, N. (1992) 'The Rational Choice Perspective: A Theoretical Assessment', *Rationality and Society* 4(3): 381–410.

Smith, A. D. (1973) *The Concept of Social Change*. London: Routledge & Kegan Paul.

Smith, A. D. (1976) *Social Change*. London: Longman.

Smith, A. D. (1983a) *Theories of Nationalism*. London: Duckworth.

Smith, A. D. (1983b) 'Nationalism and Classical Social Theory' *British Journal of Sociology* 34(1): 19–38.

Smith, A. D. (1986) *The Ethnic Origins of Nations*. Oxford: Blackwell.

Smith, A. D. (1991) *National Identity*. Harmondsworth: Penguin.

Smith, A. D. (1995) *Nations and Nationalism in a Global Era*. Cambridge: Polity.

Smith, A. D. (1998) *Nationalism and Modernism*. London: Routledge.

Smith, A. D. (1999a) *Myths and Memories of the Nations*. Oxford: Oxford University Press.

Smith, A. D. (1999b) 'Ethnic Election and National Destiny: Some Religious Origins of National Ideals', *Nations and Nationalism* 5(3): 331–56.

Smith, A. D. (2000) 'The "Sacred" Dimension of Nationalism', *Millennium* 29(3):791–814.

Smith, A. D. (2001a) *Nationalism*. Cambridge: Polity.

Smith, A. D. (2001b) 'Interpretations of National Identity', in A. Dieckhoff and N. Gutierrez (eds) *Modern Roots: Studies of National Identites*. Hampshire: Ashgate Press.

Smith, A. D. (2003a) *Chosen Peoples: Sacred Sources of National Identity*. Oxford: Oxford University Press.

Smith, A. D. (2003b) 'The Poverty of Anti-nationalist Modernism', *Nations and Nationalism* 9(3): 357–70.

Smith, A. D. (2004) 'History and National Destiny: Responses and Clarifications', *Nations and Nationalism* 10(1/2): 195–209.

Smith, A. D. (2004) 'Ethnic Cores and Dominant Ethnies', in E. Kaufman (ed.) *Rethinking Ethnicity*. London: Routledge.

Smith R. W. (1999) 'State Power and Genocidal Intent: On the Uses of Genocide in the Twentieth Century', in L. Chorbajian and G. Shirinian (eds) *Studies in Comparative Genocide*. London: Macmillan.

Solomos, J. (1995) 'Marxism, Racism and Ethnicity', *American Behavioral Scientist.* 38(3): 407–20.

(SP) (1986) *Jugoslavija 1945–1985: Statistički Prikaz*. Belgrade: Savezni Zavod za Statistiku.

Spencer, M. S. *et al.* (2000) 'Ethnic Identity Among Monoracial and Multiracial Early Adolescents', *The Journal of Early Adolescence* 20(4): 365–87.

Stone, D. (2004) 'Genocide as Transgression', *European Journal of Social Theory.* 7(1): 45–65.

Stone, J. (1979) 'Introduction: Internal Colonialism in Comparative Perspective', *Ethnic and Racial Studies* 2(3): 253–59.

Stokes, G. (1993) *The Walls Came Tumbling Down*. Oxford: Oxford University Press.

Strauss, S. (2004) *The Order of Genocide: Race, Power and War in Rwanda*. PhD thesis. University of California, Berkeley.

Sztompka, P. (1993) *The Sociology of Social Change*. Oxford: Blackwell.

Tajfel, H. (1981) *Human Groups and Social Categories*. Cambridge: Cambridge University Press.

Tajfel, H. and Turner, J. (1979) 'An Integrative Theory of Intergroup Conflict', in W. G. Austin and S. Worschel (eds) *The Social Psychology of Intergroup Relations*. Monterey, CA: Brooks/Cole.

Taylor, C. (1984) 'Foucault on Freedom and Truth', *Political Theory* 12(2): 152–83.

Teodosić, R. *et al*. 1946 *Zemljopis za III razred osnovne škole*. Belgrade: Prosveta.

Tilly, C. (1984) *Big Structures, Large Processes, Huge Comparisons*. New York: Russell Sage Foundation.

Tilly, C. (1995) *Coercion, Capital, and European State Formation*. Cambridge: Polity.

Tilly, C. (2002) *Stories, Identities and Political Change*. New York: Rowman & Littlefield.

Tilly, C. (2003) *The Politics of Collective Violence*. Cambridge: Cambridge University Press.

Tito, J. B. (1945a) 'Govor Maršala Jugoslavije Josipa Broza – Tita u Zagrebu', *Borba*, 23 May, 124(10):1–2.

Tito, J. B. (1945b) 'Maršal Tito govorio je u Sarajevu na velikom zboru kome je prisustvovalo 80 hiljada ljudi', *Borba*, 6 November, 269(10):1–2.

Tito, J. B. (1966) 'On Fraternity and Unity', http://www.titoville.com/sound/govor9.htm.l

Tito, J. B. (1975) 'Titovi govori', http://www.leksikon-yu-mitologije.net/read.php?id=618.

Todorova, M. (1997) *Imagining the Balkans*. Oxford: Oxford University Press.

Torfing, J. (2005) 'The Linguistic Turn: Foucault, Laclau, Mouffe and Žižek', in T. Janoski, R. Alford, A. Hicks and M. Schwartz (eds) *The Handbook of Political Sociology*. Cambridge: Cambridge University Press.

Tudjman, F. (1981) *Nationalism in Contemporary Europe*. New York: Columbia University Press.

Tudjman, F. (1990) *Velike ideje i mali narodi*. Zagreb: Nakladni Zavod Matice Hrvatske.

Turner, B. S. (1990) 'Conclusion: Peroration on Ideology', in N. Abercrombie, S. Hill and B. S. Turner (eds) *Dominant Ideologies*. London: Unwin Hyman.

Turpin, C. (2002) *British Government and the Constitution: Text, Cases and Materials*, London: Butterworths.

Taylor, C. C. (1988) 'Ustav Federativne Narodne Republike Jugoslavije (1946)', in *Ustavni razvoj Socialisticke Jugoslavije*. Belgrade: Eksportpres.

Taylor, C. C. (1992) *Ustav Savezne Republike Jugoslavije*. Belgrade: Politika.

Taylor, C. C. (1999) *Sacrifice as Terror: The Rwandan Genocide of 1994*. Oxford: Berg.

Uzelac, G. (1999) 'Perceptions of the Nation: The Example of Croatian Students in 1993', *Canadian Review of the Studies in Nationalism* 26(1–2): 123–38.

Uzelac, G. (2006) *The Development of the Croation Nation: An Historical and Sociological Analysis*. Ceredigion: Edwin Mellen Press.

Van den Berghe, P. L. (1981) *The Ethnic Phenomenon.* New York: Elsevier.

Van den Berghe, P. L. (2005) 'Ethnies and Nations: Geneology Indeed', in A. Ichijo and G. Uzelac (eds) *When is the Nation?* London: Routledge.

Vujacic, V. (1996) 'Historical Legacies, Nationalist Mobilization, and Political. Outcomes in Russia and Serbia: A Weberian View', *Theory and Society* 25(6): 763–801.

Vulliamy, E. (1994) *Seasons in Hell: Understanding Bosnia's War.* New York: St. Martin Press.

Waller, D. (1996) *Which Way Now?* Oxford: Oxfam.

Weber, E. (1976) *Peasants into Frenchmen.* Stanford, CA: Stanford University Press.

Weber, M. (1968) *Economy and Society.* New York: Bedminster Press.

Weinreich, P. (1983) 'Psychodynamics of Personal and Social Identity: Theoretical Concepts and their Measurement', in A. Jacobson-Widding (ed.) *Identity: Personal and Socio-cultural.* Stockholm: Almqvist and Wiksell International.

Weinreich, P. (1986) 'The Operationalisation of Identity Theory in Racial and Ethnic Relations', in J. Rex and D. Mason (eds) *Theories of Race and Ethnic Relations.* Cambridge: Cambridge University Press.

Williams, L. (1999) 'National Identity and the Nation State: Construction, Reconstruction and Contradiction', in K. Cameron (ed.) *National Identity.* Exeter: Intellect.

Wimmer, A. and Glick-Schiller, N. (2002) 'Methodological Nationalism and Beyond: Nation-state building, Migration and the Social Sciences', *Global Networks* 2(4): 301–34.

Wood, W. (2001) 'Geographic Aspects of Genocide: Comparison of Bosnia and Rwanda'. *Transactions* 26(1): 57–75.

Wolf, E. (1982) *Europe and the People without History.* Berkeley, CA: University of California Press.

Wolf, E. (1994) 'Perilous Ideas: Race, Culture, People', *Current Anthropology* 35(1):1–12.

Yack, B. (1996) 'The Myth of the Civic Nation', *Critical Review* 10(2): 193–212.

Zubaida S. (1993) *Islam, the People and the State.* London: I. B. Tauris.

Žunec, O. (1998) *Rat i drustvo..* Zagreb: Jesenski i Turk.

Index